**THE SEVEN
PILLARS OF
NONSENSE**

THE SEVEN PILLARS OF NONSENSE

MICHAEL ROSELAAR

The Book Guild Ltd

First published in Great Britain in 2018 by
The Book Guild Ltd
9 Priory Business Park
Wistow Road, Kibworth
Leicestershire, LE8 0RX
Freephone: 0800 999 2982
www.bookguild.co.uk
Email: info@bookguild.co.uk
Twitter: @bookguild

Copyright © 2018 Michael Roselaar

The right of Michael Roselaar to be identified as the author of this work has been asserted by him in accordance with the Copyright, Design and Patents Act 1988.

All rights reserved. No part of this publication may be reproduced, transmitted, or stored in a retrieval system, in any form or by any means, without permission in writing from the publisher, nor be otherwise circulated in any form of binding or cover other than that in which it is published and without a similar condition being imposed on the subsequent purchaser.

This work is entirely fictitious and bears no resemblance to any persons living or dead.

Typeset in Garamond

Printed and bound in Great Britain by CPI Group (UK) Ltd, Croydon, CR0 4YY

ISBN 978 1912362 158

British Library Cataloguing in Publication Data.
A catalogue record for this book is available from the British Library.

*For my wife, Rachel, without whose love
and support nothing would be possible for me*

and

*To the memory of my oldest and dearest
friend, the late Professor David Casson,
for a lifetime of friendship and for
correcting most of my speling mistakes.*

Contents

A New Career	1
Mixed Fortunes	5
All Those Wasted Hours	8
The Man Who Was Not	13
À Propos Je Ne Sais Quoi	18
The Fire	22
A Window on the World	26
Recession and the Dog	30
To the Right of Genghis Khan	33
God's Hobby	38
Grace and Favour	42
The Principal	45
An Essential Skill	50
Murder in Colchester	55
Food, Glorious Food	57
Only Shakespeare?	62
Another Life	67
Deep Thoughts	70
A Curious Arrangement	73
The Case of Siggy Fraud	77
Sheer PAP	80
This Could Be Dangerous	83

A Case of Compulsive Digression	86
Success is Everything	89
A Calming Influence	92
A Desirable Property	95
Ups and Downs	101
A Helping Husband	104
Foreignisation of the Language	107
A Duty of Care	110
Sam Clemens's Disease	112
God's Greatest Hits	115
A Visit From the RSPCHP	119
Lenin, McTrotsky and the Revolution	124
I'm No Oxymoron	127
Never to Return	131
Very Special Education	137
The Servant Problem	140
History and All That	143
Eureka	146
A Case of Lingomalignus	150
The Rites of Rong	154
Luddites of the Modern World	157
Here's a How-de-doo!	160
Heavenly Thoughts	165
Heaven Forfend	170
How to Get Rich	173
Perfection	176
Caesar Answers	179
Purrfect Rapport	182
Truth Will Out	185
The Message	189
God's Direct Line	195
Tell Me Why	198
A Downside to Everything	201
Here's Looking at Euclid	204

A Secret Life	208
The Tearaway	214
What is This thing Called Love?	217
Fine Words Butter No Parsnips	221
Great Moments in History: How to Make Fire	224
Long Life	228
Lord of the Flies	232
Ewe and I	236
Insolence and Effrontery	239
Just Give Your Name	242
A First Glimpse of Second Sight	245
The Big Idea	248
Respect for the Aged	254
An Eventful Day	257
Life is What Happens	263
The Wreath Lectures	267
Catocracy	271
What About Tennis?	274
Ignarus Quaestio Repitito	278
Adam's Story	282
A Great Turn-Off	286
The Speed of Light	289
In His Image	292
Parents are People	295
Bilingual Dog	298
Fabian Memories	302
Rock-a-Bye Baby	305
Premium Bond	309
God's Lucky Day	314
Harry Stophanes and the Birds	318

A New Career

It all started with a visit to the celebrated physician, Dr Magnus Fell.

I started by outlining my problem very simply.

"I have what I suspect is a particularly rare condition. I do not have a dog."

"That is not at all rare," Dr Fell interrupted. "You have no need to worry about this at all. Lots of people don't have dogs. Many of them are very happy that way. You can live a very satisfactory life without owning a dog. On the other hand, if you suffer from not having a dog, the condition is easily curable. You can buy a dog."

"I don't want to buy a dog."

"As I say," he continued undeterred, "you don't have to have a dog. People without dogs can get along perfectly well. Many of them hold down responsible and well-paid jobs. Some of them do not even like dogs."

"I don't like dogs very much," I admitted.

"Then you are halfway cured," Dr Fell insisted.

"Perhaps you will let me describe my condition," I suggested tentatively, intimidated by his reputation.

"This could help," said the great man.

"I keep talking to him," I confessed.

"It is good to talk," said Dr Fell. "To whom do you talk?"

"To my dog," I replied guiltily.

"Lots of people talk to their dogs. When there is nobody else around, they find it helps to speak their thoughts aloud. It helps them to relax. Sometimes it helps them to talk about the things that are worrying them. Dogs look as if they understand you. They have very expressive faces. You need not worry about talking to your dog."

"You forget, doctor," I reminded him, "I do not have a dog."

"Ah," he commented meaningfully.

"You see why I am worried?" I continued. "I talk for hours on end to a dog who does not exist. I call him Caesar."

"Why is that?" Dr Fell asked.

"It's his name," I said helplessly.

"I still don't think you need to be too worried," said the good doctor. "You know that the dog exists only in your imagination."

"Of course."

"Then there is not really a problem. Lots of children invent imaginary characters. They talk to them, play games with them and involve them in their plans and dreams. No one has ever suggested there is anything wrong or abnormal about this. It is part of the process of growing up and of trying to make sense of the world."

"I am in my late fifties," I reminded him.

"There is nothing to be ashamed of in that."

"I am just pointing out that I am not a child trying to make sense of the world."

"But you do try to make sense of the world?" Dr Fell asked.

"Of course," I said. "Don't we all?"

"Indeed," he replied. "It's a bad business."

"My talking to my imaginary dog?"

"No," he said. "The world."

There was a pause, while I contemplated the state of present day society. It had not improved by the time we resumed speaking.

"There is something else," I said at last.

"There often is," he said sadly.

"It's not just that I speak to Caesar."

"To the dog you mean?"

"Yes, it is not just that I speak to the dog. He speaks to me."

"That's not so good. To talk to an imaginary dog is one thing. To have him reply is something else again."

"He can be quite entertaining company."

"Even worse."

"What should I do?"

"What does he talk about?"

"All sorts of things. The other day he was discussing cornaceous trees and shrubs."

"I beg your pardon."

"He was particularly interested in dogwood – a European shrub with clusters of small white flowers and black berries: the shoots are red in winter. It also grows in North America, where it has beautiful red autumn foliage."

"How very interesting."

"I thought so," I said. "Caesar's interest had been aroused by a nature programme he saw on television. I had to look it up in an encyclopaedia."

"What made you discuss this with the dog?"

"Oh, I didn't start the conversation," I replied. "I didn't see the TV programme. Caesar watched it and came into the kitchen, where I was preparing some food for him, and he told me about it."

"You were preparing food for an imaginary dog?"

"He gets hungry."

"And he told you about a TV programme you'd not seen?"

"Sometimes I think he watches too much television," I said.

Dr Fell eyed me suspiciously.

"Don't you believe me?" I asked feeling hurt.

"That he watches too much television?"

"No. Don't you believe what I have been telling you?"

"Believe you? Of course I believe you," he said expansively. "I don't earn a comfortable living from disbelieving my patients. Have you told anyone else about this?"

"Do you think I am mad?" I exclaimed.

He avoided the question.

"If you are implying that you have not told anyone else," he said, "then I consider that wise."

"You think they might misunderstand?" I suggested.

"There is a greater danger that they might not misunderstand," he said firmly.

I thought about this for a while.

"What shall I do?" I asked at last.

"Have you tried to give him up?"

"I don't think I could."

"Then I doubt if we can cure you," he declared. "The best we can hope for is to disguise the condition."

"I don't follow you," I said. "Am I ill?"

"It all depends what you mean by illness. Certainly it is not normal for a man of your years to converse with an imaginary dog. Have you ever written anything?"

"I used to write applications for jobs."

"I meant have you written anything creative?"

"My job applications were quite creative sometimes – and imaginative."

"That is the answer."

"I don't follow you," I confessed.

"You should take up creative writing. If you relate your conversations with Caesar in the guise of short stories or dialogues, you might manage to pass as almost normal."

"That is the nicest thing anyone has said to me for a long time," I said. "Do you really think I could manage to pass myself off as a creative type of person?"

"I don't see why not," said Dr Fell, "the dividing line between creativity and insanity is sometimes a very fine one."

Mixed Fortunes

Yet another anniversary of the birth of the great German humourist Karl Mix provides the excuse for a new biography. Georgio Fantasia's fascinating study draws on previously unknown correspondence with his great admirer, king of the Hollywood western, Tom (Grumpy) Mix. "From the moment I picked up your book until I put it down I was convulsed by laughter. Some day I intend reading it," wrote Tom of Karl's uproarious *Ee By Gum but It's Capital*. Although the two men never met, a close friendship was nurtured by the regular exchange of letters over a period of some twenty-five years. "He is a cousin," claimed Karl, "though not mine you understand."

Tom set a trend that was to last for more than a hundred years, as generation upon generation of earnest young men intended reading Karl's work and never did. Karl would become the least read best selling author in the world and his influence would turn humourists the world over into convinced Mixers.

It was Karl's partnership with Fred Dangles that first propelled him into the best-seller lists with the publication of their *Comedy Manifesto*, destined to be turned into the most successful soap opera in the history of radio or television. In Russia it would run for more than seventy years and indeed even today repeats are still being shown in Cuba and North Korea.

Tom's career meanwhile was flourishing. After winning a national riding and rodeo contest he had rapidly become the most popular comic cowboy in Hollywood. Known professionally as Grumpy, because that is how he was, he made one film after another. When particularly in demand, he reversed the process and made one film before another.

Tom of course had four famous sisters, one of whom, Millie – nicknamed Gumbo after her favourite food – was entirely unknown. The eldest, Leonora – known as Cheeky because that is what she was – appeared in many of Tom's films, famously tearing up her contract for *A Knight on Horseback at the Opera* because there was no clause giving her time off for Christmas. Karl was a great admirer. "I particularly liked the bit with the hard boiled eggs," he wrote. "Who would have guessed such things were possible?"

The second sister, Adolina – known as Harpy because that is what she was – had speaking parts in many of Tom's silent films and silent parts in many of his talkies. She was renowned as a talented horsewoman. "What Harpy can do on a horse has to be seen to be believed," wrote Tom. Owing to the censorship imposed by the Hays Code, her prowess was not to be recorded on film.

The last sister, Bertha, was known as Zexy because no one in the family could spell. After the premiere of *Destry Rides Again*, Tom wrote, "Zexy caused a sensation by turning up for the party dressed only in horse feathers."

Karl wrote back, "Horses don't have feathers."

"Think about it," replied Tom.

Karl now moved to London, setting up home in the reading room of the British Museum. After failing to arrange a meeting with Sidney – the World Wide – Webb, Karl departed for a meeting of the Comedy International. This was to prevent his attendance at Tom's wedding, which took place in the following week. Karl had found the proceedings so hilarious that he could not stop laughing for several days and was unable to travel. "If ever you get the opportunity to see Mickey Bakunin," he wrote, "don't miss it – pure anarchy."

Tom had never expected to marry. "Do you think you will ever find a wife?" Karl had asked him in one letter.

"I have found many," Tom replied, "but they always seem to belong to someone else. Also, I could never marry any woman who would accept me as a husband." This was before he met Lydia, the tattooed lady. "We are perfectly suited," he wrote to Karl. "She understands me and I can read her like a book."

By this time Karl, much to his annoyance, had been buried in Highgate cemetery. He had been picking flowers at the time. As so often, Fred Dangles came to his aid. "It was not the first time Fred has dug me out of a hole," he wrote to Tom.

"Don't blame the man who buried you," Tom replied, "He thought you were dead. How was he to know his watch had stopped?"

One of the strengths of Fantasia's book is in the way he compares the humour of these two great friends. Unlike Tom, Karl had a serious side and often wrote his sketches twice, the first time as tragedy and the second time as farce. Hardly known in his lifetime, he is now on the way to being completely forgotten. Tom on the other hand – or Grumpy as the present generation always think of him – has become increasingly popular since the release on video of his last film, *Snow White*, where he played a small part.

The book is full of small anecdotal asides. Among the more surprising is the revelation that Mickey Bakunin also got himself into films, after emigrating to the United States and changing his name to Mouse.

All Those Wasted Hours

"I realise now," I said after several glasses of wine, "I have wasted hours and hours tidying the house. It was quite unnecessary."

"How is that?" Lionel asked, continuing the vain attempt to balance his head steadily on the top of his neck.

"Well," I said, slurring my words in order to produce what I thought was an attractive drawl, "sometimes, in the evenings I clear the dishes, load the dishwasher, put away unwanted newspapers and books, and generally make everything shipshape." I paused. "Shouldn't that be houseshape?" I wondered aloud, as I got out of my chair and swayed around the room offering more wine to everyone except Cynthia, who would be driving home and was drinking coffee.

"S'no such word," Lionel told me authoritatively, while pushing his glass towards me. "There should be, but there isn't."

"Pity," I said. "Anyway," I continued, "the point is, sometimes this is what I do. Before we go to bed, I make sure everything is shipshape – it still seems a silly word, but there it is: that is what I do – and when I come down for breakfast in the morning, everything is clean and tidy."

"Good for you," Lionel muttered approvingly.

"That's what I thought – jolly good for me – but the point is, I don't do it every evening and, even when I don't, everything is still clean and tidy in the morning."

"That is because I do it," Emmeline pronounced indignantly.

"Do you?" I asked in surprise. "That is awfully good of you."

"You are impossible," she retorted.

"I have a wonderful wife," I told Lionel, "one in a million – she told me so herself."

"You don't deserve her," Cynthia interrupted.

As Cynthia views the world, no man deserves his wife. She discovered feminism late in life and promotes her extreme version with all the zealous commitment and intolerance of a convert. Cynthia is married to Lionel. I regard Lionel as one of my dearest friends; Emmeline – for reasons I find quite incomprehensible – is equally attached to Cynthia.

"And Lionel does not deserve you," I replied, slurring my words for greater effect. "He has always led a blameless life."

"I don't know how you put up with him," Cynthia said, turning to Emmeline. This was the usual way in which Cynthia communicated with me – through Emmeline, as if I were not there. It was extremely unusual for her to speak to me directly, as she had done a moment earlier.

Emmeline smiled sweetly at me; she is the most affectionate of wives.

"Nor do I," she replied to Cynthia.

Lionel meanwhile was concentrating on the liquid in his glass. "Have I?" he said.

There was a pause, while we all waited for him to finish his question. It was Cynthia who broke the silence.

"Have you what?"

"Have I led a blameless life?"

"You cannot expect a wife to know a thing like that," I intervened. Emmeline gave me a most unfriendly look, implying she would speak to me later.

"S'suppose not," Lionel muttered. "I used to play in goal, you know? Soccer. At school. Always got the blame when we lost. Nearly always lost. Not my fault really. Always got the blame. Good preparation for marriage."

"What are you implying?" Cynthia demanded imperiously.

"Just speaking generally. Not implying anything, old sport."

"I am not an old sport." This was said slowly and deliberately.

Lionel took a deep breath. He was about to speak. Then Emmeline spoilt it all. "I think we all need some coffee," she said and then, turning to Cynthia, "Would you like to give me a hand?"

The two of them disappeared into the kitchen.

Lionel slumped back in his armchair. "I suppose a man should always be ready to take the blame," he said after a brief pause. "It's fundamental to civilised society that a man takes responsibility for his own actions."

"And a woman?"

"Hardly ever. There is something unnatural about a woman taking responsibility for what she does. In the normal course of events it is not expected."

Disloyally, my mind turned to that morning, when Emmeline had gone to the shops with the specific purpose of returning a pair of shoes of unsuitable colour. She returned in less than an hour. It was an unsuccessful expedition. She had forgotten to take the shoes, which had been in a bag in the dining room. It was my fault. She had asked me to accompany her and I had said I was busy. That is what made her forget to pick up the bag. I had wasted her morning. How could I be so inconsiderate?

I did not mention this to Lionel. Instead, I told him his opinions would have been more suited to the nineteenth century, when the law recognised that a crime committed by a wife was the responsibility of her husband.

"That is taking things too far."

"Murder wasn't included."

"Even so, I wouldn't go for that. There is no saying where it might end."

"I suppose we should take the blame for our wives. After all, we married them."

"That is true," Lionel agreed, "but they married us, so it follows equally that our wives should take responsibility for us."

"And so we do," said Emmeline coming back into the room carrying cups and saucers on a tray. "I doubt you would survive without us."

"Nonsense!" I exclaimed with unthinking bravado. "I, for one, could be totally self-sufficient – if I wished."

Cynthia had brought the coffeepot and heard this. She turned to Emmeline and whispered loudly enough for us all to hear, "You have no excuse now."

"No. I haven't, have I?"

Emmeline smiled mysteriously, as she poured coffee for all of us.

I have learned to be wary of Emmeline's mysterious smiles. I sipped my coffee in silence. Why should Emmeline need an excuse? I was not going to ask. I recognised an incipient threat. Perhaps, if I kept quiet, it would go away.

"When were you last in Paris?" Cynthia was addressing Emmeline.

"Not for years. The last time was soon after we got married. I always meant to return."

"Now is your opportunity. It is beautiful in April."

Emmeline looked at me thoughtfully. "Why not?" she smiled.

"Sorry," I said. "I have several people I promised to see throughout April. I couldn't possibly get away."

Cynthia gave me the kind of look she might bestow on an injured dog.

"You'll be busy then?" Emmeline asked.

"Very."

"Good. Then you will not miss me."

"Why should I miss you?"

"Because I am going to Paris."

"You can't do that," I said in a tone of mystification.

"Why on earth not? It is not as if you are not able to look after yourself. You said you could be self-sufficient. Here is your opportunity to practice it. I am going to have a holiday."

Lionel, to my extreme annoyance, seemed to find this very funny. "Careless talk costs lives," he said chortling.

"I don't see the joke," I said sternly. "In any case," I said, addressing Emmeline once more, "you cannot go for a holiday to Paris on your own."

"Quite right," Lionel laughed. "You put your foot down."

"Yes," Emmeline agreed disarmingly. "He is quite right. I couldn't possibly go alone. I won't go alone."

"Good," I said. "That settles that."

"I never intended to go alone," Emmeline said meekly. "I am going with Cynthia."

Lionel stopped laughing.

The Man Who Was Not

This is the story of a young man who woke up one morning to find he did not exist. He got out of bed in the usual way, stretched his arms above his head, bent down to touch his toes and then looked in the mirror. There was no sign of him. All he could see was the wall behind his head and one chair. His first thought was that he was dreaming. He turned his head toward the bed. He was not lying in it. The bed was empty and showed no signs of anyone having slept in it that night.

He went into the bathroom, showered quickly, checked his wardrobe, selected his clothes and got dressed. He took his wallet, small change and keys from the bedside table and put them in his pockets. He put on his watch and looked in the mirror once more. He was not there. At least he might have expected to see his clothes but there was nothing, just the furniture and wall. He wondered if his clothes disappeared when he put them on and went to the wardrobe to find an item he could hold up to the mirror. The wardrobe was empty. He looked around the room again. There was a bed, though not the one he had slept on and covered by a quilt he had never seen. There was a wardrobe that was not his and was not that from which he had chosen his clothes only a few moments earlier. There was also an empty chest of drawers. There were no personal effects and no sign of occupation. There was no bedside table.

He returned to the bathroom. It looked as he had found it when they first moved to the house – old cast iron bath with shower attachment, large cracked white tiles and lavatory in a separate room. There was no sign of recent use.

He checked his wallet. His money was intact, as were his credit cards with his name, Fabian Beale. Reassured, he descended the stairs and entered the morning room. He found it as always, with the table ready laid for breakfast. After Lucy had left him, he had determined to tidy up each night before he went to bed and to lay the table ready for the morning. It would have been so easy to lapse into casual squalor, had he not imposed strict discipline upon himself. Having a routine for all the things needing to be done about the house was important. He filled the electric kettle with water and switched it on to boil. He took a bottle of milk from the refrigerator and placed it on the table.

He went to the front door to collect the morning newspaper. It had not been delivered. It was nearly nine o'clock. It was absurd he should pay extortionate delivery charges if the paper was not to arrive in time to be read while he consumed his breakfast. Recently, it had been arriving late more and more. He waited for the kettle to boil and then made himself a cup of instant coffee. Then he took his address book from the sideboard, looked up the telephone number of the newsagent, picked up the telephone and dialled.

"My newspaper hasn't arrived," he said, after the usual introductory remarks.

"I am very sorry. I'll try to check. What name did you say?"

"Beale."

"Address?"

He gave his address. There was a pause.

"I am very sorry," came the voice, "we don't seem to have any record of your name or address."

"No record?"

"No. Are you sure you are on to the right newsagent?"

"Of course I am sure."

"Well, we don't seem to have any record. Perhaps you could come in to the shop to sort it out."

He made some unintelligible reply and put the telephone back on its stand. He finished his coffee and decided he did not want to eat anything.

"I'll wash up later," he thought, and went into the hallway to fetch his anorak. He put it on and was about to go out of the front door, when he remembered a book he needed to take back to the library. He would have time to take it in after work. He returned to the morning room, which had now changed beyond recognition. Gone were his oak sideboard, table and chairs – in their place, a Formica-topped kitchen table, three bentwood chairs and a Welsh dresser that had seen better days. An old man sat at the table, huddled over a copy of the *Daily Mail* and clutching a mug of tea. The smell of frying bacon wafted in from the kitchen, from whence soon emerged a small, dark, elderly woman, wearing a tattered housecoat.

"The bacon will be ready in a minute," she announced, looking at and through Fabian, before turning her attention to the old man.

"Who are you?" Fabian blurted out.

"Don't overcook it," the man muttered in a tired voice.

"Do you want it raw?" she replied angrily, again looking in Fabian's direction. "Who's your friend?" she said.

"I'm not his friend," Fabian said.

"I won him in a raffle," the man replied, "at the club."

The woman walked past Fabian. Stopping at the dresser, she picked up a child's teddy bear. "Just what you need."

Fabian withdrew into the hallway and towards the front door.

From the end of his road, he caught a bus, which dropped him outside his office door – except that now it was not there.

To be precise, the office was there but instead of *Fabian Beale – Mortgage Adviser*, the sign on the door proclaimed *Newlook Design Services*. The lights were on. Fabian opened the door and went in.

"Can I help you?" A young, smartly dressed young woman addressed him.

"I was looking for someone else," Fabian mumbled.

"I beg your pardon?"

"I thought this office belonged to a different organisation."

"You must have the wrong address. We have been here five years."

Five years. It was little more than five years since Fabian had started his business here.

"Have you heard of Fabian Beale, the mortgage adviser?" he asked.

"Sorry. I can't help."

Fabian retraced his steps, descending the stairs from the first floor office. Larry Warman, who occupied offices on the second floor, was coming in the other direction.

"Excuse me," Fabian said as they drew level, "have you ever seen me before?"

Larry stopped and looked at him carefully. "I don't think so. Should I have done?"

"I don't know." Fabian shook his head sadly and moved on. He had known Larry since University days; they were regular tennis partners.

To the left of the front door, just inside the building, there was a large mirror. Fabian looked for his image. There was no reflection.

Outside, he hailed a taxi and travelled uneventfully to Jason Square. He stepped out of the taxi and examined his wallet to pay the fare. When he looked up, the taxi was gone. He shook his head woefully and, replacing a ten-pound note in the wallet, noticed that his credit cards and all identifying documents were now missing. He entered the bank and approached a desk, where a receptionist sat.

"I have an appointment to see the Manager at ten-thirty. I am afraid I am a little early. Is there any chance he can see me now?"

The receptionist, who was new to him, smiled brightly.

"Mr Beale, did you say? I'll go and see." She returned a few moments later. "There doesn't seem to be any note of an appointment. I am afraid Mr Loomis is busy, but Mr Nightingale, the Deputy Manager is free. Would you like to see him?"

"I am sure he can help."

The receptionist led the way to a small office. A tall youngish man stood up as he entered and offered his hand. "Frank Nightingale."

"Fabian Beale." Fabian had not before had occasion to meet the Deputy Manager, though he knew his reputation as an efficient high-flyer tipped for early promotion.

"Please take a seat. Now, what can I do for you?"

"I am thinking of expanding my business. I want to discuss my overdraft limit."

"I see. Where is your account held?"

"Here."

"Here? Fabian Beale did you say?" Frank Nightingale turned to the computer on his desk. He appeared to be checking the database. After a few moments he looked up with a puzzled expression. "Are you sure your account is with this bank?"

"Of course I am."

"Well, according to our records you do not exist."

Frank Nightingale looked up from his desk and examined the empty room. There was a knock on the door and Maurice entered.

"Are you busy? I wanted a word."

"Yes, come in. It is a funny day. I haven't seen a soul all morning."

À Propos Je Ne Sais Quoi

(A Consultation from the Casebook of Dr Magnus Fell)

- Bonjour Dr Fell.
- *Good morning. What brings you to me?*
- I was hoping we could have a tête-à-tête about my condition. I am sure you will be simpatico.
- *I shall try. Tell me about it.*
- You may know that I am a member of an organisation, the raison d'être of which is the promotion of good English. I have long been regarded as the organisation's enfant terrible, my particular bête noire being the use of foreign words and phrases. Recently, however, I have been using them myself – ad nauseam. My bona fides is being questioned and I am in danger of being declared persona non grata.
- *Are you able to compose a sentence not containing a foreign word or phrase?*
- That I cannot is a source of considerable angst. I am beginning to wonder if I am quite compos mentis.
- *No, you are quite sane but you do appear to be suffering from lingua franca internationale.*
- I am au fait with the name. I am told that my babushka suffered from the same complaint.

- *Your grandmother, really? The condition is not thought to be hereditary. It is probably just a coincidence but you had better tell me something about her. How well did you know your grandmother?*

- She was one of the nouveaux riches in the years after the First World War and was considered a femme fatale among the beau monde. She associated with the crème de la crème, enjoyed la dolce vita but then had a torrid affaire de coeur, left my zeider...

- *Your grandfather?*

- Yes, she left him and was involved in a ménage à trois with a famous artist and his model. My zeider was a mensch...

- *A man of integrity and honour?*

- Indeed: he felt that revenge was de rigueur and, in a fit of rage, he shot the artist. It became quite a cause célèbre.

- *What happened?*

- The artist, who by the way was a real schlemiel, recovered. I don't think I mentioned it but the shooting took place in la belle France. French juries are, or were, often sympathetic to the crime passionnel and my zeider was acquitted.

- *And what happened to your grandmother?*

- The artist would have nothing more to do with her and so she sought a rapprochement with my zeider.

- *Did he take her back?*

- He said she had chutzpah to ask him and he never wanted to see her again. The last anyone in the family heard of her, she had become a chanteuse, singing songs with rather risqué lyrics in nightclubs that were not quite kosher.

- *It's a sad story.*

- C'est la vie.

- *It is very interesting but I don't think it could have any bearing on your case.*

- Prima facie, what do you think could have started me off like this?

- *Have you had anything worrying you?*

- Au contraire. I have had an annus mirabilis. My wife presented

19

me with a new bambino; my magnum opus on the history of La Belle Époque has been accepted for publication and my income per annum has virtually doubled.

- *I did know that you have had several books published but I have never seen your name in print.*

- I write under a nom de plume.

- *I should have guessed.*

- I don't write for the hoi polloi but my books are highly regarded by the cognoscenti.

- *We don't seem to be getting anywhere.*

- I can see that we are in a cul-de-sac but this is a cri de coeur. If things don't return to the status quo ante – and pronto – my career will be kaputt. Already some of my colleagues are beginning to regard me as a dummkopf.

- *Tell me about your diet. The food we eat can often explain the most unexpected things.*

- I have to confess to being something of a bon vivant, with a particular liking for cordon bleu cooking. I am very fond of a rather chic French restaurant near my home – not far from the palais de danse – where they have a superb à la carte menu and a delicious range of hors d'oeuvres.

- *Ah!*

- I used to go also to a rather avant-garde Italian place in the City, where they served an escalope de veau par excellence. Recently I find it has become somewhat outré and to go there would be rather infra dig, though I must say that it is still frequented by the paparazzi.

- *I see. I take it you had a classical education?*

- Yes, I am an alumnus of both Eton and Oxford.

- *I should have spotted it earlier. I know of one other case of lingua franca internationale brought on by an excess of foreign food overlaying an education in the classics.*

- Sacré bleu.

- *I shall have to put you on a diet.*

- Do you mean you will put me en route for a cure: you can restore my joie de vivre?

- *If you follow my instructions.*

- You have carte blanche to lay down the rules as you wish.

- *It is very simple. You must stick firmly to simple English food – no foreign food whatsoever – and avoid restaurants where the menu is written in French. You will also have to give up all foreign wines.*

- Not even a soupçon of Cabernet Sauvignon? Ah well, que será será. Is it wise for me to try to carry on with my normal routine, or should I remain incommunicado for a while?

- *Just carry on as usual. Come back and see me in three weeks' time and we will see how you are getting along. Good luck.*

- Au revoir. Tempus fugit.

- *Sayonara.*

The Fire

Scene 1

THE RECEPTION ROOM IS EMPTY, SAVE FOR THE RECEPTIONIST SITTING AT A BENCH BEHIND A HALF-OPEN GLASS SCREEN.

THE OUTSIDE DOOR IS FLUNG OPEN. A MAN RUSHES INTO THE RECEPTION ROOM.

Man   Help! My house is on fire.
Receptionist   The doctor will see you now.

THE MAN LOOKS WILDLY ABOUT HIM AND STUMBLES THROUGH ANOTHER DOOR LABELLED "DOCTOR".

Scene 2

THE DOCTOR, SITTING BEHIND HIS DESK, LOOKS UP AS THE MAN ENTERS.

THROUGHOUT THE SCENE, THE MAN BECOMES INCREASINGLY MANIC, WHILE THE DOCTOR SPEAKS QUIETLY, SLOWLY AND DELIBERATELY.

Man Help! My house is on fire.
Doctor Good morning. Please take a seat.

THE MAN HESITATES, THEN PERCHES HIMSELF ON THE TIP OF THE CHAIR IN FRONT OF THE DOCTOR'S DESK.

Doctor That is it. Make yourself comfortable. Now, tell me all about it.
Man My house is burning down.
Doctor I see. You think your house is burning down.
Man It is burning down.
Doctor And what makes you think so?
Man The flames. There are flames everywhere.
Doctor I see. Flames. And you associate these flames with a fire?
Man And smoke. Smoke is pouring out from all the windows.
Doctor Smoke as well? How interesting. Can you say for how long this has been going on?
Man I don't know. I was coming home from the shops, when I saw the flames. It was just a few minutes ago.
Doctor And you felt nothing before that?
Man Why should I?
Doctor Just so.
Man Please, you must hurry. This is an emergency.
Doctor You feel it is urgent something is done?
Man Of course.
Doctor Do you often feel this sense of urgency?
Man I don't think so.
Doctor And why do you suppose it is different now?
Man Because my house is on fire.
Doctor I see. Has this ever happened before?
Man What? Has what happened before?
Doctor Have you ever before had the feeling the house was burning down?
Man I have never had a fire before.

Doctor Not even a small one? In the kitchen, perhaps?

Man No.

Doctor How about in the garden? Burning rubbish? Guy Fawkes night?

Man Not for years and years. Why on earth is this important?

Doctor That is what we are trying to find out. Do you miss not having fires in the garden?

Man No, not at all. Don't you understand? My house is burning down.

Doctor I hear what you say. I understand perfectly. Has this ever happened to anyone else in your family? Parents? Brothers or sisters? Uncles or aunts?

Man Does this matter?

Doctor Family history can often be very significant. Has anything like this ever happened to any member of your family?

Man My great aunt was bombed out during the second-world war.

Doctor Excellent. Now we have something to get hold of. Did you know your great aunt?

Man Not very well. I was still very young when she died. My parents told me about it.

Doctor So you don't feel guilty about not being there to help?

Man How could I?

Doctor Just so.

Man Are we just going to sit here?

Doctor It is the way I usually work. Why? Do you want to lie down?

Man Of course not.

Doctor Just as I thought. The important thing is for you to relax.

Man How can you expect me to relax when my house is burning down?

Doctor You have to try, if we are to get to the root of all this.

Man There isn't any root. All you need to understand is that my house is being destroyed by fire.

Doctor Things are not always as simple as they seem. These days we try to treat problems holistically – to deal not only with the physical manifestation but, also, with the psychological needs underlying it.

Man I don't know what you are talking about.

Doctor Not to put too fine a point on it: why did you need a fire?

Man Need a fire? Why in heaven's name should I need a fire? All my possessions, all my business records are in the house.

Doctor Ah!

THERE IS A LONG PAUSE, WHILE THE MAN AND THE DOCTOR STARE AT EACH OTHER INTENTLY.

Man Are you accusing me of arson?

Doctor My dear sir, I accuse you of nothing. I am a doctor not a policeman. Now, think very carefully before you answer this question. Have you told anyone else about this?

Man I didn't have to. There was a great crowd watching from the other side of the street. As soon as I saw what was happening, I came straight to you.

Doctor That was probably the wisest thing you could do. But you have not consulted me before. Why did you come to me rather than to your regular doctor?

Man I live next door.

Doctor Ah.

THE SOUND OF FALLING MASONRY CAN BE HEARD. IT GROWS LOUDER. PART OF THE WALL TO THE SIDE OF THE DOCTOR'S DESK COLLAPSES. FIRE AND SMOKE CAN BE SEEN.

A Window on the World

At school, we used to make jokes about it. Imagine my surprise, then, when I read about the new degree in Fenestrology at the University of Duffborough. I telephoned for information; I could hardly wait to get hold of the Prospectus. I had to wait. In spite of a promise to send it the next day by first class post, it took two weeks to reach me.

"Fenestrology: A Window on the World," it announced. Fenestrology, I soon learned, amalgamates a wide range of disciplines. It allows one to look through the great walls, which stand between the Arts, the Sciences and the Social Sciences, as well as those between theoretical and practical studies. Art and Architecture, Physics and History, Building Science and Mathematics, Religion and Domestic Science: all of these and other studies are brought together in this new and exciting degree programme – the first of its kind in the world.

I wrote for an interview and, three weeks later, found myself in the office of the Director of Studies, John Casement. I had explained I was a writer and wanted to publish an article about the new Course.

"We always welcome publicity," he told me.

I nodded.

"I don't think I have heard your name before."

"How interesting," I said enigmatically. "Has no one previously offered a course in Fenestrology?"

"Duffborough is at the cutting edge of academic innovation."

"So you have practicals in glass cutting," I joked.

"Naturally," he replied seriously, "also in glazing and window cleaning. There is even a module dealing with the problems of cleaning the windows of high-rise buildings. We use our own tower block to practise."

I asked how the idea for the Course arose.

"You may see Fenestrology simply as the study of windows," Professor Casement replied, having decided to follow his own agenda for the meeting. "We see it as the ultimate unifying discipline, encompassing elements of all branches of knowledge. In Chemistry we study the techniques of glass manufacture. In Physics we examine the physical properties of different kinds of glass, their refractive qualities, their tensile strengths. Art and Architecture are, of course, at the core of our studies, with Architecture leading on to Mathematics and Engineering. The importance of windows in Church architecture must not be forgotten. Windows thus have a significant place in religious worship and so we study Religion. As you know, the very word Fenestrology comes from the Latin word for window, *fenestra*, and is closely related to the French *la fenêtre* and to the Welsh *ffenestr*, so we have to study foreign languages, both modern and classical, with particular reference to the links between Celtic and Latin. The Francophile wing of the Department, still feel the subject should be called Fenetrology rather than Fenestrology, while there was even a rather silly proposal that the name should be spelt Ffenestrology. It is an area of academic dispute in which feelings run quite high. I have written a paper on it myself, which will appear next month in *The Journal of Languages – Ancient and Modern*."

"It is quite a list of subjects," I commented.

"There is no end of them."

"Economics?" I suggested playfully.

"Do you not recall the Window Tax, levied in England between 1695 and 1851? Its abolition was linked to the Public Health movement and brings us on to important elements of Economic and Social History. We also look at the economics of double-glazing, which brings us on to matters of energy conservation and environmental matters generally."

"Psychology?" I asked tentatively.

"Another major area of study. Have you ever thought about how people are affected by living or working in rooms without windows? We have a special subject in Part Two of the Course dealing with modern retailing and the ways workers in shopping malls are affected by spending all their working lives in areas totally devoid of natural light. Elsewhere, we discuss how the window provides an analogy for the Jungian concepts of extroversion and introversion. A window allows you to look out at all of Nature's wonders, but it allows you also to look in. The views are entirely different."

"There must be some academic studies not encompassed by Fenestrology," I suggested. "Geography?"

"Another core subject. You realise how much architectural styles vary around the world. Differences in climate were very important. Our module on Archaeology explains it. A window is simply an opening to let in light and air. From the earliest times, such openings were filled with stone or wood. Later there were iron grills. In ancient Egypt, windows were covered with matting: the Romans used panes of glass; in the Far East windows were covered with paper."

Professor Casement went on to explain the place of English Literature in Fenestrology. "Nineteenth century heroines are always sitting under a window sewing or reading." This year's Literature lectures would also cover E. M. Forster's *A Room with a View* and J. M. Barrie's *A Window in Thrums*. Thrums was Barrie's home town, where he grew up. Film Studies analysed

Fritz Lang's *The Woman in the Window* and, of course, Hitchcock's *Rear Window*.

"Surely there is some discipline you don't take in?"

"I think not," the professor replied.

"Sociology?"

"Not a discipline," he asserted grandly, "more of an indiscipline, if you ask me."

"Computing?"

"Obviously."

"Law," I suggested finally.

"Covered in our lectures on Crime and Punishment. Thieves often gain access to homes, shops and offices through windows. Cars are broken into through windows. We study the nature of these crimes and the appropriate deterrents and punishments. Often the thief is a mere child, which brings us into the realms of Family Law, Social Service provision and Education. We look also at prevention – the use of safety glass and toughened glass – which brings us back to design and technology." Professor Casement said he hoped I could now see that not only did Fenestrology cover all areas of genuine academic study but provided a window of opportunity through which they could be integrated. Where Duffborough led, other Universities were sure to follow.

Editor's note: Since this article was written, Professor Casement has been dismissed from the University and the course has been cancelled. The Vice-Chancellor – Dai Evans, previously head of the Social Science Faculty – has refused to comment.

Recession and the Dog

"Stop making that noise," I yelled at Caesar. "I am trying to read."

"And I am trying to find something I lost," barked Caesar, continuing to forage under the furniture and pushing aside anything that got in his way.

"What have you lost?" I sighed.

"I don't remember, but I'll know it when I find it."

"That is ridiculous. Go and play somewhere else and leave me in peace."

"You are very grumpy today," he growled.

It seems to me there is something profoundly wrong with a world in which your dog can tell you are being grumpy, and I told him so in no uncertain manner. I concluded my remarks by telling him he should show more respect to his master.

Have you ever seen a look of incredulity on the face of a dog? It is wondrous to behold and not a little disconcerting.

"You are suffering from recession," he told me.

"What are you talking about?"

"I heard all about it on television." – He watches too much television. – "You are not into a depression yet but you are deeply recessed."

"People can't be recessed. It is economies that go into recession, not people."

"Aren't economies what you make when you buy me those cheaper tins of dog food?"

"Yes, but that is not what I am talking about."

"What are you talking about? You don't seem to be able to explain yourself very clearly."

"I don't really expect a dog to understand," I said witheringly. "Just go away and leave me in peace."

"I don't like to do that. I would be shirking my responsibilities."

"Really?" I said coldly. "And what responsibilities do you think you have?"

"Someone has to look after you, particularly when you are not feeling well."

"I am feeling perfectly well. At least, I was feeling perfectly well until you started to irritate me with all your noise and your nonsense."

"If I am responsible for your not being well, it must be my responsibility to look after you."

"I am perfectly well," I shouted. "I do not need looking after. I never need looking after by you. You wouldn't have the foggiest idea how to look after someone who needed looking after."

"I still think you are recessed."

"That is because you are a very stupid dog." I should not have said that. Caesar looked crestfallen. The truth hurts. "I don't know why I waste my time talking to you," I continued.

"Well you will never find another dog you can have a conversation with."

This was the first sensible thing he had said, even though he did end his sentence with a preposition. I wish it were a habit I could get him out of.

He looked at me sadly for a few moments, then turned away and resumed his search for he knew not what. Now he did it more quietly and I was able to get back to what I had been about to read – a review of a book called "How Not to Write a Novel." That is easy, I thought. Don't write it. Don't even think about it.

Certainly don't start to write it. It is not as if writing a novel is something that happens to you when you are not expecting it. You don't wake up after taking a nap in the middle of the day and find you have already written half a chapter. A book on how not to get electrocuted when changing a light bulb would be more useful. It might be a very short book, I thought. Probably it would need to be padded out with chapters on how not to do a few other things. A yelp from Caesar disturbed my reverie.

"Help me out," he called. "I'm stuck." He had climbed into a gap between the sideboard and the study wall.

"I've got it," he panted. "I knew I would find it." There was a moment of quiet. "I can't get out."

I could just see his head. He had a small rubber duck in his mouth. Somehow he had managed to get into a space from which he was unable to extricate himself.

"I think I am in a recession," he said.

To the Right of Genghis Khan

Clifford had said something quite outrageous, politically that is; it was not unusual.

"You really are to the right of Genghis Khan," I said, with my customary show of originality.

"You may not approve but it matters not; your approval is of no worth," he said imperiously. "You see, I know what I am talking about, while your opinions seem to be a product of ignorance unsullied by learning of any kind."

"That is no way to talk to anyone," I reprimanded him, "least of all an old friend."

"On the contrary, you can talk to someone like that, only when you have known him for more than forty years and went to school with him. One can say what one likes to old friends; that is one of the joys of growing old."

I had to admit there was a grain of truth in this.

"Of course it is true," he persisted. "If it were not so, you would have taken umbrage at what I said and would have walked out on me."

"I hardly think I would have walked out," I said. "It is my house."

Clifford coughed and admitted this was a fair observation. "You are probably correct in your analysis. It must be a pleasant and novel experience."

"You are at it again," I complained. "You really must stop it."

"I quite agree. We should get back to the matter in hand."

"What matter in hand?"

"The fact that you don't know what you are talking about."

"I may not always know what you are talking about, which I suppose gives us something in common," I paused for effect, "but I don't put words together just because they sound nice. If I say something, I mean it and I know what I mean."

"Patently untrue," Clifford declared. "You just said I was to the right of Genghis Khan."

"A witty and accurate observation."

"In terms of wit," Clifford said sadly, "the remark was well up to your usual standard."

"That bad?"

"I am afraid so."

I took this seriously. Clifford would not joke about such matters.

"Now let us examine the accuracy of your statement," he continued.

"Obviously true," I said happily. Your politics are a joke."

"Where does Genghis Khan come into it?"

"It's just an expression."

"Ah," he said meaningfully. "Just an expression."

"It means your politics are so far to the right as to be a caricature of conservative thinking."

"Why does it mean that?"

"Because that is what it means. You might as well ask why 'a table' means a table."

"Ah," he said again. When Clifford says "Ah," it sounds both sinister and threatening. "You don't know," he continued. "Why right? Why not left, or up or down?"

"Ah," I said. It sounds quite different when I say it, altogether softer and more passive. "Shall I make some coffee?" Such deft changes of subject always divert Clifford and make him lose the thread of his argument.

"Why not leeward or windward, or wet or dry, or long or short?" he continued, shaking his head. "I presume you are not admitting that conservative means right, in the sense of correct."

"It is a traditional meaning."

"I shall put you out of your misery," Clifford said generously. "The terms left and right originated in the French National Assembly of 1789. The Nobles took up what they regarded as the position of honour on the President's right; the Third Estate, that is not the nobility or the clergy, sat on his left."

"Oh, I knew that," I said. Clifford raised his eyebrows. "I used to know it."

"It had slipped, what you are pleased to call, your mind," he prompted.

"It is a small point. Would you like the coffee now?"

"I haven't finished with you yet," he replied. "You still haven't told me about Genghis Khan."

"Do I have to?"

"You brought him into the conversation. The least you can do is tell me why. I suppose you think he was a member of the French National Assembly in 1789."

"Now you are being silly. Everyone knows Genghis Khan was a Mongrel emperor."

Clifford gave me a wicked smile. "I can see you are an expert," he said. "I suppose you think he lived in Barking and was President of the Canine Defence League. He was a Mongol emperor."

"That is what I said," I declared, with an absence of truth.

"When did he live?"

"A long time ago," I replied confidently.

"How long?"

"Are you sure you wouldn't like some coffee?"

"I would like some coffee very much," Clifford answered, "and while you are making it, you can prepare to tell me why you think Genghis Khan was to the right of the political spectrum."

I retired into the kitchen, where I measured two heaped

teaspoons of ground coffee into a filter paper, filled the machine with water and pressed the electric switch to start the filtering process. I put two cups on a tray and waited for the coffee to be ready. Meanwhile, I took stock of all I knew about the Mongol emperor. I put the jug on the tray and rejoined Clifford in the lounge.

"Well?" he said.

"He lived in Mongolia," I said. "He was an emperor. It was a very long time ago," I added, elaborating on my previous answer."

"Is that all you know about Genghis Khan?" Clifford fumed.

"Many people get by on less," I suggested. "Oh, yes, and he was very much to the right politically."

"He was born in 1162, give or take a few years, and died in 1227," Clifford told me, as I poured the coffee – black for both of us.

"You are merely putting an academic gloss on what I have already said."

"He created a Mongol empire that stretched from the Adriatic Sea to the Pacific coast of China," Clifford continued.

"Quite correct," I said approvingly.

"His original name was Temujin. He was proclaimed Genghis Khan in 1206. The name probably meant Universal Ruler."

"How interesting," I yawned.

"Both as a military leader and as a ruler, he was considered to have been of genius."

I perked up. "A man of genius? You mean he was not right wing?"

"He was certainly vengeful and cruel to his enemies, though perhaps not more than was normal for the times. He was also adaptable, a man who learned and developed. He changed the world. His conquering armies found more advanced civilisations and from these brought to the empire both law and an alphabet. In many ways he was a reformer."

I had to admit this was all new to me and that my knowledge of Genghis Khan had left much to be desired.

"Fortunately," said Clifford generously, "you have one saving grace."

"Really?" I asked, surprised by such commendation.

"Certainly," he said. "You serve excellent coffee."

God's Hobby

"I have a bone to pick with you," I said to God one day.

He sighed a long celestial sigh.

"It is about these weeds," I explained.

"Which weeds?" He asked in a tired sort of way and with no show of interest.

"In my garden. I pulled them all out last week and now you have put them all back again."

"Do you think I have nothing better to do than plant weeds in your garden?"

Actually, I had been thinking more of the way He designed things but, now He had raised the matter, I was prepared to say what I really thought.

"If you put it that way," I said, "I suppose you haven't got anything better to do."

"You forget yourself," He roared with empyrean grandeur.

"Don't get me wrong," I said. "It is just that since you retired…"

"Retired?" He roared. The earth moved.

"Yes," I continued bravely – I can be quite brave at times – "I thought that since you retired, you didn't seem to have much to do. I suppose planting weeds might be some sort of distraction for someone like you."

"Poor foolish mortal, do you not realise my work is never done? I shall never retire."

"But you do stop from time to time. I seem to remember you rested on the seventh day. I suppose you were tired?"

"I am the Almighty. I never tire."

"Oh, you don't have to be defensive about it. If you did get tired from time to time, there would be nothing to be ashamed of. It would be perfectly natural."

"For you it would be natural. I am supernatural," He reminded me.

"Still," I said, "there are times when you are not working. What do you do with yourself?"

"I keep busy. As someone who thinks he can write stories, you are supposed to have a bit of imagination. What do you suppose I do?"

This rather put me on the spot. I did not want to offend Him, which might be risky. He can be quite violent at times, smiting this one and that one with gay abandon.

"I suppose you have to listen to all those prayers," I hazarded.

"You cannot imagine how dull so many of them are," He said sorrowfully.

"It's your own fault," I told Him bluntly, "you encourage it."

"I suppose I do, but it is too late. There is nothing I can do about it now." This from an omnipotent God.

"Never mind," I suggested, "it may be boring but it doesn't sound like very hard work. You only have to listen. It is not as if you actually do anything."

"It has been known."

"Yes but not recently, otherwise the world might not be in the mess it is."

"Your problem," God told me, "is that you have no religion. You have no sense of wonder at the mysteries of the universe I created. You have no gratitude for the wonders of existence. You are entirely negative in your approach to life. Where others praise me for my work, you are forever finding fault. Others give thanks for the magnificence of creation; you offer only petty criticism."

I did not think this was fair. I always try to be constructive.

"Everyone needs a little criticism," I told Him.

"I am not everyone," He boomed, as I found myself thrown to the ground with considerable force. "I am your God."

Really! I never knew anyone more status conscious. It makes normal conversation almost impossible. Sometimes I wonder why I bother with Him.

"I am only thinking of your good," I said, picking myself up. "You should relax more. You should get yourself a hobby."

"A hobby? And what sort of a hobby do you think would be appropriate for Him, the creator of all things?"

Now He was talking of himself in the third person. Julius Caesar used to write about himself in the third person. I wondered if either of them had influenced the other. Probably not. I don't think they were acquainted.

"How about philately?" I suggested. "I mean, you get around. You could probably get stamps from nearly everywhere."

"And what would I do with a stamp collection?"

"God knows," I said carelessly.

"I see you are learning."

"It doesn't have to be stamp collecting," I said. "I suppose any solitary activity would be OK."

"Solitary?"

"You couldn't exactly play competitive golf."

"I suppose not. It would not be fair."

I had never before known Him show any concern for matters of fairness, but I let it pass.

"No, it would have to be something you could do on your own. Do you read much?"

"It is not necessary."

I had forgotten He is omniscient. I supposed, in a way, not

having to read was a bit like not being able to read. It certainly limited his options.

"It does," He agreed.

"Do you really have no hobbies?"

"I admit I do go in for a little landscape gardening from time to time."

So that is how He thinks of earthquakes and volcanic eruptions. But I am sure He has another hobby – planting weeds in my garden.

Grace and Favour

Emmeline does not blame me for everything.

"I have never said you were responsible for the Vietnam war," she said generously, "nor for the decline of British shipbuilding."

I was pleased to be exonerated. Vietnam had been weighing on my mind. It had been a bad show.

"I do however blame you for the state of the garden," she continued.

"I haven't been near the garden for months," I said defensively.

"Exactly." Emmeline was triumphant.

"You should blame the gardener," I said.

"We haven't got a gardener."

"Exactly," I affirmed smugly. "That is where all the trouble begins."

"The garden is your responsibility," Emmeline informed me.

"Are you sure?"

"Of course."

"I have never seen it in writing."

"What are you talking about?" She was beginning to lose patience.

"Is it contractual?"

"Yes," she snapped.

"Show me," I challenged. "I never signed anything to do with gardens. I deny any obligation. I shall fight it in the highest court in the land. With whom is this contract supposed to have been made?"

"With me," Emmeline answered.

"I don't recall seeing anything like that," I answered thoughtfully, "let alone signing it."

"It wasn't written down, in so many words. It was implicit; it was part of the whole deal."

"What deal?"

"Marriage," she said.

"We didn't have a garden, when we got married," I objected. "We lived in a flat."

"You are impossible," she said irritably, closing the conversation.

There was work to be done. I sat down at my desk and studied the coloured fish swimming across the screen of the computer. They were no more interesting than usual. I nudged the mouse and the fish were replaced by a single sentence of text. *The secret of a happy marriage,* I had written, *is mutual support and understanding.* Well, I thought, it is a start, not a very funny one but that might come later. The important thing was to get started. After that it was just a matter of determined application.

I looked out of the window. The sun was shining and I could see several birds sitting in the branches of the apple tree. I stood up, pushed the net curtain aside and inspected the garden. I wondered what Emmeline had meant when she said she blamed me for its state. What was its state? Perhaps I should go and inspect.

I went out through the patio doors of the dining room. I supposed that the grass was a little long but it was still wet from overnight rain. There was a creeper growing up the side of the shed. I was sure I had never noticed it before. As I surveyed the scene, there seemed to be several things I had never noticed before. How curious, I thought. I wandered idly around looking at the flower beds as if for the first time. I had to admit that in some places they were very untidy and absent-mindedly I began to stoop down and pull out some of the weeds. After a while, I warmed to the task and fetched an old cardboard box from the shed, which I soon filled with weeds.

It was time for lunch. I went into the house and washed my hands. I found Emmeline in the living room having a cup of tea and reading the newspaper.

"I have done some gardening," I said, expecting her to leap out of her chair and fall at my feet in grateful thanks.

"Good," she replied without expression and without taking her eyes from the newspaper.

"I thought you would be pleased," I said, somewhat put out.

"It's your garden."

"I pulled out all the weeds by the back fence," I said, still looking for approval. "They were particularly untidy there."

"Where?" Emmeline asked, looking up.

"By the back fence. They were growing all over the place there."

"Those were the flowers I planted last year."

"They looked like weeds."

"Can't you tell the difference?"

"What's for lunch?" I replied.

"I had some soup and a sandwich," Emmeline answered.

"What shall I have?"

"Take what you like."

"I thought you'd get it for me," I said. "You do usually."

"Grace and favour," Emmeline replied. "It's not part of the contract."

It was late afternoon before I returned to my desk. I looked at what I had written so far: *The secret of a happy marriage is mutual support and understanding.* I continued. *Some division of labour will be conducive to absolute harmony.*

The Principal

The last chords of Mozart's Linz Symphony faded as the Principal eased his car into his reserved parking place. His speed as always had been perfectly judged; the Violin Concerto in A might have got him there fifteen minutes earlier, Tchaikovsky's String Quartet in E Minor five minutes later. He was well pleased with his journey.

Breakfast had not been so successful.

"Don't forget that Penny and Sigmund are coming for dinner this evening," his wife had instructed.

"No dear."

"Don't be late home."

"No dear."

"Remember to pick up a couple of bottles of wine."

"I will."

"And you'll have to clear up the lounge. You left your papers and books all over the place."

"Yes dear."

"Put the rubbish out before you go."

"I haven't forgotten."

"Don't forget the old newspapers."

"No dear. Any more orders?"

"You're lucky you don't have one of those wives who tells her husband what to do," she had said.

"Good morning," he greeted the girl at the reception desk, as he always did, as he had done for nearly twenty years. Girl? She must be nearly forty by now. They had started at the College at almost the same time. He remembered; she had been just out of school. He had been young then. He had thought of himself as young, full of energy, ready to make his mark. His predecessor had been awarded an MBE for services to education. What might he achieve?

Now he looked back and wondered. There were more students, more courses, more staff, more buildings – everything just grew around him. He had happily taken the credit but, in solitary moments, he couldn't think quite what he had had to do with it.

"I suppose it is all to do with leadership," he told himself. "The ability to inspire others, to get the best out of people: that is what counts."

His secretary was busy typing. They greeted each other.

"There are several messages for you," Beryl said, getting up and following him into his office.

He took off his raincoat and sat at his desk. It was a large desk, positioned so that he was facing the door through which they had just entered. His swivel chair was made of leather and comfortable enough for an afternoon nap. To guard against this possibility there was a framed cartoon on the desk showing two executives talking in a plush office. One was saying to the other, "I dreamed recently that I was attending a Board meeting – then I woke up and found I was."

"Peter wants to see you," Beryl said. "He says it's urgent."

Everything was urgent for the Head of General Education.

"I trust you told him I am in China and will stay there for the next three months – and I must not be disturbed."

"I said you would see him at ten o'clock."

"I suppose I must," he groaned. "What else?"

"The Director of Finance asked if you had any thoughts

about the paper he wants to table at the meeting of the Academic Board tomorrow evening. I said I was still typing your comments."

"Thank you. I promise I will let you have them this afternoon."

"The President of the Students' Union came in to say that the Students' Union will be calling for a boycott of the refectory every Tuesday until further notice, as a protest against the rise in the price of tea and coffee. He said he thought you would like to know."

"That was handsome of him."

"I referred him to the Vice-Principal."

"The Vice-Principal likes to deal with the Students' Union," the Principal commented approvingly. "Is that it?"

"Quite a few things more. A reporter from *The Gazette* wanted to know if we had any problems with drugs. I passed that to the Vice-Principal as well."

"Good."

"The Premises Officer wanted to know which wallpaper you had chosen for the redecoration of your office."

"I've been thinking about that. I thought I would let you choose."

"I did. He needed a decision immediately."

There was a knock on the open door. The Vice-Principal was beaming.

"Isn't it a lovely day," he said moving towards the window and settling himself into an easy chair.

Beryl retreated into her office and closed the door.

"It's raining and the forecast is for snow," said the Principal grumpily.

"But inside, Steven, inside. Isn't it lovely indoors?"

What on earth was the man talking about?

"Not when Peter 'I-don't-want-to-worry-you-but' wants to see me as a matter of urgency."

"I can guess what that is about," said the Vice-Principal. "He is unhappy about Astrology."

"I wouldn't have expected him to give it a second thought. Doesn't he call himself a rationalist?"

"Exactly. That's the problem. The Head of Adult Education is advertising a course on Astrology. Peter thinks it demeans the Institution. He says an educational establishment should not be a purveyor of mysticism."

"What does he want me to do about it? Adult Education has a pretty free hand."

"He wants you to put your foot down."

"More likely he wants me to put his foot down."

"He has a point."

"Apparently there is a demand for the class. It will be self-financing and, in any case, I can't order the Head of Adult Education how to run his patch."

"It's your decision."

"You tell him, Dave. He is coming up here at ten o'clock. By the way, did you remember to send your comments on the draft finance paper to be tabled at tomorrow evening's Academic Board?"

"I gave Gerry a paper last week," the Vice-Principal replied coldly. "That was when he wanted it."

"Of course. I expect we will have another busy day, but I'll see you for lunch."

Beryl returned as the Vice-Principal left.

"When Peter arrives," the Principal said, "tell him the Vice-Principal will see him. Also, you won't need to bother with the memo to Gerry. Tell him I agree with the Vice-Principal's comments and have nothing to add."

"Would you like tea or coffee?" Beryl asked.

"Coffee would be nice," he replied, "or maybe tea for a change."

"I'll make coffee," she said, "and don't forget you have to contribute to the induction programme for new staff next week."

"I'll just say the usual thing."

Beryl had brought him a cup of black coffee, no sugar and with two biscuits. He sat alone in his room looking out of the window at the traffic building up at the roundabout. The day had started well, he thought.

An Essential Skill

I was back at Duffborough, the most innovative of the new universities.

"Please don't use the word innovative," Professor Magpie pleaded. "It rather contradicts the spirit of what we are trying to do."

What are they trying to do?

"We are trying to ensure our graduates have the knowledge and skills they will need when they enter the world of employment."

Fergus Magpie had for the third year in a row been voted the most popular lecturer in the University. Designed for the Creative Studies and Journalism degrees, his lectures each week attracted more than four hundred students from every discipline. Why do lectures in Plagiarism excite so much interest?

"It is the scope of the subject," Professor Magpie explained modestly. "Students see its vocational relevance."

"So you demonstrate how to spot plagiarism and how to avoid it?"

"Heaven forbid!" Professor Magpie threw up his hands in horror. "I can see you don't know anything about it. Plagiarism is the key to success in nearly every field of human activity. We analyse its various manifestations and its uses, and we send forth our graduates as qualified and skilled practitioners of the art. Like much else, the idea comes from America. The inspiration was provided by Tom Lehrer."

I remembered Tom Lehrer had taught at Harvard. "Wasn't he a mathematician?"

"Well remembered," Professor Magpie smiled, "but I am referring to his more important work: in particular to his seminal study on Nikolai Lobachevski. Do you remember what he wrote? 'Plagiarise, plagiarise. Let no one else's work evade your eyes.' I have never forgotten it. It inspired the writing of my first novel, *Four Men in a Canoe (to say nothing of the cat)*."

Fergus Magpie had grown up within sight of what is now Duffborough University's main campus in the days when it was still Duffborough College of Technology. After attending the Siggy Fraud Comprehensive School, it was at the College of Technology that he took a degree in General Studies. Why General Studies?

"At that time, I had no particular interests." He smiled again. I was not sure if he was joking.

His post-graduate studies were in the University of Life. He went to London, found a bed-sit in Camden Town and took employment first as a waiter, then as a mini-cab driver, and then teaching English as a foreign language. Within three years, his first novel had been accepted for publication. Several other books followed. Now a successful author, he was invited to return to the new University of Duffborough to join the Department of Interdisciplinary Studies.

"Plagiarism is going to take off in a big way in the twenty-first century," the Professor assured me. "It is a complex field of study, with many branches."

I had not realised.

"Consider Quotation, the oldest form and simplest form of Plagiarism. You take a section of someone else's work – often quite a large section – and incorporate it into your own work. The advantages of doing this are many and various. If the quotation is short and well known, it provides the reader with a reference point, a comfort factor. He is flattered that his understanding and learning are acknowledged. If the quotation is obscure and attributed, then he is impressed with your wider knowledge and with the breadth of your reading. It assures him of your expertise. If you take large segments of someone else's work, you have two possibilities. Firstly, if the work is familiar, then again you provide the comfort factor – familiar ideas are less likely to shock and disturb the reader. Secondly, if the work is unfamiliar, you are performing a public service by rescuing forgotten ideas.

"Of course," he continued, "the main branch of study is Recycling."

"Recycling is plagiarism?"

"Journalists do it all the time. The ability to rewrite essentially the same article time and time again is one of their core skills. If it were not for recycling, Sunday newspapers would be small enough to fit inside your jacket pocket. It is just as important in Literature. Think of Shakespeare. None of his plots is original. Good plots, I grant you, but recycled. He did it so well, people are still recycling the same stories.

"Think of the cinema," he continued. "Hollywood was built on recycling in all its various forms. Films based on books or plays, films based on other films – adaptation, tribute, sequel – these are all forms of Plagiarism."

I expressed surprise that it had not previously been subject to formal study.

"Oh, but it has been," he replied. "I am sure you studied Précis at school. You take something written by someone else and rewrite it in your own words, in shortened form, while being careful not to add any ideas of your own. Pure plagiarism: you can call it nothing else."

Why was there so much interest from students outside the Creative Studies and Journalism courses?

"There are very few jobs where people are required to be

truly creative or original," Professor Magpie explained. "What are wanted are team players, people who go by the rules, people who can be understood by their peers. No one wants a maverick. In most organisations, when top management looks for the solution to a problem, it wants something it knows will work, not some new idea that may throw up as many problems as it solves. The qualified Plagiarist knows exactly where to look for ideas, as well as how to dress them up so that they look fresh and exciting. This is why industry is showing such interest. We have plans to set up a post-graduate programme, an MPA or Master of Plagiaristic Applications. We see it as a powerful rival to courses in Business Administration. I have no doubt that all of our graduates will find suitable employment at the end of their course."

"What sort of employment?"

"Think of the fashion industry — never a new idea. Four new plagiaristic variations each year — one for each season — constantly recycling the styles of an earlier age. Then, when the top designers have displayed their wares and have decided whether to return to the nineteen-twenties or the thirties or the sixties, when they have decided whether skirts are to be long or short, where the waist is to be and so on, the producers of clothes for the mass market get busy making their copies. There is no better example of serial plagiarism."

"Surely the fashion industry is rather special," I suggested. "After all, there are only so many places you can put a waist line."

"That may be so, but almost any field you can think of requires good plagiarists. As you might expect, many go into teaching, journalism, and the media, but you find Plagiarists in all the sciences, in engineering, computing, art, music — in almost everything."

"I hadn't realised this," I admitted.

"Nor have most people, but only because they never think about it. The engineer applies well-worn theory to practical problems: plagiarism. The computer programmer gathers together procedures that perform this or that function – none of them new or original – and produces a *new* program: plagiarism. In practical terms, what would you call the opposite of plagiarism?"

"Originality?"

"In practical terms, it is experiment. Would you want to be the subject of medical experiments? Would you like your doctor to be experimenting on you? I am sure not. You want a doctor who is a plagiarist, who prescribes cures and carries out procedures that have stood the test of time. The trouble is," he added in a confidential tone, "the word carries pejorative associations."

"Really?" I feigned surprise.

"It is quite unjustified. Original ideas – in music, art, politics – no one wants them. They want old comfortable ideas, dressed in new clothes, but familiar and accessible."

I was beginning to appreciate the force of his arguments. In what profession were the skills of the plagiarist most needed, I wondered.

"The humourist needs them most," he told me. "Everyone knows there is no such thing as a new joke."

Ever since we parted, Fergus Magpie's words have been worrying me.

[First published (in amended and shortened form) in *Education, Public Law and the Individual (EPLI) – Vol. 7, Issue 1, May 2002.*]

Murder in Colchester

Anna was dead. Of that, there was no doubt. Neither was there any doubt that Sasha was responsible for her death. He had admitted it freely but no charge had been laid and I was allowed to interview him. I travelled to Colchester, where he still lived.

"You killed her," I said.

"Yeah," he replied gravely. "I was provoked."

"One is not supposed to do that sort of thing – not in England."

"I suppose not, but I had no choice."

"She was your wife, after all."

"No," he roared. "We were not married. I would never have married her."

"Well then, she was your common law wife."

"Not even that. We were strangers. We had hardly met."

"Then I don't understand," I said.

"She was foisted on me. She was infiltrated into my home and behaved as if she lived there. I could see she had no intention of leaving. She behaved as if she owned the place. She behaved as if we were married."

I wondered if she did the housework.

"Not a scrap. She was one of these feminists – do what she

wanted, when she wanted and to hell with any mere male who got in her way."

"I see."

"Then to crown it all, she expected me to make love to her."

"And you weren't inclined?"

"Look, I am as macho as the next guy, but she only wanted me for my sperm. I wasn't drawn to her and she wasn't attracted to me. She said so. She wanted to use me. She said so in so many words. She said I was a pretty poor specimen, but she wanted a baby and I was her only chance."

"So, what happened?"

"Well, she came on at me and I just cracked. I got hold of her round the throat and in less than a minute she was dead. It was sort of self-defence."

"You severed her windpipe."

"Well, yeah."

"With your teeth."

"Yeah."

"I must ask you if you think this is a normal method of self-protection."

"It is where I was brought up."

"Where exactly were you brought up?"

"In Siberia."

"People don't fight with their teeth in Siberia."

"Tigers do."

"Well then?"

"In case you haven't noticed, I am a tiger – a Siberian white tiger."

I took my glasses off to clean them; then I stared into his cage. He was quite right. It explained so many things.

Postscript: Sasha remained at Colchester Zoo until his death eleven years later in December 2010 (aged 15).

Food, Glorious Food

"The cuisine will be of the finest tonight." Clifford asserted, as we walked towards a restaurant he had discovered only recently. He was celebrating a particular success at work and I was to be his guest. "I hope you are hungry," he said.

"I am rather," I admitted.

"I shall provide you with aliment," he said.

"Are you sure?"

"It is but pabulum," he assured me.

"Surely pabulum is a word usually reserved for the food of plants, or of animal organs or organisms. I understood it was used rarely with reference to higher animals."

"I have never thought of you as a higher animal," he replied thoughtfully.

I ignored the comment.

"By the way," he said, "they know me here, so it will not do for you to eat your peas with a knife."

"I never eat my peas with a knife."

"If you say so," he conceded with a show of surprise. "You may, of course, choose any dish you like but I recommend their speciality."

"What is that?"

"Food."

"What sort of food?"

"The edibles are excellent."

"I am pleased to hear it."

"The sustenance is equally good, as is the peckage."

"I would expect no less."

"You might prefer viands."

"They would suit me equally well," I admitted.

"Some speak very well of nouriture."

"I am encouraged."

"Some provender, would you like that?"

"I am not so sure."

"Or simple fodder."

"I don't think so."

Clifford thought for a few moments.

"I suppose nosh is more in your line," he suggested.

"High class nosh?"

"Basic rations."

"I am not sure I am looking forward to this," I said.

"Surely you don't regard yourself as a friand," Clifford said.

"I am not sure," I admitted.

"I mean, you will eat any sort of grub, won't you?"

"Well, not any sort."

"Never fear," he assured me, "tonight you will be provided with nourishment."

"I suppose so."

"And nutrition."

"I am not into healthy eating," I told him, "at least not when I go to restaurants at someone else's expense."

"Your sentiments do you great credit," he said admiringly. "Ah, here we are."

We had stopped outside a small Italian restaurant. Clifford beckoned me to precede him and we entered. Most of the tables were occupied. A waiter approached.

"Good evening," Clifford said. "A table for two, please. I did book." He gave his name and we were soon seated comfortably at a table against the far wall. The waiter brought menus for each of us.

"The chow is excellent," Clifford commented, as I surveyed the list of offerings. "You are a carnivore," he said. "Would you like some fried chawdron or chitterling?"

"It sounds awful."

"Offal, actually."

"No thank you."

"Some crowdie to start, if you would prefer a vegetarian meal."

"I don't particularly like porridge for dinner."

"You will need some fosterment."

"Undoubtedly."

"The one dish you may not like is the gallimaufry."

As I like to know what I am eating, I promised to avoid it.

"Otherwise the mungaree is excellent."

"You are sure about this?" I asked.

"You can even have mush, if you prefer."

"Thank you," I said without enthusiasm.

"But avoid the stodge."

"As you frequent this place," I said, "I think I shall let you order for me, I will have whatever you have."

"An excellent choice," Clifford replied. "Then I suggest we start with the comestibles, served with nutriments on the side. We could follow that with a regale and then, as a main course, we can have oven-baked esculent with mixed victuals and a delicacy on the side. To finish, we can have a confection covered in embamma."

"It sounds excellent."

"And I will order some liquid refreshment to go with it." He called the waiter and translated.

"This," Clifford promised me, "will be a khana."

It was, indeed, and a meal to remember.

[As Clifford is in the habit of using many words we lesser mortals would avoid, a Glossary of terms is appended.]

aliment – something that nourishes, supports, or sustains the body
chawdron – a kind of sauce containing chopped entrails, spices, etc.
chitterling – the smaller intestines of a pig or other animal prepared as a dish, and sometimes stuffed with minced meat as a kind of sausage
chow – food
comestibles – articles of food
confection – any sweet preparation of fruit, nuts, etc., such as a preserve or a sweet
crowdie – a porridge of meal and water or a cheese-like dish made by straining the whey from soured milk and beating up the remaining curd with salt
edibles – things fit to eat
embamma – a sauce or dip to enhance the appetite (particularly for an invalid)
esculent – anything edible
fodder – cattle feed, esp. hay, straw, etc.
fosterment – food
friand – a person having a dainty taste in food – an epicure
gallimaufry – a hash made of odds and ends of food
grub – food
khana – a meal
mungaree – broken meat and scraps of bread
mush – a kind of porridge
nosh – food – a meal
nourishment – food
nouriture – nourishment – food
nutriments – food
nutrition – that which nourishes – food

offal – the edible internal parts of an animal, such as the heart, liver, and tongue
pabulum – food, most often the food of plants, or of animal organs or organisms
peckage – food
provender – any dry feed or fodder for domestic livestock – food in general
regale – a feast or banquet
stodge – heavy, filling, starchy food
sustenance – the means of sustaining life – food
viands – a type of food – a delicacy
victuals – food

Only Shakespeare?

(From The Casebook of Dr Magnus Fell)

- Good evening. Lovely weather we are having.
- The moon shines bright.
- Indeed. *What seems to be the trouble?*
- When I was sick, you gave me bitter pills.
- *I am sorry the taste was unpleasant but I trust they made you well.*
- Canst thou not minister to a mind diseased?
- *What do you think is wrong?*
- A heavier task could not have been imposed
Than I to speak my griefs unspeakable.
- *You must not let things get you down.*
- Everyone can master a grief but he that hath it.
- *True but you must try.*
- I could a tale unfold, whose lightest word
Would harrow up thy soul.
- *Try to tell me about it.*
- My grief lies all within:
And these external manners of laments
Are merely shadows of the unseen grief
That swells with silence in the tortur'd soul.
- *Have you had trouble eating?*

-With eager feeding food does choke the feeder.

- *It is important to take your time but you must eat well. Have you ever felt depressed or suicidal?*

- Against self slaughter
There is a prohibition so divine
That cravens my hand.

- *I am glad to hear it. Do you have any trouble sleeping?*

- He that sleeps feels not the toothache.

- *Indeed. Do you dream much?*

- A dream itself is but a shadow.

- *Exactly. That is what Hamlet said.*

- I have had a dream past the wit of man to say what dream it was.

- *Ah, Bottom in "A Midsummer Night's Dream". I recognise your problem.*

- Unfold it.

- *You appear to have a serious case of Bardic Literitus.*

- What's in a name? that which we call a rose
By any other name would smell as sweet.

- *True but the name is quite accurate. The condition is not uncommon among those who received a grammar school education.*

- Thou hast most traitorously corrupted the youth of the realm in erecting a grammar school.

- *I am sure you don't mean to blame me personally but I catch your drift. Did you not like school? What sort of a pupil were you?*

- The whining schoolboy, with his satchel,
And shining morning face, creeping like a snail
Unwillingly to school.

- *Were you not popular with your schoolmates? What did they say to you?*

- Away with him! away with him! he speaks Latin.

- *That can't have been at all pleasant for you.*

- I cannot but remember such things were.

- *I can understand that but there must also have been happy times, times when you laughed?*

- Mirth cannot move a soul in agony.

- *Your condition seems to have deep roots. Has it been evident for long?*
- O! call back yesterday, bid time return.
- *You were OK yesterday? Perhaps this is not as serious as I feared. It may pass.*
- There are many events in the womb of time which will be delivered.
- *We need to see if we can discover the cause of your condition. Have you received any shocks in the last few days?*
- The thousand natural shocks that flesh is heir to.
- *Nothing out of the normal then?*
- There is something in this more than natural, if philosophy could find it out.
- *Have you any other symptoms?*
- Dogs bark at me, as I halt by them.
- *That is not necessarily related. You say this really worries you? You don't think you could learn to live with it?*
- Intolerable, not to be endured.
- *We will have to try a cure. I cannot guarantee that it will work. We may fail.*
- We fail?
But screw your courage to the sticking-place,
And we'll not fail.
- *First I will have to ask you what sort of things you normally read, apart from Shakespeare.*
- Words, words, words.
- *I might have guessed. OK try reading this text. Don't say anything until you have finished. Let us hope that this will cure your misery.*
- I thank you, doctor.

(Pause)

- The secret of being miserable is to have the leisure to bother about whether you are happy or not.
- *Well, that's not Shakespeare.*

- It would positively be a relief to me to dig him up and throw stones at him.

- *That is not advised. I hope you are not really tempted to do anything silly like that.*

- I never resist temptation, because I have found that things that are bad for me do not tempt me.

- *I think you need a rest. Take a holiday.*

- I enjoy convalescence. It is the part that makes illness worthwhile.

- *Oh, no – George Bernard Shaw. I am afraid my worst fears are justified. You are cured of Bardic Literitus but instead have caught something far worse. I am sorry to tell you that you have contracted Shavian Witicitus. It is incurable.*

***

For those who wish to examine more closely the symptoms of *Bardic Literitus* and *Shavian Witicitus*, the origins of each manifestation is given below, in the order in which it appeared.

The moon shines bright – *The Merchant of Venice* – V,1.

When I was sick, you gave me bitter pills. – *Two Gentlemen of Verona* – II,4.

Canst thou not minister to a mind diseased? – *Macbeth* – V,3.

A heavier task could not have been imposed… – *The Comedy of Errors* – I,1.

Everyone can master a grief but he that hath it. – *Much Ado About Nothing* – III,2.

I could a tale unfold… – *Hamlet* – I,5.

My grief lies all within… – *Richard II* – IV,1.

With eager feeding food does choke the feeder. – *Richard II* – II,1.

Against self slaughter there is a prohibition so divine… – *Cymbeline* – III,4.

He that sleeps feels not the toothache. – *Cymbeline* – V,4.

A dream itself is but a shadow… – *Hamlet* – II,1.

I have had a dream… – *A Midsummer Night's Dream* – IV,1.

Unfold it. – *Henry V* – III,6.

What's in a name? that which we call a rose By any other name would smell as sweet. – *Romeo and Juliet* – II,2.

Thou hast most traitorously corrupted the youth of the realm… – *Henry VI, Part II* – IV,7.

The whining schoolboy… – *As You Like It* – II,7.

Away with him! away with him! he speaks Latin. – *Henry VI, Part II* – IV,7.

I cannot but remember such things were. – *Macbeth* – IV,3.

Mirth cannot move a soul in agony. – *Love's Labour's Lost* – V,2.

O! call back yesterday… – *Richard II* – III,2.

There are many events in the womb of time… – *Othello* – I,3.

The thousand natural shocks… – *Hamlet* – III,1.

There is something in this more than natural, if philosophy could find it out… – *Hamlet* – II,2.

Dogs bark at me… – *Richard III* – I,1.

Intolerable, not to be endured. – *The Taming of the Shrew* – V,2.

We fail?… – *Macbeth* – I,7.

Words, words, words. – *Hamlet* – II,2.

I thank you, doctor. – *Macbeth* – IV,3.

The secret of being miserable… – *Misalliance* – Preface.

It would positively be a relief… – *Dramatic Opinions and Essays* – Vol. II.

I never resist temptation… – *The Apple Cart* – II.

I enjoy convalescence… – *Man and Superman* – I.

Another Life

Caesar stood in the doorway of my study, wagging his tail and looking happy.

"What are you doing?" he asked casually.

This was unusual, very unusual. Caesar's interest in what I do normally manifests itself in ways physical. He doesn't ask; he just gets involved. He will move things around, hide objects under furniture, and generally – as he puts it – help me to keep things tidy. He likes to feel that he makes a difference and he does make a difference – everything takes longer when Caesar is helping. I would never tell Caesar this; it would hurt his feelings. I appreciate his motives; I recognise the warmth of feeling that leads him to try to help. I could never resent his efforts, however ill directed.

However, today he just asked me what I was doing. He made no attempt to jump onto my lap or disturb my position in any way.

"I am writing," I said.

"What are you writing?"

"I am writing a story."

"Why?"

"I thought I could try to get it published."

"For other people to read?" Caesar asked. "In a magazine or a book?"

"Yes."

"What sort of story?"

"It is about Cleopatra," I said. "It is about what she told me."

"You are writing about a cat!" he exclaimed incredulously. "What rubbish! You do waste your time! Do you think anybody is going to be interested in a *cat*?"

"A lot of people like cats."

"Really?"

"You needn't pretend to be so surprised; and anyway Cleopatra is a very unusual cat."

"I suppose she is OK as cats go," Caesar said grudgingly, "but she is not exactly interesting. She doesn't do exciting things. How on earth can you make up a story about Cleopatra?"

"I'm not making it up," I said. "It's about the things Cleopatra believes."

"What about?"

"Reincarnation," I replied, "Cleopatra has some very interesting views on reincarnation. She says that sometimes she has the strong feeling that in an earlier life she was Queen of Egypt."

"I always thought she had delusions of grandeur."

"She says she has the feeling that in her earlier life she knew someone with your name. There was also someone called Antony. She says she had kittens by both of you."

Caesar spluttered uncontrollably.

"I mean by both of them," I corrected myself. "By Caesar and Antony."

"The Queen of Egypt had kittens?"

"I am quoting her. She probably means children. She also remembers someone called Ptolemy. Ptolemy was the Queen's brother."

"And that's it?"

"Not all of it," I replied. "Cleopatra has a morbid fear of snakes. She claims that this is because of some experience she had in her earlier life. Legend has it that Queen Cleopatra committed suicide by causing a poisonous snake, an asp, to bite her breast."

"And you believe all this?" Caesar sniffed the air, as if to say that I was even less intelligent than he had believed.

"Of course I don't believe she has been reincarnated. We are rationed to just one life. That is all there is."

"I agree." Caesar seemed to think I was in need of his approval – just in case I had any lingering doubts. He is a strange dog.

"If you don't believe in reincarnation," he continued, "then it seems to me you've not got much of a story. Of course I'm only a dog," he said with unaccustomed modesty, "but I don't see how you can develop a story about something you think is impossible."

"The story," I explained patiently, "is about Cleopatra's belief. It is about what she thought she remembered and about how she explained it to me."

"She explained it to you," he repeated patiently.

Caesar eyed me with pity.

"Let's get this straight," he said. "You are going to write a story about your having conversations with a cat."

"Is there anything wrong with that?" I asked, a little uncertainly.

"Is there anything wrong?" Caesar jumped up and down with excitement. "Is there anything wrong? You must be barking mad. You are going to write a story about a talking cat who believes in reincarnation, and you ask if anything is wrong!!!"

Deep Thoughts

Albert Onejug settled himself in my most comfortable armchair and accepted a cup of coffee.

"Normally, I drink tea," he said, "without milk or sugar. Ten cups a day helps to protect you against heart disease."

I had recently appointed Albert as my Independent Scientific Adviser.

"Why *Independent*?" I had asked.

"Because I get no government funding," he replied. "Just like nearly all other scientists in Great Britain these days," he added.

We both laughed – bitterly in his case.

"What is the problem?" he asked me now.

"Life," I replied simply. "It is not what we thought it was."

"Was it ever?"

"I am the one supposed to be asking the questions," I objected. "You are supposed to provide the answers. You are advising me."

"Ask me a question then," he said bravely.

"What is life?" I asked simply.

"Ah," he said slowly, looking around the room and seeming to measure the distance between his chair and the door. "Is that all?"

"Won't it do to get us started?"

"I suppose so," he said reluctantly, "but I should warn you

that I am not authorised to deal in some of the most popular products purporting to provide answers to your question."

"What products?" I asked, sitting up straight in my chair.

"The religious ones," he replied. "I should point out that they are very popular and have millions of satisfied customers but I am not allowed to deal in any of them. I am afraid that any explanations I provide will have to be based on other than religious teachings."

"Then you don't recommend them?"

"I am not telling you not to buy their ideas. I am only saying that I am not authorised to speak one way or the other about them. Some of the ideas are very interesting but they have not been subject to any independent testing under laboratory conditions."

"I see," I responded uncertainly. "I must say that I expected that an Independent Scientific Adviser would be able to give me a summary of all available theories."

"Only the bona fide scientific ones," he confirmed. "Tell me, is there any particular aspect of life that is worrying you at the moment?"

"Lots of things," I admitted, "but I'll just mention the particular news item that provoked me to call you in."

"Yes, do that," he said looking at his watch.

"I had just about got used to the idea that I was descended from a monkey."

"Not just you," he said reassuringly.

I paused for a few moments, wondering whether to call the interview to a close. I decided to give him another chance.

"I have accepted that there are millions of microbes and bacteria, all over the place and invisible to the naked eye – some of them living right inside me. I have accepted all of that. I do not say I am happy about it – given the choice, I might have had it otherwise – but I have come to terms with it."

"It does you credit," Albert murmured.

"However," I continued, "I thought that one thing was

beyond doubt. I thought that all life was confined to the surface, or very near the surface, of the planet and that life could not exist in extremes of temperature or of pressure."

"I see," Albert commented understandingly.

"And now what do I read?"

"Indeed, what do you read?" Albert's tone was sympathetic but I couldn't help wondering if he was really as well up with the scientific press as he should be.

"You know what I read," I said, putting my unworthy thoughts aside. "First I read that pogonophora have been found under the seabed near underwater volcanoes."

"Worms," Albert said. I wasn't sure if he knew or if he was guessing.

"That wasn't all," I said.

"So true."

"Bacteria," I said, "living three and a half kilometres below sea level, seven hundred and fifty metres below the seabed. It is not life as we know it or as we have understood it."

"You are quite right about that."

"And hence my question. What is life?"

"It is a good question."

"Thank you. And what will happen to these bacteria."

"I can tell you that," said Albert. All my suspicions melted away. "Some of them are at Bristol University."

"I suppose they must have got exemption from the normal entry requirements," I said.

Albert sat looking at me in silence for a long time after that.

A Curious Arrangement

- Mary?
- *Yes, Joe?*
- I've been thinking.
- *That's nice.*
- Why do we have to wait?
- *No, Joe. That's not nice. You know I don't want to be pressured.*
- But we will be married quite soon.
- *Then we can wait. You know I love you.*
- But why?
- *You know I want to go under the chuppa* [the wedding canopy] *as a virgin. I wouldn't feel right if you knew me before the wedding.*
- If it is not important to me, why is it so important to you?
- *It could be very important to both of us.*
- No one cares about these things any more. Perhaps in the old days but not now.
- *The boss says it's very important.*
- My boss?
- *He's my boss too.*
- I suppose he's everyone's boss really.
- *I suppose he is.*
- Anyhow, what is it to do with him?
- *He says it is because one day I am going to be as famous as Madonna.*

- You'd never be like that.
- *He says that all over the world people will have pictures of me.*
- I'm not going to let you pose for pictures like that.
- *No, my dear. I'll keep all my clothes on.*
- Why should you be famous then? Why will everyone want your picture?
- *Joe?*
- Yes, my sweet.
- *Dearest, I think there is something I need to tell you.*
- About the boss?
- *Well, it does concern him.*
- He's a funny old cove, you know. He asked to see me today.
- *Oh! What about?*
- It was very odd really. He started by saying what a high opinion he had of me – not just of my work but of me personally – and of you, and how he would look after us.
- *Look after us?*
- Yes. He wasn't very specific but he did say that, when our first child is born, we should have to worry for nothing; he would always see that we were OK.
- *He said that to you?*
- Yes. I was very surprised. Why do you think he said that?
- *Well, Joe. I think it is because of what I am going to tell you. You do like the boss, don't you?*
- Of course I do. We all love him. He has done so much for us all.
- *And you do love me?*
- You know I do. You are my whole life.
- *You know I wouldn't do anything wrong?*
- You wouldn't know how.
- *It is true, Joe. It is true. I would never do anything wrong or anything to hurt you.*
- I know dear. What is this all about?
- *I am trying to tell you.*

- Then tell me.
- *I'll try. Joe, have you noticed anything about me lately.*
- You are prettier than ever.
- *You haven't noticed that I am getting – well, getting bigger.*
- I noticed you had taken to wearing loose dresses and I thought that you might be putting on a little weight. It suits you.
- *I am going to have a baby.*
- I hope so my darling. When we are married we will have lots of babies, if the boss allows.
- *He has allowed this one. He has willed it. I am carrying his baby.*
- What baby? Whose baby? What are you talking about?
- *Don't get excited, Joe. Everything will be all right.*
- You're pregnant? You, who wanted to be a virgin on your wedding night. You, who wouldn't let me touch you.
- *Joe. I am a virgin.*
- And I'm Nebuchadnezzar. Pull the other one. What sort of a fool do you take me for?
- *I am telling you the truth, Joe. You said you loved me. I thought you trusted me.*
- I did trust you. I never expected…
- *Listen to me Joe. Let me tell you what the boss said.*
- I trusted him as well. I didn't dream that he would get you in trouble.
- *He says this is an honour, Joe.*
- He would say that, wouldn't he?
- *He says it is an honour for you and for me.*
- I know that women are attracted to rich and powerful men but I never expected this of you.
- *I never think of the boss as a man, not as just a man like other men.*
- No more did I. Now I don't know what to think.
- *It is the boss's child, Joe. He chose me to carry it for him. I didn't have to do anything. I just woke up one morning and there it was inside me.*
- Just like that?
- *He said he will tell you himself. He wants to acknowledge paternity but*

he wants us – both of us Joe – to bring up the child. He says that if we do this, we will be remembered and honoured for ever.

- And we bring up the baby?
- *When he is born…*
- He? It might be a she.
- *The boss says I will bear his son.*
- How can he know that?
- *He seems to know these things. He says that, when the boy is born, he will arrange for some rich men to bring gifts – gold and frankincense and…*
- Mmm.
- *No dear. It is pronounced myrrh. How did you know?*
- And what do you suppose is going to become of a boy brought up by a carpenter but known to be the boss's son?
- *That is the wonderful thing. When the boy is old enough, the boss will make him a partner.*
- A partner! That is something. Then one day, he will run everything and we will have brought him up.
- *Yes, Joe.*
- And he told me he would look after us. He said we would have nothing to worry about.
- *That's right, Joe.*
- Do you think he will help us get a hotel room when we go to Bethlehem?
- *I don't think we can expect that Joe. It will be Christmas.*

The Case of Siggy Fraud

- Today we are privileged to welcome Dr Magnus Fell, author of a new biography of Siggy Fraud, often considered to be the surrogate father of modern psychiatry. Good morning Dr Fell.
- Good morning.
- May I ask you first why you decided to write about Siggy Fraud?
- Yes.
- Why did you?
- Why did I what?
- Why did you decide to write about Siggy Fraud?
- I thought you would never ask. I got interested in his work after treating a number of patients with unusual psychiatric disorders. I found myself going back to his writings and felt more and more that his work should be better understood.
- Can you tell us about some of the cases that sparked your interest?
- I am afraid not. It would be totally against medical ethics for me to discuss actual cases. You can read all about them in my next book, "The Casebook of Dr Magnus Fell", to be published in the autumn by the University of Duffborough, price £25.00.
- You say in the biography that Siggy Fraud was the child of Austrian, Chinese and Italian parents.
- No. Although widely believed at the time, it would have been impossible in those days for him to have had three parents. He

was known as a difficult colleague and this was a way in which colleagues, who found him impossible, sought to explain his character. He was certainly very unusual.

- *In what ways was he unusual?*
- His interest in sexual experimentation was unusual.
- *Surely that is not uncommon.*
- It is at the age of three.
- *What was it that made him special?*
- I am in no doubt about that. Siggy had an extraordinary ability to empathise with his patients.
- *Can you give me an example?*
- Certainly. In my book I describe the time when he was asked to treat a twelve-year old boy, who had developed very strange behaviour. He would dress himself in a nappy and demand that the housemaid fed him from the breast. He was quite unmanageable until she complied.
- *How did Siggy handle the case?*
- In a most original manner. He copied the boy's behaviour. He dressed himself in a nappy and demanded that his receptionist breast-feed him.
- *What was the outcome?*
- Siggy said that it was fantastic. He told the boy that he was on to a good thing, to keep in touch and to let him know if he had any more good ideas.
- *You have some interesting things to say about some of his most famous theories.*
- Yes. For instance I felt that previous writers had not understood the origins of his Edie Perce theory. This is that all men go through a phase when they want to slip their hands up the skirts of any pretty girls they meet. He named the theory after his first girlfriend, who rather liked the practice.
- *I understand that he was a great humourist.*
- Indeed he was. As a young man he spent several weeks studying in Paris under Jack Charcoal. It was then he developed

his interest in hysteria. It influenced his style and much of his writing is now regarded as hysterical.

- *You have new things to say about Fraud's approach to the unconscious mind.*
- This is true. Siggy believed that if you could free the unconscious mind, you could then pour into it the memory of all sorts of experiences that may or may not have occurred. This was called free association, probably in the hope that his patients would forget how much he was charging them.
- *Why did he want to fill the mind with the memory of events that had not taken place?*
- He was ahead of his time. He realised that people by and large have dull, uninteresting lives, or memories they would rather do without. By putting new memories into their heads, he was enabling them to have a happier old age, remembering pleasures and triumphs they had never enjoyed. Well, now they could enjoy them.
- *How did his attitudes to sex fit in with this?*
- Perfectly. By giving his patients new memories, they were able to look back on a life of carnal pleasure, even if they had remained celibate all their lives. Siggy was a real friend of the elderly.
- *Do you have much to say in your book about Siggy Fraud's colleagues, associates and rivals?*
- I do concentrate on Siggy but the story would not be complete without mentioning the split with Karl "Gusty" Rong. I have discovered that the real reason for their moving away from each other was that Siggy kept on misspelling Gusty's name, that and the fact that Gusty pretended that he wasn't as keen on sex as was Siggy.
- *You also mentioned new discoveries about Alf Alder.*
- Yes. The only reason why Alf developed the Inferiority Complex was because he wasn't as famous as Siggy Fraud.
- *Thank you very much Dr Fell. I enjoyed talking with you.*
- Consciously or unconsciously?

Sheer PAP

A ban on the right of children to hit their parents moved a step closer recently, when the European Court of Human Rights ruled in favour of a 34-year old father. The court ruled that the father received treatment "sufficiently severe" to reach the level prohibited by Article 3 of the European Convention on Human Rights. This states that no one shall be subjected to "torture or to inhuman or degrading treatment or punishment".

The application to the European Court was made after an eighteen-month-old baby girl had been acquitted of causing actual bodily harm to her father by hitting him about the face, pulling his hair and scratching his face. The father, who cannot be named for legal reasons, needed two stitches in his right cheek and has since found it necessary to undergo psychological counselling. He and the child's mother separated four years ago, less than eighteen months after the court case, which had put severe strains on their relationship.

The girl, now aged six and a half, today lives with her 29-year old mother, recently remarried and who was shocked even by the decision to refer the case to the Court. The father had "run riot" from the moment his daughter had been born, she claimed. He was never in the house when the baby needed him, seldom read her stories and frequently just pretended to be playing with her, while in reality he was watching television. Dana [not her real name] just reacted, "as anyone would", to obtain her legal right not to be ignored.

The father, on the other hand, argued this was an unprovoked assault – the worst of many such – when he had picked the child up to take her into the kitchen for her evening meal.

"She never liked me," he said. "She wanted her mother for herself and resented having to share her with me. Well, let's see how she likes it. She got rid of me but now she is going to have someone else in the house. It will serve her right."

Lawyers acting for the child had contested the case vigorously, insisting that "English law coincides with common sense" and that reasonable chastisement of parents can always be justified in the cause of maintaining family discipline and, therefore, ultimately in aid of family solidarity and harmony. The father had reacted quite unreasonably and disproportionately, they argued. He had been subjected only to "reasonable punishment". The Court did not accept this.

The Government was quick to indicate that they had no intention of introducing a complete ban on the rights of children to strike their parents. The Minister for Health said: "We are determined to ensure that our laws protect parents against abuse. But let me make one thing absolutely crystal clear: we are equally determined to ensure that nothing undermines a child's right to discipline a parent within a caring and loving environment. This Government believes in the need for disciplined parenthood." The vast majority of children, he said, knew the difference between a proportionate response to provocation and the "savage beating that occurred in this case".

On the other hand, the decision was welcomed unreservedly by a spokesman for PAP (Parents Are People). "This is a landmark decision for parents – the first step towards confirming that parents have the same rights as children to protection from violence under the terms of the Convention on Human Rights."

Teachers' Unions were equally supportive. "The lesson needs to be learned from the very beginning," said a spokesman. "Violence by children against adults cannot and will not be tolerated." Assaults by children upon teachers had become far too common. Let "Dana" be an example to show that violence will never pay.

[First published in *Education, Public Law and the Individual (EPLI)* – *Vol. 3, Issue 3,* December 1998.]

Readers may be interested in the following information published by the Council of Europe:

"The European Court of Human Rights has challenged the concept of 'reasonable' chastisement by parents. In September 1998, the Court unanimously found that corporal punishment of a young English boy by his stepfather was degrading punishment in breach of Article 3 of the European Convention on Human Rights (A v. United Kingdom, 1998). Prosecution of the stepfather in a UK court had failed on the grounds that the punishment was 'reasonable chastisement'. The European Court found that the United Kingdom Government was responsible because the domestic law allowing 'reasonable chastisement' failed to provide children with adequate protection, including 'effective deterrence'. The Court ordered the UK to pay £10,000 compensation to the boy, who had been repeatedly hit with a garden cane. The 'A v. United Kingdom' judgment cites articles of the UN Convention on the Rights of the Child, including Article 19 which requires states to protect children from 'all forms of physical or mental violence' while in the care of parents and others."

This Could Be Dangerous

A Script for Radio

(There are two characters, a GIRL in her early twenties and a much older and obviously well-educated MAN.)

GIRL   Good evening.
MAN   Young lady, is it your habit to accost strangers in public places?
GIRL   No but...
MAN   Do I know you?
GIRL   I don't think so.
MAN   Have we met before?
GIRL   No but...
MAN   Did your mother never warn you about the dangers of speaking to strange men?
GIRL   I don't see...
MAN   That is the trouble with your generation; you don't see. You don't think about the consequences of your actions. You live for the moment and don't give a thought to the future.
GIRL   I don't think...
MAN   Exactly. I am pleased that you can admit it. That is the first step along the road to a cure.

GIRL   I don't know…
MAN   Of course. Of course. You don't know what you should do to change.
GIRL   How…
MAN   You must give up this habit of going up to people you have never met and trying to engage them in conversation.
GIRL   I was…
MAN   Indeed you were and you understand that you must not do it again. Don't you read the papers? Don't you watch television? Don't you realise that this could be dangerous?
GIRL   Do you…
MAN   Of course not, though this is one of the things that is still different for a man. There are not the same risks involved.
GIRL   I don't understand…
MAN   I blame your mother.
GIRL   What has my mother got to do with you? Anyway, my mother died many years ago. I don't want to talk about my mother.
MAN   I understand. I have been too hard on you. It is not your fault.
GIRL   I am just trying to earn a living. Now would you…
MAN   My poor child. I did not realise. Of course everyone must eat. You are not to blame. Whom does one blame? Parents? Schools? Politicians? Society at large?
GIRL   I don't know what you are talking about. I just want to take…
MAN   Your fair share of what the world has to offer. And so you should. It is a hard world. We are born into unequal opportunities and, for many, life can be nasty, brutish and short. Life is not fair. You are entitled to want the best for yourself but is this the best that the world has to offer?
GIRL   I don't know about the world but it's the best you can get round here.
MAN   How terribly depressing.

GIRL   It is very popular.

MAN   A sad reflection on the state of current morality.

GIRL   What has morality got to do with it?

MAN   Oh, my dear, morality should be at the heart of all our actions. Do unto others as you would have them do unto you. Just as you must not exploit others, you must not let others exploit you.

GIRL   Prices are very reasonable.

MAN   Price has nothing to do with it. If something is wrong, then it is wrong.

GIRL   There is nothing wrong here. I have never known a customer to complain.

MAN   Life is all about making choices. Make one choice and therein lies happiness. Make another and it will lead you to misery and torment. But you must never mistake temporary gratification for happiness. Beware temptation.

GIRL   I always avoid fatty foods. Now, would you like…

MAN   Give him half a chance and Lucifer will lead you into the path of damnation.

GIRL   I don't know Lucifer. I don't think he comes in here.

MAN   Beware.

GIRL   I'll keep my eyes open. Now, have you finished?

MAN   I think we understand one another.

GIRL   Then you can give me your order?

MAN   I think I'll start with the soup and then, for a main course, perhaps the fish with…

A Case of Compulsive Digression

(A Consultation from the Casebook of Dr Magnus Fell)

- Good morning Dr Fell.
- *Good morning.*
- Yes it really is. We seem to get more and more of them these days. The weather is so much better than when I was a boy. I was only saying the other day...
- *Indeed, indeed. Now what can I do for you?*
- What can you do for me? Have you ever thought what an open question that is? It sets no parameters, no limits, and yet that surely is not what any of us ever mean when we ask, 'What can I do for you?' Somehow, on both sides of the conversation there is an implicit understanding that the range of legitimate answers will be constrained by the context in which the question is asked and by the relative status or position of each of those engaged in the conversation. The word 'position' is interesting here...
- *I am sure it is. May I ask why you have come to see me?*
- My wife suggested you would be able to help me. Do you know we have been married for thirty-two years? I remember we went to Rome for our honeymoon. There were so many things...
- *What is it that is worrying you?*

- Ah! That is a question. There are so many things to worry us all in this modern world.
- *Why do you think you need to see a doctor?*
- As I told you, my wife suggested it. She said I had symptoms from which my family and friends were suffering. For myself, I feel perfectly fit. I walk three miles every day – twice right around the park. It is fascinating to see the trees and gardens change with the changing seasons. I usually stop and feed the ducks. I am quite interested…
- *We are trying to discuss why you are here.*
- Yes, of course. And I very much appreciate your giving me the time to discuss the matter fully. These days, so few people seem to have time for anything. Everyone is always rushing. There is no sense to it.
- *You seem to have difficulty in keeping to the subject in hand.*
- Do you really think so? It is a very interesting word, that word 'subject'. It can mean a number of quite different things. The subject of a conversation is the predominant topic or theme around which the rest resolves. That, I believe, is the sense in which you have just used the word. In other quite different senses, you are a British subject; you are also the subject of this sentence. In music, the subject of a movement of composition will be its principal theme or phrase. I could relate numerous other meanings.
- *I don't think it will be necessary. It is quite clear you have a severe case of CD.*
- Surely not. I don't even have a CD player. You see I have so large a collection of old gramophone records, I can see no reason to replace my record player. I started collecting when I was in University. You may be interested to know…
- *I don't think so. Your complaint has nothing to do with music. You are suffering from Compulsive Digression, CD for short.*
- Are you sure? I have never noticed it. Mind you, they do say one is always the last to know, but I think they are talking about something else. I really can't remember. I suppose it is age. I don't

remember things the way I did when I was young. Do you think that is the problem?

- *Do you find you talk more than you did?*

- Not at all. Even at school I had a reputation of being able to talk on any subject. There was one occasion when the local Member of Parliament visited and wanted to be shown around by one of the boys. I was selected to be his guide. We didn't just talk about the school. I told him all about my ideas for reforming the electoral system and how we could stem the influence of American culture in England. Of course, that was before the Internet. It would be more difficult now.

- *I see. It is likely your reputation as being able to talk on any subject was misguided. CD is a compulsion to talk off any subject. It is possible you have had this condition for a very long time.*

- Can it be cured?

- *Very rarely. What is your occupation?*

- I am a politician.

- *Oh, in that case a cure is quite unnecessary.*

Success Is Everything

"Publicity Officer for a secret Government think tank? That is absurd," I said.

"Not at all." James Spinner told me. "It is part of our drive towards open Government, freedom of information and all that sort of nonsense."

"Nonsense?"

"Yes. It is nonsense to suggest we don't believe in all that sort of thing."

"But the think tank is secret?"

"That is why we need a Publicity Officer. If there were no secrets, there would be no need to control the spread of information."

"So your job is to conceal and to restrict the spread of information?"

"Not at all. All publicity is good publicity."

"I don't understand," I admitted.

"Excellent." James Spinner smiled broadly. "Would that everyone were like you."

"I believe your think tank is concerned with education," I said.

"That is something I could not possibly admit."

"So it is true?"

"Of course."

"Surely you could give me some idea of the things you deal with," I suggested.

"In confidence?"

"Naturally."

"Well then, as long as I have your word that this will go no further."

"I guarantee it," I affirmed, checking that my tape recorder was still running.

"Examination results," he said. "We are working on examination results."

"You must be very pleased. They seem to be improving."

"Year on year, better and better in every stage of education. This is something for which the Government can take the credit."

"Are you saying the improvement in exam results is a product of Government policies?"

He eyed me curiously. "I am saying the Government can take the credit."

"Not quite the same thing."

"Not exactly but you have to remember that, whenever things are going right, a Government will claim the credit, just as whenever things go wrong, an Opposition will pretend the Government is to blame. That is life. Who are we to knock it?"

"So your job is to make sure the Government takes the credit for improving examination results?"

"No, no – much more than that. We expect improvements to carry on for some time, but what then? That is where we come in."

I expressed puzzlement.

"Let me put it this way," he said, "what happens when examination pass rates increase?"

"Tell me."

"It is simple: failure rates go down. If the current trends are sustained, we can look forward to a time when failure will all but disappear. It will be identified as deviant behaviour and we will have to take steps accordingly."

"Remedial help?"

"Hardly." James Spinner shuddered. "We have to face the fact that there will be an irreducible minimum of young people and adults who are unwilling or unable to respond to the harangues and homilies of Ministers and even of the Prime Minister. Such villains are surely guilty of a lack of patriotism and thus worthy of no sympathy. The full force of the law must be brought down upon their heads."

Was he saying that to fail would be a crime?

"Certainly. In our brave new world, there will be no place for failure. A modern technological society will not be able to afford failure. Those who fail to understand this will be punished. We will legislate and let the judges do the rest."

"How can you punish people for failure?" I asked in amazement. "What sort of punishment?"

"Indeed. What would be appropriate? Why should good, hardworking citizens pay to sustain those unwilling to help themselves by being successful? We have begun to search Government records to discover whether there are any residual colonies to which these miscreants could be transported. We look forward to a time when the county is populated entirely by successful people and," he added, "when our social security bills are lower."

I can understand why his is a secret think tank.

[First published in *Education, Public Law and the Individual (EPLI)* – *Vol. 4, Issue 3,* December 1999.]

A Calming Influence

Caesar lay on the rug in front of the television watching the six o'clock news.

"That," he said when it had finished and I turned it off, "that was very interesting."

"What in particular?" I asked.

"The political bits. The bits about the economy and about building regulations."

"Not everyone would agree with you," I told him. "Many people are bored by politics. Even at election times most people are bored."

"I have always thought people are strange animals," Caesar said, standing up and shaking himself. "You may not care but I want to know about employment prospects."

"It will hardly be a problem for you," I said. "You won't need to worry where your next meal is coming from."

"There is more to life than the next meal," declared Caesar uncharacteristically. "There is fulfilment, self-expression," – he looked me straight in the eye – "the satisfaction of knowing that one makes a difference."

He must have been talking to the cat.

"You have been talking to Cleopatra," I said.

He looked away.

"I am interested in employment prospects because I am going to get a job," he informed me.

"I suppose you are going to join the police," I said sarcastically.

"I am going to work in an office."

"You could not work in an office?" I blurted out. "You can't read."

This was wrong of me. Caesar was aware I knew he couldn't read but it was something we never mentioned. It was one of the few things about which he was sensitive. On this occasion he seemed not to notice.

"Dogs don't get jobs in offices," I said more gently.

"I met one that did," Caesar replied. "His name is Red; he worked for *Vogue*."

I said I didn't believe him. Caesar is not above wild flights of fancy, when the mood takes him. I wonder sometimes where he gets his ideas.

"Red did work for *Vogue*," Caesar continued. "I think he was some sort of advertising executive. He had a big office on the fifth floor; he showed me a photograph."

"He had a big office to himself?" I asked unbelievingly.

"He shared it with two women," Caesar said, "but Red was in charge. He said lots of dogs worked there. He was not the only one."

"What did he do?" I was intrigued in spite of myself.

"I'm not sure exactly. The women pottered around all day, having meetings and speaking to people on the telephone. He used to tell them what to do and generally keep them in order. He was very good at sizing up visitors and didn't get involved in detail. He said that was always the sign of a good manager."

"You're making it up," I insisted.

"Not at all," Caesar said indignantly. "As far as I can understand it, the office would never have functioned properly without Red. He said the people there could get very excited and agitated when things are not going to plan. He never got excited. He calmed them down and helped keep things in a proper perspective. He said people get too involved, too emotional. If a sale fell through, he never let it worry him. He still demanded to be fed at the usual time so that normal routines could be maintained. If someone seemed to be particularly upset by something, he would go and look soulfully at her – we dogs are experts at looking soulful – and this usually cheered her up."

"I would have expected a dog to get in the way," I said unkindly.

"You haven't thought about it," Caesar reprimanded me. "Isn't a dog man's best friend? When things are going badly, don't you want a friend there to support you? When things are going well, don't you want to share your triumphs with a friend?"

I had to admit he had a point.

"I had another reason for listening to the political news," Caesar said. "I wouldn't be at all surprised if the government insisted soon that all new office buildings have special facilities for dogs."

A Desirable Property

"Good morning." The estate agent smiled warmly by way of introduction.

"I want to buy a house."

"Then you have come to the right place." He stood to shake hands, smiling unctuously as he beckoned her to sit opposite him, and watching carefully as she settled herself into the chair. In his business, it paid to observe your clients, to get to know them, to get a feel for their likes and dislikes. Damien Piccard had been an estate agent for five years, recently having passed the last of his qualifying examinations. He was good at his job and prided himself that he was a good judge of people.

His customer appeared to be in her late twenties or early thirties. She was of medium height, with short dark brown hair and was dressed in a dirty anorak and tattered jeans. She wore no rings – not that that meant anything these days – but Damien could tell she was unmarried. She had the look of someone who lived alone.

"May I take down a few details?" he asked. He held a pen poised above a pad of questionnaires. "May I have your name?"

"Jimbal," she replied. "Mrs Selina Jimbal."

Having obtained her name and then her address and telephone number, Damien then asked her about the sort of property she was seeking.

"My husband and I have very special requirements," she said.

"Of course," he murmured. "We are here to find you exactly what you want." There was no shortage of modern three-bedroomed semis on the market, just the sort of thing she would like.

"We need something large," she said, "old and with plenty of character."

"That could be quite expensive," Damien told her. He could tell now, she was a schoolteacher, somewhat unworldly, and probably had no idea of property values.

"Just find us what we want," she said curtly. Perhaps her husband was a builder or decorator. They would be looking for something they could renovate and then sell at a profit.

"It doesn't need to be in good condition," she continued, confirming his thoughts but then adding, "Possibly you can recommend a builder, if any structural repairs are needed."

"You don't mind if it needs structural repairs and alterations?"

"It will probably be necessary."

It was becoming clear. Mrs Jimbal was a teacher or a lecturer at the local College. She wanted a large house to convert into flats for students. You could make a packet doing that; he would do it himself, if he could borrow the capital.

"You'll want to be near to the town centre?" he suggested.

"Not particularly. That is not important."

"With good public transport?"

"It doesn't matter. We both drive."

"Easy access to primary and secondary schools?" Damien had realised there must be at least three or four children in the family.

"We live alone."

"Ah." That was it. Once you listened to a woman talk for a little while, it was easy to guess the sort of man she would have married. Her husband was a long distance lorry driver, often away from home for days at a time. This would explain why there were no children. She would not be able to hold down her job and cater for a family. She was not the sort of woman who would want someone else looking after her kids.

"You did say you wanted a large house?" Damien asked, for one brief moment unsure of himself.

"That is what I said. I doubt if we can find what we need in anything small."

"I am sure you are right," Damien smiled. "You don't find many small houses with five bedrooms." A joke always went down well; it helped relax people. Buying a house was a stressful business.

She grimaced. Damien had noticed that people often did this when he said something funny. It must be a way of avoiding the embarrassment of laughing in a public place. In spite of her scruffy mode of dress, this woman was obviously shy and conservative.

"I am sure we have what you want," Damien concluded.

"I haven't told you yet," she said sharply. "What we must have is a ghost."

"I'm sorry," Damien coughed. "I thought you said a ghost."

"Exactly. We would be prepared to live almost anywhere, so long as there is a resident ghost."

"Any sort of ghost?" Damien found himself asking.

"Preferably quiet and friendly," she said, "someone for my father to talk to, someone to keep him occupied."

"I thought you said there were two of you, just you and your husband."

"That is right, just the two of us."

"And your father is interested in the supernatural and would come to visit you?"

"Oh, no. He is with us all the time. He died three years ago."

For the first time in his life, Damien felt out of his depth. He had often been out of his depth but never before had he realised it.

"I don't understand," he said for the first time since leaving school.

"It's not really my father who lives with us," Mrs Jimbal declared. "It is his ghost. Didn't I explain?"

"It wasn't exactly clear," Damien stammered, "but if you've already got a ghost, why do you want another one?"

"Well, you see," the woman replied, "my husband and my father were always very good friends. My father made a joke once and threatened to come back to haunt us, when he died. My husband said that would be fun and my father took him at his word. At first, we rather liked it. We had the pleasure of his company, without having to cook for him and clear up after him – he was always very untidy – and we all got on very well together. Of course, it could be a bit embarrassing when he materialised at the wrong time, but he soon got used to our routines. Unfortunately, it turns out that there is very little for a ghost to do, not much to keep him occupied. Did you realise, a ghost cannot read a book?"

"I didn't know that," Damien admitted.

"You see, he can't turn the pages. That's the trouble with having no substance. He can walk through walls to his heart's content but he cannot pick up even a piece of paper. I suggested he watch television but he never liked it. He wants to talk all the time. We don't mind in the evenings but my husband works from home and my father's ghost keeps interrupting him, when he is busy."

"Wouldn't two ghosts make it worse?" Damien had regained his composure.

"Not if we get the right ghost," Mrs Jimbal replied, "someone my father's ghost can talk to."

"Very well," Damien said. "We should be able to fix you up without too much trouble. There are some very nice ex-council houses not far from the centre of the town."

"Haunted?" Mrs Jimbal asked in surprise.

"I should say so," Damien confirmed. "The ghosts of old Labour are all over the estate these days."

Mrs Jimbal shook her head sadly. "I don't think that would

suit my father. He was very conservative in his views. Have you anything else? Something with a nice traditional sort of ghost?"

"If you want a traditional ghost, I am sure we can find one for you. Male or female?"

"I hadn't thought. Do you suppose it matters?"

"That depends on what your grandfather is – was – is like," Damien replied, once more in full control. Once the customer started asking him for his opinion, he could be sure things were going well.

"I haven't got any experience of female ghosts," Mrs Jimbal confessed. "Perhaps a male ghost would be safest."

"There is a very nice ghost in Mengelev Close," Damien suggested. "Highly cultured. He was a quite well-known actor in his day – before he was murdered that is, gassed. The house had gas lighting in those days – middle of the nineteenth century. They never discovered who did it. The ghost has threatened – you might say promised – to stay in the house until his murderer is revealed."

"I don't know," the teacher said, shaking her head. "It might suit father but I don't like the thought of living in a house where someone was gassed."

"It is all electric now," Damien told her.

"Even so, I don't think I would be happy. Can you suggest something else?"

"We have got a property with two ghosts," Damien said, after checking a list on the corner of his desk. "Two children, twins, who died from neglect when only seven years old. Pleasant well behaved children. They spend most of their time in the attic, so they wouldn't interfere with your husband when he is working."

"My father didn't have much patience for young children, as he got older. I think he would want someone he could converse with on his own terms."

"I've got just the thing," Damien said, "a Victorian detached house, fully modernised with four bedrooms and two bathrooms, and with a ghost inherited from an earlier property built on the same site. Elizabeth the first had him executed for treason, which he denied. They say he knew Shakespeare."

"It sounds ideal," Mrs Jimbal agreed.

Damien gave her details of its exact location and of the price, and they settled on a time to meet her and her husband the next day, at the house.

"This will be something for you to tell your students," Damien told her.

"What students?"

"At the College. Don't you teach there?"

"Heavens no," she laughed, getting up to leave. "I'm a stripper at the club across the road. I thought you recognised me. Aren't you one of our regular customers?"

After completing the paper work, Damien went into the back office, where the secretary worked.

"Could you get on to *Apparitions Incorporated* for me?" he asked. "Tell them I want the sixteenth century, headless ghost at Spectral Gardens tomorrow at two o'clock. You know that dark-haired stripper, who works across the road? As soon as I saw her come in the office today, I knew she would go for that property."

Ups and Downs

"It says here," said Clifford.

"It is rude to read the paper, when you are supposed to be entertaining a guest," I said firmly.

He looked up. "Usually that would be true, but in this case there are extenuating circumstances."

"Such as?"

"It is quite excusable, indeed it is to be recommended: when the guest is poor company, the host should cut his losses and turn his attention elsewhere."

"I presume the same goes for a guest?"

"You presume too much. A guest should know his place and show proper appreciation of the honour bestowed on him."

"What honour?" I asked.

"The honour of being invited into my house."

"Ah! I see. This is all about you."

"And you. I wouldn't dream of taking this attitude to anyone else, nor would he deserve it."

This is the sort of conversation you can have only with a very old friend, and Clifford is even older than I am – by a few days. I sat for some moments in quiet contemplation, while Clifford returned to his newspaper.

"What are you reading about?" I asked.

"It says they can go down as well as up."

"That is life."

"No. It is value of your investments in the Stock Market."

"It is bound to be so. You know what they say: what goes up must come down. Indeed, where there is an up there is always a down."

"You go too far," he told me sternly. "What you say is not true. You can update something. You cannot downdate it. You can be upset; you cannot be downset. You can have an upbringing but not a downbringing."

"You can be brought down."

"You can, but that means something entirely different – just as downright has nothing to do with upright, or write down is not the opposite of write up."

"You will probably write something down if you are writing it up."

"You are changing the subject. I am discussing some of the deficiencies, indeed the illogicalities, of the English language."

"The language of Shakespeare."

"No doubt he would do something about it, if he were still here. I suppose it is now up to me."

"Or down to you?"

"I suppose so."

"I had feared as much."

"You see the problem? What you said earlier ought to be true. What goes up should be able to come down, and yet you have uproar but not downroar. The result of some happening is its upshot; failure to achieve a result should be the downshot. The opposite of upkeep should be downkeep. If you can be upstanding, then why not downsitting, uptight or downloose, up-and-coming or down-and-leaving. What is required is a total upheaval in the language."

"Not a downheaval?"

"I shall have to write a book to promote the virtues of logical language, to uphold common sense. You cannot downhold common sense and my words are bound to be uplifting and not downlifting. The uptake – never the downtake – of my ideas could start a revolution or, at least, an uprising. I can say with confidence there will be no downfalling. This is the crux of the matter. Uplift and downfall should be opposites and they are not. Their meanings are quite unrelated."

Clifford was getting quite excited. I suggested he calm down.

"I certainly cannot calm up," he replied.

"I am not trying to knock down your ideas," I said, "nor to downplay them. I just think you should be more down-to-earth."

"I see. You don't want me to be up-to-sky, but nor do you want to knock up my ideas or upplay them. But never mind. I am not downcast, nor am I upcast. I shall write my book. It will be original and up-to-date."

"I doubt you will find a publisher," I told him, "but if you do, try to get a down payment upfront."

A Helping Husband

I was just putting on my overcoat.

"Are you busy?" Emmeline called.

"I was just about to go out."

Emmeline came into the hallway. She was looking particularly fetching, dressed as she was in old slacks, apron, rubber gloves and with a scarf tied around her hair. A smudge of dirt on her forehead suggested she might have been busy.

"Anywhere important?"

"I thought I ought to take the dog out for a walk."

"We haven't got a dog," she reminded me patiently. "We have never had a dog."

"That's not his fault. You can't use that as a reason for depriving him of exercise."

"Let him go alone," she said humouring me.

"Let who go alone?"

"The dog," Emmeline replied firmly.

"You said we haven't got a dog," I answered.

"Your imaginary dog," she explained, clearly confused.

"Is it possible to send an imaginary dog for a walk on his own?"

"I imagine it is," she replied irritably.

"I see," I said meaningfully. "You imagine we have a dog."

"I do nothing of the kind." She sounded quite angry. "You are the one who imagines he has a dog – or maybe you don't and you are pretending just to annoy me."

"I'd never do anything to annoy you – not intentionally."

"Or to help me."

"Of course I would help you. Nothing would give me greater pleasure."

"Fine," Emmeline said triumphantly, "you can come and do some work in the house."

"What about my walk?"

"That can wait," she said decisively.

"Caesar won't be pleased. By the way, he seems to have disappeared. Did you see where he went?"

"I have never seen him," Emmeline exploded. "He doesn't exist. He is imaginary."

"But he doesn't like it when I let him down."

"If that is your biggest problem, you are extremely lucky."

"I don't think you like Caesar," I said sadly.

Emmeline raised her eyes to the heavens. She said nothing.

"Is there something you want me to do?" I asked after a pause.

"Have you seen the tiles in the bathroom?"

"I suppose I must have done. They were here when we bought the house. They are green and white aren't they?"

"Just go and look at them," she said despairingly.

I went obediently into the bathroom. It looked just the same as always. I went back to find Emmeline. She was in the kitchen removing the rubber gloves.

"Have you finished then?" I asked.

"I have," she replied, putting heavy emphasis on the first word.

"I was right," I said. "They are green and white. Was there anything else you want me to do?"

"The bathroom tiles."

"I looked at them. They are all there."

"So clean them."

"Do they need cleaning?"

"I thought you just looked at them."

"I did. You didn't say anything about looking to see if they needed cleaning."

"Don't you ever notice anything about you?" Emmeline asked in exasperation.

"How do I clean tiles?"

"How long have we been living in this house?" Emmeline responded.

"Twenty-nine years." I tried to make the connection with my earlier question. "I suppose tiles would get a little dirty in all that time."

"I've been cleaning them up until now," she shouted. "As you are taller than I am and as you obviously have nothing more important to do, it seems right to me that you take over that particular chore."

"I agree entirely. You should have mentioned it before. How do I do it?"

"You put some bleach in a bucket, add some water and wipe the tiles with a cloth."

"That sounds easy. Where is the bleach?"

"Look for it."

I started to look. It was quite interesting to discover all the things that Emmeline had stored away. She was very well organised.

"Don't forget to wear rubber gloves," she shouted to me.

"I don't have any rubber gloves," I said, going into the kitchen where she was peeling potatoes.

"Then you had better get some. You are going to need them for a lot of jobs I have you marked down for."

"I'll go and get some immediately," I said happily. "I'll just walk down to the local shops."

"Good," said Emmeline.

"Oh," I said, "and I might as well take the dog with me. He needs some exercise."

Foreignisation of the Language

A correspondent writes: "I do get annoyed by writers. I don't mean *you*. I mean the well-educated writers who went to fancy schools and learned how to spell. What was I saying? Oh yes, I remember, I was telling you that I get annoyed by writers who insist on infiltrating foreign words into what otherwise would be perfectly sound English prose. Why do they seek to subvert the Queen's English? Is it a republican plot? Are they wanting to bring back the grammar schools?"

The answer to all of these questions is almost certainly in the affirmative. This, however, has nothing to do with the problem. The fact is that many of the so-called foreign words complained of are either misspellings or *foreignised* – that is, the reverse of anglicised – versions of perfectly good English words and phrases. The following selection is typical:

ad hoc – This is a simple misspelling commonly found in cookery books and should be written *add hock (or other white wine)*.
aficionado – Again from cookery books, a corruption of *a fishy on hard dough* meaning *fish baked on a bed of crushed biscuits*.
aide-mémoire – *help my mother*. Another example of the difficulty foreigners have with English spelling.
apparatchic – *a baby parrot*.

avant-garde – *lacking protection* as in *avant-garde sex*.
bête-noire – A term used in roulette meaning *bet on the black*.
comme il faut – *here comes the enemy*.
cri de coeur – Literally *the dog is howling*.
derrière – *an Irish tune*.
entente – *in a tent* as in **entente cordiale** – *having a drink in a marquee* – from the Hindustani for camp refreshments.
errata – A corruption of *hurrah, ta* – meaning *thank you, well done*.
faux pas – *father is against (me)*. To commit a **faux pas** is to make an enemy of one's father.
force majeure – *the Conservative Party in the 1990s*.
gestalt – *an alternative guest, someone who is invited to a dinner party at the last minute*.
gravitas – A Yorkshire expression: **he has gravitas** meaning *he has the gravy, he has*.
herrenvolk – *fish eaters*, a corruption of herring-folk.
infra dig – An archaeological term indicating willingness to get ones hands dirty: e.g. We spent the weekend **infra dig**.
ingénue – *a new engine*.
jeune fille – Entry prices tend to rise in the summer for many outdoor entertainments and facilities. This is known as the *June fee* or **jeune fille**.
karaoke – *a good Indian meal*.
lèse majesté – *without the Sovereign*.
lingua franca – A type of *French pasta*.
mañana – *a small Spanish banana* mainly found in Mexico.
manqué – *like a monkey*: hence **un peintre manqué** is *a painter whose work is similar to that produced by a chimpanzee*.
nisi – As it sounds, e.g. he has a cataract in one eye but has one **nisi**.
nom de plume – Originally **non de plume** meaning *without feathers*.
paparazzi – *father is a sailor*.
quid pro quo – *quids in* or *in profit*.

raison d'être – Literally *a debt of raisins*. What this is actually supposed to mean is lost in antiquity.

soupçon – *the food is nearly ready.*

tour de force – *army service overseas.*

tout de suite – *sing with dulcet tones.*

A Duty of Care

Lawyers are agreed that it was only a matter of time before someone brought such a case. Jack Ne'erdowell is suing his old University for stress and loss of earnings consequent upon the grade of degree he was awarded.

"It was perfectly obvious to everyone who knew me that I had a third class mind. I did not deserve an upper second and the University had no right to award it," he says bitterly. "My life has been ruined; I was catapulted into a world where I had no place and where I was out of my depth."

Mr Ne'erdowell, then a student at the University of Duffborough, had the offer of a post with a merchant bank, dependent on his obtaining the upper second in his finals. "I don't blame the Bank," he says. "They were entitled to expect someone with an upper second to be able to cope with the work. I couldn't cope; I struggled from the very beginning. The University, by giving me this degree, had expressed the opinion that I could do this sort of work. I was young and naïve enough to believe them. I stayed late at the office each evening; I went in at weekends; I found I had no time to think of anything else. My girl friend left me; my friends deserted me; I became morose and depressed and eventually had a complete breakdown."

Now unemployed, Mr Ne'erdowell claims damages, together

with compensation for loss of earnings from the job he would have taken, had the University awarded him the lower class of degree, as he deserved. The standard of teaching was far higher than one could reasonably have expected, he argues, and this was compounded by a system of marking made deliberately easy so as to enhance the results of students in an effort to attract funds into the department.

Had his degree not qualified Mr Ne'erdowell for the post at the Bank, he would have joined in partnership with an old school friend to run a market stall in Stevenage. Selling bric-a-brac obtained from the clearance of old houses, the business was soon making a clear profit of twelve thousand pounds a week, leading to its take over by one of London's leading auction houses. As a partner, Mr Ne'erdowell would by now have received shares in the new company, worth half a million pounds, together with a seat on the board.

Mr Ne'erdowell claims the University had a duty of care, which it failed to exercise. It was irresponsible to award him a good degree, without considering the effects that this could have on a man of his limited ability.

No one from the University was willing to comment.

[First published in *Education, Public Law and the Individual (EPLI) – Vol. 3, Issue 2,* August 1998. The editor of that august publication felt it necessary to warn readers: *This article is not to be taken too seriously nor in any way to detract from the genuine nature of many negligence claims.*]

Sam Clemens's Disease

(A Consultation from the Casebook of Dr Magnus Fell)

- *Good morning. You have not been to see me for quite a long time. What is the trouble?*
- The report of my death is an exaggeration.
- *As your doctor, I am pleased to hear it. Actually, you are looking very well.*
- I can live for two months on a good compliment.
- *I know what you mean but you would also need to eat.*
- Part of the secret of success in life is to eat what you like and let the food fight it out inside.
- *If you adopt that attitude, your life might be successful but it is likely also to be short. You do seem to have put on a lot of weight since you came to see me last.*
- The only way to keep your health is to eat what you don't want, drink what you don't like, and do what you'd rather not?
- *I didn't say that but, if you want to stay healthy, you should eat a balanced diet and not in excess. Oh, and drink plenty of water.*
- Water taken in moderation cannot hurt anybody.
- *I remember you gave up smoking.*
- It is easy to give up smoking. I have done it a hundred times.
- *That sounds like Mark Twain.*

- Some of his words were not Sunday-school words.

- I see. *Everything you have said was a quotation from Mark Twain. Are you able to speak without quoting him?*

- Better to keep your mouth shut and appear stupid than to open it and remove all doubt.

- *I suppose, as long as you quote Mark Twain, no one will think you are stupid. Many of his books are classics.*

- A classic is something that everybody wants to have read and nobody wants to read.

- *Yes, I am sure: you are suffering from Sam Clemens's Disease. As you know, Mark Twain was the pen name of Samuel Clemens. I presume you admire his writing?*

- Good breeding consists in concealing how much we think of ourselves and how little we think of others.

- *Did you know that Mark Twain was the first author to submit a typewritten book manuscript?*

- I would rather have my ignorance than another man's knowledge, because I have so much more of it.

- *I am sorry. I thought you would be interested. I believe we have a mutual friend who is quite an expert on Mark Twain.*

- An experienced, industrious, ambitious, and often quite picturesque liar.

- *I thought you liked him.*

- I admire him I frankly confess it; and when his time comes I shall buy a piece of the rope for a keepsake.

- *I am bound to say that I find him charming, considerate and entirely honest in every way.*

- Few things are harder to put up with than the annoyance of a good example.

- *I suppose you are entitled to your opinion.*

- It is by the goodness of God in our country that we have those three unspeakably precious things: freedom of speech, freedom of conscience, and the prudence never to practice either of them.

- *Such prudence does not seem to be among your principles; you have been extremely blunt in expressing your opinions.*
- Principles have no real force except when one is well fed.
- *But you eat very well. We have established that. Perhaps there is something in your lifestyle that is affecting you adversely. What work do you do these days?*
- Work consists of whatever a body is obliged to do.
- *What about exercise? Do you play golf?*
- Golf is a good walk spoiled.
- *An interesting view.*
- The radical invents the views. When he has worn them out, the conservative adopts them.
- *How else do you relax? Are you interested in music?*
- I have been told that Wagner's music is better than it sounds.
- *Some think it quite heavenly.*
- I don't like to commit myself about heaven and hell – you see, I have friends in both places.
- *I am afraid I can think of no treatment for your condition. Sufferers from Sam Clemens's Disease often find it wears off after a while. It may take some time. Do you think you can cope in the meantime?*
- All you need in this world is ignorance and confidence; then success is assured.

God's Greatest Hits

"Someone in the United States is planning to bring out a volume of my greatest hits," remarked God during one of our occasional chats.

"A record?" I asked.

"A book," He said, "though we are bound to have record sales."

"You think so?" I said.

"I know so. I am God."

"So what are your greatest hits?"

"You know them as the ten commandments. There will be little stories about each commandment and testimonies from famous people about how their lives have been affected."

"You're kidding. No one takes much notice of your ten commandments any more. I remember reading that two-thirds of Britain's vicars have actually forgotten many of them. If ever they were any use, they have certainly passed their sell-by date. In my opinion they are much over-rated."

The earth trembled slightly. That is one of the troubles with God. He cannot contain his emotions.

"I was rather proud of them," He responded in a subdued manner. "Don't you like any of them?" I think He was rather hurt.

"My mother was very fond of number five," I said to cheer

Him up. "She felt that honouring thy father and thy mother was the secret of a happy life."

"I've always liked number one," He said. "I am the Lord thy God and so on. You shalt have no other gods before me."

"Advertising," I said. "Nothing but advertising."

"There is no need to knock advertising. It helps to turn the wheels of commerce. A people without advertising is a poor people."

"True, in some circumstances. But you seem here to be on an ego trip, like in number three about not taking your name in vain. It is sheer self-aggrandisement."

"I suppose that you are going to object to number two as well."

"Certainly I am. First you ask people not to make graven images, effectively not to create statues and, I suppose, by implication pictures, representing any living thing. You thereby put a veto on art and a severe limitation on education. The bit about not bowing down to images is OK but then you go on another ego trip about how jealous you are and start threatening revenge not only on the one who offends you but on his children and his children's children. Frankly, that is not very nice."

There was a period of silence.

"What about my fourth commandment, about remembering the Sabbath day and keeping it holy?"

"Not wholly bad," I said, "not bad in its time. I suppose it helped to get working hours reduced. Certainly useful to many people these days for washing cars and watching football matches."

"You are being flippant," He roared. "I have addressed serious matters. Thou shalt not steal, number seven; thou shalt not commit adultery, number eight."

"I'll give you number seven," I said generously, "though even in your injunction against stealing a little elaboration might have been useful. But you must be joking about adultery. Your attempt to get that banned is your greatest failure not your greatest hit.

Even in biblical times you were not all that successful. Today? Well! Was it not Saul Bellow who wrote about 'the increasing triumph of Enlightenment – Liberty, Equality, Adultery'?"

"Even you cannot disagree with number six," He said testily. "Thou shalt not kill."

"I wasn't sure that you really meant it," I countered.

"Of course I meant it," He thundered. "I don't say things I don't mean; I'm not human."

"Then why do we always find your representatives going around blessing the soldiers on all sides in any war they can find?"

"I have never signalled approval of such action?"

"Have you ever given any sign you disapproved?"

"Let us keep to the subject," He said, avoiding an answer. "Do you approve of the teaching?"

"Thou shalt not kill? What about in self-defence? People differ in their understanding of what you intended."

"You think I should put in some detail on this one?"

"Certainly, if you want it to have any real influence. You could make it something like 'Don't kill other people, except possibly in self-defence.' Also you should give a lead on euthanasia and on whether or not you are referring to unborn foetuses."

"And then you will be satisfied?" He asked wearily.

"There is still the question of animals," I suggested. "Some people have taken you to mean that one should not kill anything. But elsewhere you talk about keeping milk and meat separate. Clearly you don't advocate vegetarianism."

"OK," God murmured, "I get your drift. How do you like my ninth?"

"I prefer Beethoven's ninth."

"I helped him with that," God said proudly. The thought seemed to have improved his mood.

"I am against bearing false witness," I said. "Your number nine is fine but number ten is a dog's breakfast. All this stuff about not coveting your neighbour's servants suggests that you are quite out of touch with today's world. And as for your neighbour's ox and ass, really!"

"I suppose I could update it."

"You will need to be careful," I warned. "You said earlier that advertising helps to turn the wheels of commerce. It could also be argued that covetousness is the engine of enterprise. Without it we might all still be living in caves."

"What do you suggest?"

"Why not something modern like 'Thou shalt not make unauthorised use of thy neighbour's computer software'?"

"I'll consider it for the second edition," He said.

A Visit From the RSPCHP

Oh, the ignominy of it all. I was visited by an official of the RSPCHP. Such a thing has never before happened to any member of the family – not in my lifetime – unless it was kept from me. I suppose that is always a possibility: no one tells me anything. I think people are afraid I will write it all down and it will be used in evidence against them. Really, I think that is very silly. I can keep a secret as well as the next man. Take the time Clifford got drunk after going to the opera. I have never told anyone, nor would I.

Anyway, it happened last Thursday afternoon. I was sitting quietly at home thinking of all the jobs I needed to do around the house, when the doorbell rang. I opened the door. Before me stood a respectable looking middle-aged man, holding a briefcase. He addressed me by name, thrust forward an official looking card with a photograph and introduced himself by name, which I forgot immediately.

"We have received a report, which we have to follow up. I hope this is not an inconvenient time."

I thought of the jobs to be done. "Not at all," I said.

"This may take some time. Do you mind if I come in?"

I led him into the sitting room and we both sat down.

"The RSPCHP." I repeated the acronym he had uttered. I

did not like to admit I had not heard of it – not for myself, you understand, but I did not want to hurt his feelings.

"The Royal Society for the Prevention of Cruelty to House Plants," he offered helpfully.

"Of course."

"You may not have heard of us."

I pursed my lips in a way that indicated an acceptance of this possibility.

"It is strange how few people know about us," he mused, "even though we were founded in the reign of George III. Actually, King George himself was the driving force behind our creation. It was in the early seventeen-nineties, not long after his first attack of porphyria. You know about that?"

"I could learn more," I admitted modestly.

"At the time they thought he had gone mad. Now we know he was suffering from this malady characterised by an excess of purple-red pigments in the blood which, as well as causing great pain and other unpleasant symptoms, induces delirium. In George III's case, this manifested itself in his talking to trees. The interesting thing is that, when he recovered, he claimed to have a new understanding of and sympathy for plants. In his illness, he said, he had gained an appreciation of how delicate were the sensibilities of plants and how impressionable they were. He said one should never underestimate the umbrageousness of plants."

I raised my eyebrows.

"He meant they were prone to take offence; they were easily offended. Now you probably know that George was already very interested in agriculture and was a keen supporter of what we call the agrarian revolution. Not for nothing was he known as Farmer George. He called together an assembly of the great and the good, and the RSPCHP was born. It was early in 1793. Three days later the French sent Louis XVI to the guillotine."

"Good gracious! Was there any connection?"

"Not that we know of but you can never be sure with the French. They are a strange people."

I presumed the model was the Royal Society for the Prevention of Cruelty to Children.

"Good gracious no," he exclaimed. "This is England. Plants came first. In 1793, George III founded the RSPCHP – Pitt and Fox both gave support, as did Beau Brummell. Rothschild, of course, provided the finance. It was more than thirty years later, in 1824 that William Wilberforce and others met at the Old Slaughter's coffee house in St. Martin's Lane to launch a society 'for the purpose of preventing cruelty to animals'. The RSPCA was born two years later and the Metropolitan Police three years after that. The National Society for the Prevention of Cruelty to Children was not incorporated until 1895 – a *National* Society note, not a *Royal* Society."

"This is all very interesting," I said, "but I am sure you did not come here just to give me a history lesson."

My interlocutor stiffened and adopted a serious demeanour. He shook his head sadly.

"I am afraid not," he said. "We have received a serious complaint."

"I doubt if I can help you," I apologised. "I know nothing about plants."

"That may be the root of the problem." I grimaced but he continued undeterred. "But ignorance is no excuse. You see, the complaint is about you."

"About me?" I feigned incredulity.

"We have received a number of reports about your mistreating your houseplants. I am very sorry but I have to ask you if I may have a look about the house."

"This is absurd."

"We try to keep things on an informal basis, if we can, and we hope people will co-operate. If you are not willing to help us with our enquiries, it is possible for us to get a search warrant."

"Do you actually do that?" I asked in amazement – this time not feigned.

"Not often. Usually it is not necessary. It can be quite unpleasant – a big official van drawing up outside the house, all the neighbours coming out to see what is happening."

"Would you like to have a look around?" I offered amicably.

He opened his briefcase and withdrew a notebook. He spent a few moments writing in the book and then stood up. He continued making notes throughout the remainder of our conversation.

"Do you have many plants in the house?" he asked.

"Quite a few. I have never really noticed."

He shook his head sadly.

"I think there is one just behind the chair on which you were sitting."

He looked behind the chair. "What is – was – this?"

"I think that is a green one," I told him helpfully.

"It shows no signs of having been watered for several weeks. Do you know the names of any of your plants?"

"I know we have a cactus in the dining room – or is that a cactus?"

We wandered through the house, looking for plants. I was quite surprised how many there were, at least one or two in each of the downstairs rooms, as well as in the windows on the stairs and landing and in the bathroom. There was even one in my study, though I knew about that as I often had to move it to get to the bookcase. It was another green one. When we had completed our tour, we returned to the sitting room.

"I am bound to say, this is a very serious case," he began. "Out of twenty-three plants, only one looked reasonably healthy."

"The cactus."

"Exactly. That hardly ever needs watering. All the others showed serious signs of starvation. Do you ever feed your plants?"

"My wife does that but for the last several weeks she has been staying with our daughter. I have been flitting backwards and forwards."

"So she left you in charge of the house?"

"Yes."

"And all its contents?"

"Yes."

"And she told you to water the plants?"

"Now you mention it, I believe she did."

"You must understand you are *in loco parentis* to these plants. For a first offence, we would issue a formal warning and come back to check that you were performing your duties appropriately. The problem is: this has happened before."

"Has it?"

"You will remember several years ago one of your colleagues confiscated a houseplant from your office. You had neglected it so badly that he could not tell if it were alive or dead. It took three months of his tender loving care to nurse it back to health."

"I didn't buy it."

"That is no excuse."

"It was given to me by people who must have known I did not possess a watering can and knew nothing about houseplants."

"Once you had accepted the present, you were responsible for it."

"It was given to incriminate me. The present was a plant."

"Exactly, and it deserved your care and compassion. I find your lack of contrition quite disturbing," he told me sternly. "I shall make a full report to my superiors. Good morning."

With no further ceremony he departed and left me wondering what happens next.

Lenin, McTrotsky and the Revolution

One of the enduring images of the twentieth century is of John Lenin returning to Russia in a sealed railway carriage to lead the Beatlevik Revolution, which had been started by accident.

"Nobody told me," he complained.

It was winter and John was away from Russia, playing a gig in a cave in Liverpool. His dramatic return to centre stage occurred in the winter, when fans stormed the Palace Theatre in Petrograd and demanded he take top billing.

These events form the heart of Georgio Fantasia's new book, *Lenin, McTrotsky and the Revolution*.

Ignoring all documentary evidence, Fantasia has based his memoir entirely on folk memory. In a lengthy introduction, he argues that this approach returns History from professional historians to the people, to whom it justly belongs. It is not what happened in the past that affects our lives, he argues, but what we perceive as having happened. Our lives are shaped by how we remember events, rather than by the events themselves.

Did Lenin really proclaim, "Hard times are over," when he first entered the doors of the Kremlin? No matter – that is what people remember. Other historians may point to his middle class origins, but for the people he was a true Working Class Hero.

"Give peace a chance," he proclaimed as he struggled to extricate his people from either the First or the Second World War. (Folk memory is not very clear on the distinction between these two events.) Soon there was peace, except for the people who were still fighting. The Beatleviks found they had nothing and wanted to share it with everyone else, so John Lenin founded the *Comedy Turn*, a nightclub where he could sing his own songs and strum his own guitar. Having lost his watch, John Lenin had no time to run the club himself, so appointed Greg Zinoviev (better known as George Martin) to run it for him. Zinoviev would later become famous as someone who did not write his own letters.

Paul McTrotsky also missed the start of the revolution. He had been in New York arranging for the Beatleviks' first American visit and trying vainly to set up a recording contract. "We don't think they will do anything in this market," said the head of Capitol Records, rejecting their approaches. Dejectedly, McTrotsky purchased a ticket to ride and returned to Russia where, much to his surprise, Lenin told him, "I proclaimed Power to the People and said, 'Yes, I'm your angel, stand by me.' With a little help from my friends, we are more popular than Jesus now."

"Imagine," McTrotsky murmured admiringly. Soon he too had immersed himself in the revolution and was composing Variations for the Red Army Band.

According to Fantasia, folk memory is a little hazy about the other Beatleviks. The Ringo Kid, of course, was a star in his own right, having impersonated John Wayne in the Hollywood film, *Stagecoach*. When his predecessor was drummed out of the Central Committee, Ringo was drafted in to put the beat back into the Beatleviks. Later he would join a commune living in a yellow submarine.

"All things must pass," George Morrison would comment, before he too departed – in his case for England, where he became Home Secretary and was completely forgotten until, many years later, he resurfaced as Felix Mendelssohn's grandfather, of whom

Felix – sometimes known as Peter and a celebrated musician in his own right – was particularly proud. (Fantasia admits that this version of the facts poses certain chronological difficulties but posits no alternative theory.)

Meanwhile, with the revolution well under way, Lenin's big idea was to get serviettes used all over Russia and eventually all over the world, but other than this the Beatleviks had no idea how to run an economic policy. No guidance was to be found in the writings of either Karl or Grumpy Mix. "From each according to his abilities, to each according to his needs," Karl had written.

"All you need is love," declared Lenin. "In the future Beatlevik society there will be no money, because money can't buy you love. There will be no profit motive. No one will want wages."

"But they will want Something," George Morrison suggested, somewhat put out for previously having received no attention.

McTrotsky agreed. "Here, there and everywhere everybody wants something."

Thus did the Beatleviks argue, but always they would come together as they struggled to lead their people on a magical mystery tour, along the long and winding road to a better future. In the event, they did not abolish money, because without money there could be no Taxman.

Fantasia's story ends when Lenin joined Lucy in the sky, though whether with or without diamonds is not known.

Despite John Lenin's having labelled him the Nowhere Man, Joseph Stilton would become the new Big Cheese, while Paul McTrotsky was to marry Eleanor Rigby and settle down on the Mull of Kintyre. But that is another story.

I'm No Oxymoron

"You stole your example of a zeugma from Mr Metcalfe," said Clifford after reading something I had written recently.

"Which example do you mean?" I asked, wondering what he meant.

"I thought as much," he responded in a superior tone of voice. "You don't know what I am talking about. You don't know what a zeugma is."

"You tell me what you think it is."

"What I *think*?" He exploded. "It is not a matter of what I think. Do you recall nothing of your education?"

"It was a long time ago," I said, "but I do remember Mr Metcalfe tried to teach us English."

"He succeeded with some of us." Clifford looked me straight in the eye. "Unfortunately he did not succeed with us all. For some of us it was a waste of a good education. Nevertheless, you have now used his zeugma – 'he left the football field covered in mud and glory'."

"It was quite unconscious."

"I suppose you also use litotes without knowing it."

"Not very frequently. I have not heard of litotes."

"Just as I thought: a perfect example. If you had any sense of shame, you would avoid constructions you cannot name. Any self-respecting ignoramus would have said *seldom*. Not you; you have to affirm the negative meaning. You have to say *not very frequently*. I hope you recognise how serious this is," he continued. "Now that schools no longer teach English grammar, everyone is becoming like you. I wouldn't be surprised if you used copulative verbs without knowing it."

"I never use bad language and I've grown sick of hearing it."

"There you are!" Clifford exclaimed. You have used *grown* as a copulative verb."

"Does it matter?" I asked. "Didn't Moliere write 'For over forty years I have been speaking prose without knowing it'?"

"He did – in a play. It was a joke. It was written in fun."

"Life is full of furious fun."

"Alliteration! I don't suppose you realised."

"It was a result of unconscious deliberation."

"Oxymoron!"

"How dare you," I responded. "There is no reason for you to be rude."

"An oxymoron is a rhetorical phrase where contradictory terms are used in conjunction."

"You did I ask?"

"That is anastrophe – reversing the normal order of words."

"I'd have called it a catastrophe."

"That was either a joke," he said doubtfully, "or it was an example of catachresis."

"I'd have called it a malapropism."

"That would probably be better. It would be catachresis if you said *infer* when you meant *imply*."

"Did you have to tell me all this?" I asked.

"I suppose not," said Clifford. "I have a scrap of paper with me; I could have written you a note."

"You should save your breath and waste paper."

"That is an example of amphibology or, as some people say,

amphiboly. It is not clear whether you mean I should waste paper or whether I should save waste paper."

"You should save it always and never waste."

"An example of chiasmus: reversing the order of construction of two linked phrases. Is there no limit to your unconscious plunder of grammatical technicalities?"

"I am bound to say I find your tone a little offensive," I told him.

"By *a little*, you mean *a lot*?"

"Of course."

"That is called meiosis," he said happily. "Would you like me to give you some formal lessons in grammar?"

"I would not want you to do that; I can think of nothing I would like less."

"I suppose that is a roundabout way of saying *no*?"

"Exactly."

"Circumlocution," he cried triumphantly, "or, as we grammarians say, periphrasis."

"So you are a grammarian are you?" I said sweetly. "I was wondering what to call you."

It was some days before I spoke to Clifford again. "Mr Metcalfe was wrong," I told him.

"Impossible," he pronounced.

"It isn't a zeugma," I said. "'He left the football field covered in mud and glory' is an example of syllepsis. The verb covered is applied to two different nouns, having a different sense with each of them, but is grammatically correct with them both. In zeugma the single word fails to give meaning to one of its nouns."

"The *New Fowler's Modern English Usage* has them the other way round but in any case says that the distinction is no longer useful and the word syllepsis is no longer used."

"Does it matter?" I asked.

"I suppose not," he admitted.

"Just for once I agree with you, Cliff," I smiled.

"I object to the hypocorism," he said. "Kindly use my full name."

Never to Return

Caesar entered the room looking pale and uncertain. His usual carefree and arrogant nature had given way to nervousness and uncertainty. He shook himself vigorously and trotted to the centre of the room near to the armchair, where I was sitting reading the newspaper.

"You look as if you have seen a ghost," I said.

"I have seen a terrible thing."

"Tell me about it."

Caesar settled himself on his rug, looked up at me and began, slowly and quietly.

"You know how much the neighbours have been quarrelling recently?" he asked.

"You mean Madge and Jeremy Blewitt? They are married. It is quite natural for them to quarrel."

"It doesn't seem natural to me. I don't argue with anyone like that."

"That is because you are not married," I said.

"Dogs don't get married," he muttered, "but I go steady with the bitch at number ten."

I mused for a while on Caesar's idea of going steady. It didn't seem a good time to make fun of him. He did seem to be genuinely disturbed.

"Go on with your story," I offered.

"Last night," he continued, "they seemed to argue more than usual and then, this morning, I saw them going out together. It looked to me as if Mrs Blewitt didn't want to go and Mr Blewitt was hurrying her along. They didn't take their car but walked towards the centre of town. I followed."

"Why did you do that?"

"I was curious," Caesar answered, "and as it so happened I didn't have anything better to do."

I nearly commented that he never had anything better to do.

"OK, so you followed," I prompted.

"We walked for about fifteen minutes. Mrs Blewitt kept stopping, as if she wanted to turn back, but Mr Blewitt kept pushing her along. Finally, we came to a large building and they went in."

"And that was it?"

"Of course not," he remonstrated. "I followed them."

"No one stopped you?"

"No. I kept very close to them. People either don't notice or don't mind being followed by a dog, so that wasn't difficult. People in the building may have assumed that we were together."

"Very clever."

"It was then that I saw a terrible thing."

"Go on."

"I saw the Blewitts go together into a small room. I was standing directly outside and could see that no one else was in there. There were no windows; neither were there any other doors. The door closed and I waited right outside. Five minutes later, the door of the room opened and Mr Blewitt came out. His wife was nowhere to be seen. I could see clearly into the room and it was easy to see that it was completely empty." Caesar shuddered. "I don't understand how the room could have been empty but it was."

Caesar, who normally did not have a care in the world, was visibly shaken.

"It is an odd story," I admitted. "Are you sure that Madge didn't come out earlier, when you were not looking?" Even at the expense of upsetting him more, I had to ask this. At the best of times, he is not noted for his ability to concentrate. If a cat had come by or another dog, he would easily have been diverted.

"I wasn't waiting for long in front of the door. I was watching it all the time."

"I'll get you something to eat," I said, hoping that the usual methods would restore his good spirits. For the first time I could remember, Caesar had no appetite.

That evening there was no sound from next door, though the lights were on and someone was clearly at home. During the next few days, I did not think too much about what Caesar had told me. For his part, Caesar gradually began to recover his spirits but spent long hours standing at the front window and would bark whenever he saw Jeremy going in or out. Neither of us saw Madge and the house remained quiet.

It was eight days after Caesar had recounted his adventure, when I encountered Jeremy in the local supermarket. We exchanged the normal pleasantries.

"How is Madge?" I asked.

"Fine," he replied and started to move away.

"I haven't seen her for a while," I said hurriedly.

He gave a non-committal grunt.

"Is she OK?" I pressed.

There seemed to be a pause, as if he was making up his mind what to say.

"Fine," he said at last.

"I wondered if she could help me with something," I continued. "I've been given a houseplant that is displaying symptoms of extreme neglect and maltreatment. I know Madge is good with houseplants. Could I bring it over for her advice?"

Jeremy seemed perplexed. After a further pause, he said, "Actually, she is not at home at present."

"Oh," I said meaningfully.

"She had to go away for a few days," he said hurriedly.

"Oh," I said again with great emphasis. "Will she be away long?"

"What?" Jeremy's attention seemed to have wandered. "Yes, it is possible. We don't know."

"Is everything OK?" I said with more sympathy.

"What?" Again the loss of attention. "Yes," he said. "Everything's fine, couldn't be better."

I had wanted to ask him about the little room and Madge's dematerialisation. But how? I couldn't say my dog had told me. People begin to regard one strangely, if one says things like that. Caesar does not talk to anyone except me. He says they wouldn't understand him.

That evening, I was sitting thinking about this. What had happened to Madge?

"You see," said Caesar, "now you are worried."

"I didn't say anything."

"You don't have to," he said. "I know how he did it," he went on.

"Did what?" I asked.

"Made her disappear."

"Tell me, then," I said with genuine curiosity.

"Magic," he said decisively.

"There is no such thing," I said witheringly.

"Yes there is. I saw it on television."

"What did you see?"

"I saw a man make a woman disappear."

"That was a trick. It is not real."

"It looked real enough. First she was there and then she was gone. The audience in the studio seemed convinced."

"It was still a trick, an illusion."

"Then why did they put it on television?" Caesar complained. "It's not right. It is misleading. I'll get you to write to the BBC for me. I don't pay a licence fee to be hoodwinked by people I have never even met."

"You don't pay the fee," I reminded him. "I pay it."

"It's the same thing. The principle is the same."

"People like to watch magicians creating illusions," I told him.

"Why do they? Dogs don't. Dogs like things to appear as they are. I think dogs are wiser than people," Caesar declared.

There was a pause.

"What is an illusion?" Caesar asked. It was typical of Caesar that he would talk about something and halfway through the conversation admit he didn't know what he was discussing.

"An illusion is a false or misleading appearance," I answered. "An illusionist makes people believe that they have seen something other than what was real, like sawing a woman in half."

"Do they do that?"

"They make you think they do. It is an illusion."

"Is it always a woman?"

"Yes."

"I wonder why," said Caesar. There are some things one cannot explain to a dog. I didn't try.

"Perhaps Mr Blewitt only created the illusion that his wife had disappeared," he suggested.

"Just for your benefit?" I said scornfully.

"You don't think it's likely?"

"No."

It was two weeks before Madge returned. We saw her coming up the path to her front door. She was carrying a small suitcase and several parcels. Jeremy went out to help her with the parcels. They exchanged a long, warm kiss.

"Where was she then?" Caesar asked.

"That is their business," I said. "It doesn't do to pry into other people's affairs."

A few days later, I was out walking with Caesar. He pointed to a large building across the road.

"That is where it happened," he said.

"Where what happened?"

"Where she disappeared."

"Let's go in," I said.

There were no rooms leading off the foyer of the office building. I noticed that Trounce and Simkins, Solicitors, had their offices on the third floor. That might or might not explain things in a number of ways but it wasn't anything to do with me. Caesar, however, was my responsibility. I pressed the lift button.

"Caesar," I called, "come here."

The lift doors opened.

"Let's go in," I said to Caesar.

He took one look and ran away faster than I had ever seen him move before.

Very Special Education

Duffborough West Comprehensive School is in no way remarkable. The performance of its pupils has never been better than average. Never particularly favoured by ambitious parents, never in any way identified as a failing school, it has effortlessly and unconsciously avoided the spotlight of publicity. Indeed, DWC – as it is popularly known – could have been exactly what Alastair Campbell was thinking of when once, in a moment of political and linguistic madness, he referred to "the bog standard comprehensive". All this could change if the new Chair of Governors gets his way.

In – what he calls – real life, Dr Mark Arbiter is Senior Lecturer in Law at nearby Duffborough University.

"We were approached to nominate someone to serve on the governing body. The Vice-Chancellor knew I was interested in education – not many of us are – and suggested me."

He joined the governors three years ago and became chairman at the end of last year. The government's commitment to the development of specialist schools has given a focus for his determination to make DWC a school of which Duffborough can be proud – a beacon shedding light on its neighbours, a school like no other, leading where others will follow.

"Other schools seek to become centres of excellence in Music or Drama, in Engineering, Technology or Science, in Sport, in Foreign Languages, even in Business Studies and Enterprise. That is fine for them but a school should build on its strengths. The Green Paper proposed a new National Centre for Gifted and Talented Youth. We are happy to see others bid for that particular honour. Here, we feel we are part of the mainstream. We see Duffborough as the natural venue for a new National Centre for Ungifted and Untalented Youth. Naturally, at the centre of the curriculum will be study of the law."

"You want DWC to specialise in putting young people on the first steps to becoming lawyers?"

"Of course not! What a ridiculous idea. The profession has no place for the ungifted. But everyone needs some knowledge of the law. In this world, you need to know your rights – whom to sue and how to go about it.

"Just think about it. Every time you step out of your house, you risk tripping on a paving stone or being hit by falling masonry. You may be involved in a traffic accident; you may be the victim of an assault or invasion of privacy. If your health has been damaged by smoking, you may be able to sue the tobacco manufacturers. If you suffered as a secondary smoker in the workplace, perhaps you can sue your employer. And never forget, the less you know about your legal rights, the more vulnerable you are. What's more, the less success you have had in life, the more help you are likely to need from the law. You are more likely to have bought shoddy or faulty goods, have more about which to complain, and have more regulations to understand about all the benefits you can claim.

"That is why we will develop GCSE examinations in really useful subjects like *Civil Rights* and *Compensation Claims* – not just dry academic studies, but practical courses based in the real world. All pupils will go on an Outward Bound course, where they will develop self-awareness, self-confidence and communication skills. The object will be to exercise initiative and resourcefulness and return with a case for compensation.

"We have already carried out a pilot project," Dr Arbiter continued. "Some pupils found the course very demanding but they have risen to the task and shown great initiative. One has indicated his intention to sue his teacher for stress caused by overwork."

"Not at all what you were expecting? How did the teacher feel about this?"

"He was very proud."

[First published in *Education, Public Law and the Individual (EPLI)* – *Vol. 6, Issue 2,* September 2001.]

The Servant Problem

"Edith," I called. "Edith."

"Who is Edith?" Emmeline asked.

"The servant girl. Servant girls are always called Edith."

"We haven't got a servant girl."

"Are you sure?"

"Positive," she replied. "We have never had a servant girl."

"Perhaps it's her night off," I suggested.

"No."

"She shouldn't work every evening."

"She doesn't."

"Who doesn't?"

"Edith."

"Who is Edith?" I asked.

"You are impossible," Emmeline declared.

"I don't think I can be," I responded. "I think, therefore I exist. I exist, therefore I must be possible."

"Do you?" There was a touch of surprise in her voice.

"Do I exist?"

"No," she said gently, "do you think? I haven't seen much evidence of it lately."

Sometimes my wife says the strangest things.

"You are changing the subject," I complained.

"What is the subject?"

"We were discussing the servant girl."

"We do not have a servant girl," Emmeline said with exasperation. "We have never had a servant girl. Very few people do have servant girls these days."

"I read somewhere that there were more servant girls in England than there were cotton workers and that cotton was our biggest industry."

"That was in the mid-nineteenth century. Cotton is no longer a major industry and servant girls have all but died out."

"What about Edith?"

"There is no such person as Edith."

"It's a very common name."

"Not really," said Emmeline. "It used to be but it has gone out of fashion."

"Perhaps that is why there are not many servant girls any longer," I suggested.

Emmeline sighed.

"I wonder who cleans the bathroom floor," I continued.

"You do know then that it has to be cleaned?" Emmeline said acidly.

"So I understand. I don't know much about it."

"I have to do it," Emmeline claimed, "like most things about the house."

"That doesn't seem fair somehow."

"I couldn't agree more."

"I don't like to think about you doing all that work," I said sadly.

"What are you going to do about it?" she asked, managing to sound as if her expectations were modest.

"I could think about something else, I suppose."

"That is not going to help me."

"It would help me," I responded. "Surely any help to one of us is a help to us both. We are a couple, a partnership."

"But you'll still leave me doing all the work?"

"That doesn't seem right."

"I'm darned sure it's not right. The question is: what are you going to do about it?"

"It is an interesting question. I've not heard any like it for quite some time."

"It is a practical question and I think it is incumbent upon you to give me an answer."

"That is a posh way of putting it," I complimented her. "You really do express yourself very well."

"I am waiting," she said impatiently.

"What is it you want?"

"Put simply, so that even you can understand it," she added unnecessarily, "I want some help about the house."

"Why don't we employ a servant girl?" I suggested.

History and All That

Widely known as a man of letters – I can recite all twenty-six of them and in the order nature intended – I am often asked to explain History. Not only family and friends, but sometimes complete strangers, come up to me and ask, "What is it all about?"

Quite often I am taken off my guard – my mind on other things – and I just mutter something incomprehensible. Certainly I hope it is incomprehensible; I would not want anyone to know what I am thinking when I am off my guard. On other occasions, I explain it all, lucidly, eloquently and comprehensively. Such occasions are rare.

The time has come to write it down.

The first thing to know about history – or History, to give it its full name – is that there is too much of it, and much more than there used to be. In the old days, they did not have this problem. Take the Romans, or the Ancient Romans, as they preferred to be called. They had a few hundred years of their own history plus some scraps they had inherited from the Greeks – and that was it. There was just the right amount for them to get their minds round and enough blood and gore to maintain their interest. There were only a few people trying to write books about it and not many more who could read them. Most things that tried to pass into history came straight out the other side and were completely forgotten. Thus did the Roman Empire last for more than five hundred years.

Then some fool went and invented newspapers. This was much later, by which time there was a lot more history. Soon it was the twentieth century and all hell let loose. To tell the truth – I will try most things once – it is all the fault of the twentieth century. Never in the course of human endeavour was so much history created by so many for... so many. It is not only the newspapers I blame. I blame mass education. I blame the cinema. I do not excuse television, for with television came the repeat and without repetition history would soon wither and die.

More than all these things, I blame the fall of empire and the rise of nationalism. No sooner does a new country emerge than it demands a history of its own. Territories that had once formed part of the British Empire were very well catered for by a dose of British History. As soon as they became independent this wasn't good enough any more. They had to have a flag, an anthem and some history. It was no use explaining that no one would recognise the flag and that their anthem would very likely be confused with someone else's. It was even more futile to explain there was a glut of history and less rather than more was needed. One might as well tell them they should not have refrigerators because the Americans have already got too many.

But why blame the Americans, when we can blame the Russians? The fall of the Soviet Union was the occasion of the biggest expansion of history in – how can we best put it? – in History. Also, there has been a significant rise in the number of people – politicians for the most part, but we will call them people – who set out to make history. Such people should be put down or, at least stood down or, at the very least, sent to Coventry and ignored.

Where should we be if everybody tried to make history? Think of that – if you have nothing better to do. Alternatively, teach yourself to speak Chinese.

So there we are. There is too much of it. History is as much subject to Malthusian laws as is population. Malthus taught that population had a tendency to expand faster than the means of subsistence. History has already expanded beyond breaking point. Those wise pioneers of the art of popular History, Sellar and Yeatman, in their ground-breaking treatise, *1066 and All That*, could write that, "as every schoolboy knows" etc., etc. But that was then and now is now, and you cannot say something like that anymore. There is nothing that every schoolboy knows. Indeed, one might go further and say that there is plenty that no schoolboy knows, while the cynics among us might say there are plenty of schoolboys who know nothing at all.

Indeed, today we might question whether there is such a thing as popular History. Did anyone ever vote for it? There is no record of such a happening.

One problem remains. What shall we do about it? More History keeps getting produced and no one is willing to identify and dispose of any that is surplus to requirements. They hoard old History, in case it might be wanted at some time in the future. I propose a moratorium. No new History should be allowed without the verifiable and permanent decommissioning of old stock. This will require careful planning and execution.

I seek no special recognition for having found the answer, nor do I wish politicians and administrators to come knocking on my door asking how to implement the policy. Implementation of policy is what they get paid for. My gift, which I give freely, is in the realm of ideas.

Eureka

The first time I received a letter from Albert Onejug suggesting it was time for my annual review, I was more than a little puzzled. It was less than six months since I had appointed him as my Independent Scientific Adviser.

"I think you will come to see it is more profitable if we have two reviews a year," he said, when we met. "This is really a half-yearly review, when we take stock of concerns previously raised and check that you are comfortable with all the contingent matters."

"I am not sure what you mean," I confessed.

"You have no need to worry about that," he reassured me. "Many of my clients don't understand a word I say but, as long as they continue to pay my fee, I never complain."

I admired his generosity of spirit.

"And you think that this meeting will be to my profit?" I asked.

"I suppose it might be," he mused. "I never really thought about it."

"But you said that I would see it is more profitable to have two reviews a year."

"For me, dear boy," he exclaimed, "more profitable for me. Don't forget this is my living."

"That is worth remembering," I replied.

"It is very important to you that I have high earnings."

"Is it?" I asked doubtfully.

"Absolutely," he affirmed. "If I had come here on public transport and turned up wearing a scruffy shirt and looking as if I wondered where my next meal was coming from, would you have confidence in me?"

"I suppose not."

"Of course not. You would think I couldn't be of any use to you. You want to consult someone who is successful, who obviously is good at his job."

"You said you were an expert," I reminded him.

"And that is just what you want," he said. "It is all about confidence. Unless you have confidence in me, all my efforts to advise you will be fruitless."

"You mean I would never be sure if I needed a second opinion?"

"Exactly," he said, "but when you see me in my Armani suit and look out of the window at my new Daimler, you can feel that your affairs are in the hands of a top adviser."

"I see," I said thoughtfully.

"Last time I was here," Albert said, changing the subject, "I remember we drank a very fine single malt whisky."

I also remembered. There was not much remaining in the bottle by the time he left.

"I thought you might prefer coffee this evening," I suggested.

"I wouldn't want to put you to any trouble," Albert said considerately. "Whisky will be fine."

I fetched a bottle, a jug of cold water and two glasses.

"Only a little," said Albert, "just a small double."

We sat in silence for a few minutes, sipping our drinks.

"As I see it," he said after a while, "you are a little rusty on Archimedes' principle."

One had to admit that he did his homework.

"I've done my homework," he said. "I've examined your portfolio and Archimedes' principle clearly needs some revision."

There was no concealing the fact. I would have been hard put to bring the subject into intelligent conversation.

"Wasn't he one of those Greek chaps I met at school?" I asked.

"I didn't think you were that old," he said, demonstrating that I was not the only one who had difficulty with intelligent conversation.

I ignored the remark.

"He was the chap who said '*Eureka*'," I said.

"Very good," he complimented me. "You have a good grasp of the essentials."

"And that was when he discovered it?"

"Indeed it was. He was very pleased with himself."

"So he shouted '*Eureka*'?"

"No, he spoke Greek; he shouted '*Heureka*', meaning '*I have found*'."

"He meant he had found his principle?"

"Exactly."

"Where was it?" I asked.

"You mean where did he discover it?"

"Yes."

"In his bath," Albert told me, rather improbably I thought.

"And then he shouted '*Eureka*' or '*Heureka*'?"

"I think he got out of the bath first," said Albert. "Then he went running through the streets. That is when he shouted '*Eureka*'."

"You mean '*Heureka*'?"

"Of course."

"I suppose he got dressed first," I said thoughtfully.

"I would have thought that probable," he replied, "but many authorities think not."

"How did it get into his bath," I asked, "this principle of his?"

"It was in the water. That is what it was all about."

"Can you remind me?" I asked.

"He realised that an object immersed, or even partly immersed, in water weighs less than when it is not immersed in water."

"And so?"

"The difference is equal to the weight of the water displaced."

"And that's it? That was his principle."

"It still is."

"Was he a very principled man?"

"No, he was a mathematician," Albert informed me.

"That sounds serious," I suggested.

"It was. He died of it."

"He died of being a mathematician?"

"He was killed by a Roman soldier during the siege of Syracuse. It is said that Archimedes ignored a challenge by the soldier because he was immersed in a mathematical problem."

"He should have stayed in his bath," I said brightly.

A Case of Lingomalignus

(A Consultation from the Casebook of Dr Magnus Fell)

- Hi there, pill pusher. Long time no see.

- *My patients do not usually address me in that way. Are you trying deliberately to be rude?*

- Sorry, doc. I don't mean to be sassy. I wouldn't give you the business. I'm just trying to break the ice.

- *If I want any ice broken, I'll let you know. In the meantime, what brings you to me?*

- It's the lingo. Every time I flap my jaw, never mind it's something cosmic – playing for real, it comes out like I'm batting the breeze.

- *You mean people think you are being flippant, even when you try to be serious?*

- Yeah – they treat me like I'm some sort of bubblehead or ding-a-ling.

- *What about at work?*

- The same old shit.

- *I would rather you did not use that sort of language in my consulting room.*

- Sorry. I can't straighten out. I never used to cuss. It beats me how I got started. I'd dig the most to kick the habit.

- *When did this begin?*
- I'll start from scratch and lay it out for you. I've always been a square sort of guy – nothing funky or freaky or kooky about me.
- *I have always thought you very respectable.*
- Yeah – I'm one of them.
- *A High Court judge.*
- Sure thing – a beak, a gavel jockey.
- *Presumably you can't talk like this on the bench?*
- Ain't that my spiel?
- *So what happened?*
- I'm trying to spill the beans. If you don't butt in and step on my lines, I'll clue you in.
- *Please continue.*
- I get a lot of low lives – guys and dolls who've had the finger put on them – some of them real sleazeballs. They blow in with their mouthpiece and I have to give 'em a square deal. Sometimes I don't get the drift of their lingo. To me it sounds like gogbbledygookese – like bafflegab. Sometimes I'm quite spaced out, bamboozled, buffaloed. I knew if I was going to carry on in my racket and stay at the top of the heap, I had to wise up. You dig me?
- *I think so. You had difficulty understanding some of the things people said, who came before you in court, and you decided that you needed to study the language they used. I take it that you weren't used to people using slang.*
- No way. My neck of the woods is squaresville. I hang out with a mob of eggheads.
- *What action did you take to extend your vocabulary?*
- I picked up a bible.
- *A book?*
- Sure thing. Ain't that my drift? Yeah – I got a bible of the street talk.
- *A dictionary of slang? Did it help?*
- It really turned me on.
- *You found it interesting.*

- I was quite hooked. I hit the sack late but I couldn't get to sleepville. Eventually I must have copped a nod and when I rolled out and hit the deck, I'd shifted gears.
- *You could only speak in slang?*
- Dead on. You're on the button.
- *I am afraid that you have an unusual condition known as lingomalignus.*
- Who's she, when she's at home?
- *It is a language deficiency brought on by over-exposure to slang. It seems that you became so absorbed in the dictionary of slang that it took over that part of the brain that controls your speech.*
- How does this gel?
- *Have you ever heard the economist's expression, "bad money drives out good"?*
- Sure thing – but it's a double zero to me.
- *To put it simply, there are many forms of money – coins, banknotes, cheques and many items of value that can double as money, like precious stones, rare postage stamps and many other things.*
- Yeah. So where are you heading?
- *The theory is that people will hold on to the form of money they think most likely to hold its value and off-load, that is spend, the rest. When coins were made of precious metal, you would want to off-load those that had been shaved of some of their worth. If you find a foreign coin in your change, you will spend it at the first opportunity.*
- You've blown your lines – I'm a beak.
- *I'm sorry. Of course you wouldn't do anything dishonest. I could never think that of any member of Her Majesty's Judiciary. I was generalising. The point is that people try to get rid of their most worthless possessions, in this case the form of money least likely to hold its value. It is the same with language. Your mind had become cluttered up with substandard words and phrases and, subconsciously, you are trying to off-load them.*
- How can I wind it up, pack it in, pull the plug, choke it off?
- *It is not all that difficult, though it may take a little time. You will have to undergo a course of aversion therapy.*
- Sounds like a cool gimmick. I'll try it for size.

- *We have to associate your use of slang with something that you find unpleasant. I want you to put five pounds into a box for charity every time you use a use a slang word or phrase.*

- I'm always giving handouts. I get a kick from it. It gives me a buzz.

- *This will have to be a charity, a bona fide charity, but one that you personally would never support.*

- Like for homeless pooches – for mutts without a pad.

- *I see. I take it that in normal circumstances you would not support the Royal Society for the Prevention of Cruelty to Animals.*

- Not my cup of tea. I'd rather give my mazuma to the little guys.

- *Then the RSPCA will be ideal for our purposes. Come back and see me in two weeks' time and we can see how you are getting along.*

- That's peachy – just jake with me.

- *As you yourself might say, it's what the doctor ordered.*

The Rites of Rong

A new biography by the grandson of Siggy Fraud is surprisingly sympathetic to Carl "Gusty" Rong. Dr Claud Fraud's newest book, "The Rites of Rong" casts new light on the relationship between Siggy Fraud, the inventor of psychoanalysis, and Gusty Rong, at one time his close collaborator and most likely successor. The breach came when Gusty first began to question the inner meaning of psychoanalysis. *Psycho*, he reasoned, meant a deranged person, *anal* implied a concern with bodily waste matter discharged through the anus, and *sis* meant process. A psychoanalyst, he declared, must be able to demonstrate an insane interest in human excreta.

Siggy was appalled. The prefix *Psycho*, Siggy argued, had no necessary link with madness; it simply indicated something to do with the mind. *Analy* was a diminutive form of the word analogue – a representation of measurement. It followed that Psychoanalysis was the process of measuring how much your sister thought about it. It was fundamental to Siggy's thinking that *it* must be sex and that the word *sister* represented not just one's relation but all women. To be a successful psychoanalyst, said Siggy, one must show what in a layman would be considered an abnormal interest in the sex lives of women.

For Siggy Fraud then, sex was the key to the mind. Indeed, in comparing him to Gusty one might almost say that for Siggy sex was all in the mind. Gusty insisted that sex was not important. This was no untested theory. To validate his hypothesis he systematically slept with all his female patients. If he had the slightest suspicion that sex was important to them, he repeated the procedure until all doubt was removed. But what about the reverse hypothesis, that it was only those seeking treatment for whom sex was unimportant? Gusty was too canny to let this possibility remain untested and diligently made his female colleagues and associates act as a control group.

Even for men sex was not to be over-rated and sexual attraction – let alone love, whatever that was – was certainly not important enough to form the basis of a happy marriage. Ever true to his principles, Gusty Rong quite openly married for something he considered much more important, namely money. It was a matter of principle, the same principle that led him later to invite his senior mistress to live together with himself and his wife. He expressed it in simple terms: what is good for Gusty is good for everyone else.

A lonely child with a vivid imagination, Gusty had spent his early years observing his parents and teachers.

"Why are you looking through that keyhole?" his father had asked one day.

"God knows," Gusty had unthinkingly replied, so providing an answer that more than satisfied the elder Rong, a clergyman by trade.

The incident did much to persuade the young Gusty of the value of religion, while what he saw through that keyhole provided him his first great psychological insight. Doing it to yourself he named introversion; doing something roughly similar to someone else he called extroversion. Everyone, he declared, has tendencies in both directions.

Always a dreamer, after his break with Fraud, Gusty became increasingly irrational, keeping records of all his strange experiences. Gathering around him a group of disciples and admirers, who like him had no idea what they were doing, he developed the influential idea of the collective unconscious. Somewhere in the inherited structure of the brain, so Gusty came to believe, were stored inherited memories that made conscious thought superfluous. "Dream and the world dreams with you," he wrote, "think and you think alone." The American poet Ella Wheeler Wilcox was to develop similar ideas in relation to laughing and weeping.

According to Gusty, the collective unconscious contains archetypes. Put simply, this means that everyone from whatever culture was programmed to believe in fairies. In folk legend, such stories are full of cruelty, irrationality and arbitrariness. Gusty was convinced that it was the possession of these very qualities that would ensure his place in history. Ever boastful and with a rare show of sincerity he declared his aims, "Show me a sane man and I will cure him for you."

Besides providing these useful insights into the main body of Rong's work, this new study also tackles the controversial issue of his alleged anti-Semitism and support of Nazi ideals. Claud Fraud shows convincingly that this was nonsense. Even in 1918, he had believed that Germany held a special place in Europe. The coming of the Nazis supported this view and there was no reason for him to refuse professorships in Zürich and Basel. Without the Jews, there were fewer people qualified to fill such important posts and someone had to be willing to accept the power and the glory. After the war, he would speak out quite clearly against Hitler. His earlier writing and associations had been not the product of any philosophical sympathy with Nazi policies but simple, intelligent and self-serving opportunism. One's highest duty is to oneself, he had declared, catching the spirit of the time. As this brilliant biography shows, never did Gusty Rong cease to be true to the hypocritical oath he had sworn as a young man.

Luddites of the Modern World

Just the other day, or at any rate sometime in the last six months, Emmeline made a comment about all the jobs needing to be done about the house. As I remember it, she was quite passionate about the subject, shouting and saying something about my having to cook my own dinner. The strange thing was she seemed to think I ought to be doing all these jobs – whatever they were. I think she mentioned something about the house falling apart but that may have been a joke. She said the same thing last year and the house is still in one piece.

Be that as it may, this morning I came across a can of lubricant, intended for loosening metal joints and for preventing rust. I found it on the bookcase, where I recalled having put it two weeks earlier having found it in a cupboard. Now, just by chance, I remembered the garage door makes a very loud squeaking noise every time it is opened or closed and I had resolved to do something about it. Well, to cut a short story shorter, I decided to apply the lubricant to the joint. I read the instructions on the can and followed them to the letter. When it comes to do-it-myself, if I do it at all, I am the very model of orthodox conformity. I sprayed the joint exactly as instructed. I made sure the lubricant had covered all the moving parts and worked it into the joints by repeatedly opening and closing the door.

None of this made the slightest difference. The door still squeaks as merrily as ever. I am not surprised. It was ever like this. Do-it-myself never produces results, or at least not the sort of desirable results for which one might hope.

I remember the time I painted the carpet. I thought the speckled effect looked quite effective. Emmeline didn't agree. She said I only needed to paint the ceiling and the walls.

"Everybody does it that way," I argued. "I thought I'd be a little different."

"No one could say you are not a little different," she sighed enigmatically, "but I am not having a carpet with paint all over it."

Emmeline insisted on buying a new carpet. It was a shame I had not painted the carpet out of doors. The paint soon comes off anything I paint outdoors.

It seems to me that some people are just not designed for doing certain things. Emmeline looked at me pointedly and said some people seem to be designed to do nothing. I don't think that can be true and I don't know why she said it in that particularly censorious tone of voice, as if it were my fault. No, my point – and I made it to her – is that some people are made to do it themselves and some are not. This is as it should be. There are those in this world who earn their livings by doing it for others. Where would they be if we all did it ourselves? How would they live? Who would provide sustenance for them? Who would care for their children?

Now I think about it, I realise it is not a design characteristic that inhibits me from doing-it-myself. It is an advanced sensibility. Each time I go so far as to pick up a paintbrush, I see before me images of starving children. I see their poor mothers, ragged and gaunt. I see the squalor of the workhouse. Emmeline says the last workhouses were abolished by the 1929 Local Government Act, but my imagination has an historical proclivity. How could I bear to be responsible for all this suffering? As Eliza Doolittle might have put it, it would do me in. I have no wish to be done in. I hereby resolve never to raise a paintbrush again.

Now another image looms up before me. I see great processions of the unemployed descending on Parliament, waving their banners and demanding the return of Capitalism. "Give us back our jobs," they cry. "Down with the do-it-themselvers."

Of course! Where would we all be, if we all did it ourselves? Builders, decorators, plumbers and electricians are most at risk, but also many others. If we all baked our own bread, the bakers would be out of work. If we all grew our own vegetables, the farmers would soon be bankrupt. When Grandma knits a cardigan, does she consider the factory workers thus made redundant? When you walk to the newsagent to collect your morning paper, do you think about the news delivery boys thrown on the scrap heap? And what about all the recreational gardeners? It may be recreation to them; it could be paid employment for millions. Millions of would-be workers deprived of honest work: it is such a waste. It is so sad. Instead of praising the recreational gardener, we should recognise him for the anti-social creature he is.

I see it all now. The vogue for doing-it-yourself is dangerously subversive. The wealth of modern civilisation was built on the ability of man to sell his labour. Division of labour allows us all to concentrate on what we do best, to the ultimate enrichment of us all. If I put up a shelf, it takes me five or six times as long as it would a skilled craftsman – and it is more likely to collapse at some future time, causing considerable damage and expense. The do-it-yourselfers are the Luddites of the modern world. They must be stopped. I shall do my bit. I will become a *Campaigner to Let Others Do It*, or CLOT. Once I have given a lead, other campaigners will rush to join me. Soon there will be CLOTs all over the world. As the inspiration and founder of this international movement, I shall be recognised everywhere as a Prime CLOT. I shall travel the globe, lecturing to other CLOTs. This is important work. I must get started right away. Better still, I shall let someone else start it.

Here's a How-de-doo!

(A Consultation from the Casebook of Dr Magnus Fell)

- Good day, sir.
- *Good morning. What brings you to me today?*
- To consult you on a very important matter.
- *I hope it is not too serious.*
- My hopeless fear no soul can measure.
- *Have you any physical symptoms?*
- I have a left shoulder blade that is a miracle of loveliness.
- *Do you think this is a problem?*
- Of that there is no manner of doubt – no probable, possible shadow of doubt – no possible doubt whatever.
- *There are those who would disagree about that, unless there are other symptoms.*
- I've got a little list.
- *I think I understand. You may have some inherited complaint. I think we need to delve into your family background.*
- My family pride is something inconceivable.
- *Just as I suspected. I believe your family has lived in this County since the time of Henry VIII.*
- Spurn not the nobly born.
- *I would never do that. I remember your father well.*

- He was a kind and goodly man, and naturally prone, instead of taking others' gold, to give away his own.

- *I remember that he was very generous but I hear that he has been unwell.*

- A taste for drink combined with gout, has doubled him up for ever.

- *I am sorry.*

- He uses language that would make your hair curl.

- *To get back to your condition, you are suffering from GSM or Gilbertian Speech Malfunction.*

- Here's a how-de-doo!

- *Indeed. It means that your speech is composed entirely of quotations from the works of William Schwenck Gilbert.*

- I am anxious to avow my indebtedness to the author of the Bab Ballads.

- *It may have been caused by something you did as a young man.*

- When I was a lad I served a term as office boy to an Attorney's firm.

- *I see. Contact with the law can sometimes have strange effects on a man's character.*

- The law is the true embodiment of everything that's excellent. It has no kind of fault nor flaw.

- *Many think so but it can have the effect of inculcating arrogance among those who work as, or for, lawyers.*

- You've no idea what a poor opinion I have of myself – and how little I deserve it.

- *Have you had any thought as to what might have brought this on?*

- I never thought of thinking for myself at all.

- *I suspected as much. Have you any special talents?*

- I am very good at integral and differential calculus.

- *Anything else?*

- I can tell a woman's age in half a minute and I do.

- *That is not something that I would recommend. It could be regarded as rather rude.*

- I am as pleasant as can be.

- *I am sure you are.*

- Each little fault of temper and each social defect in my erring fellow-creatures I endeavour to correct.

- *I trust that they appreciate it. Tell me, has anything happened to upset you recently?*

- I fell in love with a rich attorney's elderly ugly daughter.

- *And that upset you?*

- Matrimonial devotion doesn't seem to suit her notion.

- *A pity. Perhaps if you settled down, this problem of yours would disappear. Marriage might be just what you need.*

- Oh, that the world would break down the artificial barriers of rank, wealth, education, age, beauty, habits, taste, and temper and recognise the glorious principle that in marriage alone is to be found the panacea for every ill!

- *You seem to know your Gilbert and Sullivan pretty well.*

- I've wisdom from the East and from the West, that's subject to no academic rule.

- *Of course.*

- Things are seldom what they seem.

- *I take it that you would like to be cured?*

- Wherefore waste our elocution on impossible solution? Life's a pleasant institution; let us take it as it comes.

- *But it may be possible to cure you.*

- Modified rapture.

- *Do you listen to music?*

- It revolts me but I do it.

- *The cure will require that you spend at least two hours each evening listening to grand opera. Wagner would be ideal.*

- I would rather hear Annie Laurie sung with feeling than the greatest singer in the world declaiming a scene from Tristan and Isolde.

- *Not one of your interests then?*

- I know merely that there is composition and decomposition.

- *I am afraid that this is the only cure there is. It is up to you.*

- Conceive me, if you can, an every-day young man: a commonplace type, with a stick and a pipe.

- *Maybe, maybe not but we should at least cure you of Gilbertian Speech Malfunction.*

- My brain it teems with endless schemes.

- *Good luck to you.*

The symptoms of *Gilbertian Speech Malfunction* are listed below, in the order in which they appeared.

The Sorcerer (1877) Act 1.
ditto
ditto
The Mikado (1885) Act 2.
The Gondoliers (1889) Act 1.
The Mikado (1885) Act 1.
ditto
Iolanthe (1882) Act 1.
Bab Ballads – Mister William.
The Gondoliers (1889) Act 1.
Ruddigore (1887) Act 1.
The Mikado (1885) Act 1.
Confessing self-plagiarism when addressing the O. P. Club at a dinner held in his honour. Printed in The Daily Telegraph, 31 December 1906.
HMS Pinafore (1878) Act 1.
Iolanthe (1882) Act 1.
Ruddigore (1887) Act 1.
HMS Pinafore (1878) Act 1.
The Pirates of Penzance (1879) Act 1.
Princess Ida (1884) Act 1.
ditto
ditto
Trial By Jury (1875) Act 1.

The Mikado (1885) Act 2.
The Sorcerer (1877) Act 1.
The Yeomen of the Guard (1888) Act 1.
HMS Pinafore (1878) Act 2.
The Gondoliers (1889) Act 1.
The Mikado (1885) Act 1.
ditto
Quoted in Hesketh Pearson, Gilbert and Sullivan, Ch.4.1.
ditto
Patience (1881) Act 2.
The Mikado (1885) Act 1.

Heavenly Thoughts

"Do you have any books in heaven?" I asked God one day.

"Why do you ask?" I could hear that He was amused by the question.

"I just wondered," I said, "There is so much I will never find the time for down here. Do you know that Trollope alone wrote forty-seven novels and an autobiography, as well as other works?"

"I know everything," God answered imperiously. One of his troubles is that He is easily irritated.

"Then there is Dickens," I continued, unperturbed, "George Eliot, the Brontës, Tolstoy and all those Russians – there is so much to read and re-read. I cannot imagine that Heaven would be heaven without books."

"If you ever get there," said God, "and it is by no means certain you will – or that you won't for that matter – *if* you get there, you will find pleasures and delights of which you cannot even dream."

"Tell me about them," I suggested.

"They are not for the telling," God replied.

"That is your big mistake," I said. "You've been very nice to me lately – I would like to give you some advice."

He laughed. He was uncommonly good tempered that day.

"How have I been nice to you?" He asked.

"Wasn't it you that saved me from getting run over last week?" I asked. "If you hadn't given me a shove, I'm sure that motor cycle would have got me. There was no one else there. Wasn't it you?"

"I can neither confirm or deny it," was God's answer.

"Why not?" I asked in surprise. "I thought you could do anything."

"I choose not to confirm or deny," God answered. "Not just this but anything."

"Do you mean that you won't take credit any longer for any good things you do? This is a new turn of events."

"It is my decision."

"How long has this been going on? In the past you were always going on about how you'd done this and how you'd done that and telling everyone that they had to praise you for it."

"You will all have to be content to praise me for things long past. No longer will I publicise what I do."

"Why on earth not?" I asked.

"Modern journalism," He said bluntly.

"I don't understand," I said.

"I'll explain it simply," He said. "If I once say that some story is true, then I will forever be asked to admit or deny every story about me that appears. If I don't issue a denial of anything that someone says or writes about me – never mind how far fetched – then everyone will assume it is true. I am not prepared to spend my eternity – or that part of it shared with the human race – issuing confirmations and denials of every silly story you and your kind can think up. Your Royal Family has the same problem and most of the time deals with it in the same way."

"So you won't tell me if you saved my life?"

"I am afraid not."

"Never mind," I said magnanimously, "I will still give you the advice I mentioned."

"That is kind of you," He said quietly. I had the impression that He was laughing at me. "What is the subject of your advice?"

"Heaven," I pronounced.

"You don't know anything about Heaven."

"Exactly. Wasn't that just what I was saying earlier? My advice is that you should give it some publicity."

"Everybody knows that Heaven is waiting for those who lead a good life. It doesn't need advertising. Ask anyone and he…"

"Or she," I interjected.

"He or she," God continued irritably, "will tell you that at the end of his *or her* life, he *or she* will be judged. The good go to Heaven; the wicked… . will go elsewhere."

"But that is all they know: no more than that. You hold out Heaven as the reward for living what you call a good life – which, for many of us, involves not doing lots of things we would rather like to do. If you don't mind my saying so, you are a bit of a killjoy and you offer us a pig in a poke as a reward for putting up with it."

"What are you talking about?" said God, not unreasonably.

"Look at it this way," I said. "When someone buys a lottery scratch card, he…"

"Or she?" God interjected playfully. That would teach me to be pernickety.

"When a *man* buys a lottery ticket," I said to escape from strangling the language, "he doesn't know what, if anything, he is going to get for his money. The point is," I continued, "he spends very little money on the ticket. He is prepared to risk a pound or maybe a few pounds on the *chance* of a big reward. Very few people would gamble all they owned. You are asking us to gamble away our lives."

"I don't ask you to give up your life," God objected.

"I mean our pleasures," I explained. "In essence you are saying give up your pleasures now for greater pleasures later."

"I suppose there is a glimmer of truth in that," admitted God, "though I could argue that the good life has its rewards here on earth."

"I might agree with you about that but it doesn't remove the force of my argument. You give us no way of judging the value of the package you are offering. Lots of people are going to take their pleasures now – a bird in the hand and all that."

"I see," said God.

"One might go further," I said. "Because you are so vague about what you have to offer, many people are put off. They are thinking 'to sin or not to sin?' You might think of them as the floating sinners. If they like your manifesto, they will vote for you. They will avoid sin and lead the good life. If they can't see anything in it for them, they'll think 'what the hell' and join the sinners' party."

"You think so?"

"I am sure of it. Your secrecy leads directly to an avoidable level of sin. Sin and crime are therefore your fault because, with a change of policy, both could be reduced in an instant."

"What about the fear of eternal damnation?"

"It doesn't work," I said. "Carrots are better than sticks. Few people believe in fire and brimstone and you are not even clear about what happens to those who don't make it to Heaven. Your message on this has changed over the years and is now quite obscure."

"Suppose," He said, "just for the sake of argument, that I accept what you say. What would you suggest?"

"Full disclosure," I answered promptly. "It is the only way. Send pamphlets into every home in the world. Advertise on television. Describe what Heaven is like. Use case studies: get some of the people – or souls or whatever you call them up there – to write up their experiences. Make documentaries or publish articles with titles like *My Afterlife in Heaven* or *First Days in Heaven – An Introduction*."

"You think that would work?" God asked doubtfully.

"It would help," I reassured Him. "Of course if you really want to make an impact you could do much more. You could organise day trips to the hereafter. Let people see for themselves."

"Very tricky," He said. "You are supposed to be dead before you ascend."

"Who says so?" I demanded.

"I suppose I do," He replied after a moment's pause.

"Change it then," I said. "After all you are God."

"I suppose I could try it," He answered.

"What have you got to lose?"

"There could be a problem," He said thoughtfully. "If you are right, there would be a big jump in the numbers winning the right to enter Heaven."

"I thought you would be pleased with that," I said. "Why is it a problem?"

"I'll tell you," He said, "though I'd like you to keep it to yourself. There isn't really room up there for a sudden and large increase in numbers. It's all geared up for steady expansion century by century. This could put all our projections out. To cope properly will entail considerable investment. I shall have to think about it. I shall have to do the calculations and calculate the costs."

"Are you telling me that your decisions are resource driven?" I gasped.

"Aren't everyone's?" God responded.

Heaven Forfend

"Why don't you use the word *forfend*?" Clifford suggested.

"For whom?"

"Instead of *Heaven forbid*, have him say *Heaven forfend*."

Clifford had moved into critical mode, having failed on this occasion to find any spelling mistakes or gross grammatical errors.

"I have never heard the expression," I admitted. "What does it mean?"

"What it always meant," he replied helpfully. "Dictionary."

"I don't believe it."

"You have to use a dictionary," he said patiently. "Then you can find out what the word means. That is what dictionaries are for."

This was not unreasonable. I moved to my desk and sat down. I completed my researches in less than a minute.

"It's obsolete," I said.

"Obsolete!" Clifford exploded.

"It says *forfend or forefend: Obsolete. to prohibit or prevent*."

"That is what you want."

"I can't use forfend. My readers won't know what it means."

"What readers?"

"Emmeline, Amos, Daniel…"

"I didn't realise you had so many friends."

"Family."

"Ah!"

There was a long pause.

"No one will know what *forfend* means," I said at last.

"They can look it up. Education never did anyone any harm. Anyway, they should know what it means. Who says it's obsolete?"

"The dictionary."

Clifford's features began to show signs of an incipient volcanic activity.

"*The dictionary?*" He erupted. "There is not only one dictionary. There are any number of dictionaries. They proliferate like heavyweight boxing champions."

"What do you know about boxing champions?"

"Virtually nothing. No more than you seem to know about dictionaries."

"I was using Collins."

"That is a good dictionary," he admitted reluctantly.

"I am sure the company will be delighted to have your approval."

"And it says *forfend* is obsolete?"

"Not in the United States."

"This is England," Clifford said grandly.

"Of course. I shouldn't have mentioned it."

"It was irrelevant but then so is so much of what you say."

I apologised.

"What does GOD say?" Clifford asked.

While I was consulting the Oxford English Dictionary, Clifford said he was glad to hear that the Americans were preserving the language.

"But *forfend* means something different there."

"Different?"

"Yes. It means to protect or secure."

"We should never have let those Americans have our

language," Clifford complained. They don't know how to look after it. They are always changing things."

"Not this time," I told him joyfully, finding the entry in the OED. "In the past it was used in that way here as well. The Americans have preserved the meaning. It is we who have lost it."

"GOD says that?"

"Indeed it does. It also confirms that the word forfend is obsolete here in all its meanings."

"This is very bad news," Clifford said. "If we cannot look to the OED to protect our language, on whom can we depend?"

"Words become obsolete when no one uses them. You can't blame the people who compile the dictionaries."

"Then I blame writers in general. We seem to have lost a fine word – short, melodious, clear – and all because writers, who have some influence in these matters, allowed it to die. You like to think of yourself as a writer. You have a responsibility in this matter."

"I'll do what I can to put matters right," I promised him.

This conversation took place some years ago. As time passed, I noticed the word coming more and more into use. I would like it to be known, I claim no credit for this.

How to Get Rich

"How can I make myself rich?" my good friend Richard asked me one day. I am calling him Richard so that you will not identify him. Were I to give his real name, most readers would recognise him immediately.

"How rich do you want to be?" I asked carefully.

"I am still a young man," he said – this was many years ago – "and I don't want to be greedy. I just want to be rich enough so that I never have to work again, can live wherever I want and can buy anything that takes my fancy."

"That sounds reasonable," I told him, "but are you sure about this? Your life could be changed very considerably."

"I am prepared to risk the consequences," he replied lightly. "I realise I am asking for information you do not normally divulge. I realise I am asking a very special favour, but we have been friends for a long time and I feel there is a special bond between us."

I felt this too and assured him that any reservation I might have about answering his question was to do with my concern for his wellbeing. Also, before I disclose such information, I always like to ensure that the person involved has thought of all the implications and has considered all the available options. Why, for instance, did he want to be rich?

"Sophie Tucker said she had been poor and she had been rich, and rich was better. I am prepared to take her word for it and risk all."

This was an indication of an entrepreneurial spirit I thought most admirable, and I said so.

"So you will help me?" he asked.

"I will need to ask you more questions first. What sort of a time scale have you in mind? Ten years? Twenty years?"

"Nothing like that. I want to get rich as quickly as possible. No doubt it will be nice to be a rich old man, but I would rather be a rich young man first. There are so many more things for a young man to spend his money on. The sooner I get rich, the more fun I will have."

"So the motivation is to have as much fun as possible."

"I should say so." Then, seeing me frown, he added, "Of course I would want to have enough to be able to go in for a bit of philanthropy. I think I would enjoy that and, of course, there are so many needy good causes, that the sooner I get started giving them something the better."

His sentiments did him credit.

"I presume you will want to feel you have earned the money? You wouldn't want it to come to you too easily, without effort on your part?"

"Wouldn't I? Why ever not?" He looked genuinely mystified.

"You might develop a conscience about it. This often happens with intelligent people who feel they have something they don't deserve. Sometimes they feel this so strongly they give it all away and end up worse off than they had been in the first place."

Richard assured me that nothing like that would ever happen to him.

I then proceeded to warn him against gambling. Though the potential profits can be considerable there can be considerable risk and there is always vast uncertainty. He said he understood that and was not really interested in any course of action where the outcome was uncertain. He had had enough of the lottery of life, where he had won no prizes. With as little effort on his part as possible and without any element of chance, he just wanted to get very rich very quickly.

"Just so long as we have your objectives clear," I told him, "there should be no problem. However, you do understand, if I tell you the secret of how to get rich, I can take no responsibility for the consequences. It will be no use your coming to me later and complaining you have so many millions you don't know what to do with. If the champagne is too warm or the claret too cold; if the Rolls Royce won't start, it is nothing to do with me."

"Of course I understand that. I would never blame you. Extreme riches could never dent our friendship."

With that final assurance I was satisfied and gave him the secret of how to get rich.

I never saw him again.

Perfection

"No one is perfect," Emmeline said.

How could she be so disloyal? What a terrible thing for any married woman to say – and in front of Cynthia. I tried to laugh it off.

"Emmeline will have her little joke," I muttered.

We were having dinner with Emmeline's friend Cynthia Phillinger and her husband Lionel Lynch, who is my friend. Lionel and I used to work together, many years earlier. We both liked Lionel. Emmeline, for reasons that I could not fathom, liked Cynthia: the two of them were bosom pals.

"Did you say something?" Emmeline asked me.

I smiled weakly.

"As I was saying," Emmeline continued, "no one is perfect."

"How very true," Cynthia agreed, looking distastefully in my direction.

"It has been said," Lionel intervened, "that the nearest to perfection a person comes is when he fills out an application form."

"How would you define perfection?" Cynthia asked.

Emmeline replied instantly. "Something is perfect if it is without fault."

"Is there such a thing?" Lionel asked.

"Certainly," Emmeline responded. "Things, objects can be perfect."

"But not people?"

"Of course not. That would be against human nature."

"Perhaps not even objects," Cynthia suggested. "Whoever thinks a faultless thing to see, Thinks what ne'er was, nor is, nor e'er shall be."

"Who said that first?" I asked.

Cynthia scowled at me. "That was Alexander Pope," she said, addressing the others.

"Very pontifical," I commented.

"Do you really think that everything is capable of being improved?" Lionel asked his wife.

"Some things more than others," she said, looking at me, "not necessarily immediately, or at a particular point in time, but eventually."

"What about a perfect number?" I challenged.

Cynthia gave me a pained look and then turned towards Emmeline with eyes full of sympathy.

"What is a perfect number?" Emmeline asked, sounding more like a crusty old judge than the solicitor that she is.

"A perfect number is an integer equal to the sum of all its factors," I told her. "Twenty-eight is a perfect number, being equal to the sum of one, two, four, seven and fourteen."

Lionel grinned. "Perhaps Pope didn't know anything about perfect numbers," he said to Cynthia.

"That is not the sort of thing we were talking about," she replied.

"Why not?" I asked. "If you only accept perfection on your own terms, no wonder you can't find it."

"Lionel," Cynthia replied, "you know very well that a perfect number is no better or worse than any other number. To discover a perfect number is to find a number with particular mathematical properties. It signifies no qualitative distinction. Emmeline and I are talking about perfection as an abstract concept, an ideal like beauty."

"Not like beauty," Emmeline objected. "Perfection is absolute – we may disagree about whether it is ever attainable – but beauty is in the eye of the beholder."

"Lucky beholder," I said looking straight at Cynthia. "Do I know him?"

"Nevertheless," said Cynthia ignoring me, "beauty, like perfection, is an ideal. Concepts of beauty may change over time; one person's vision of beauty may differ from another's yet, for any person and at any time, beauty remains an ideal. One may describe something or someone as beautiful but never as epitomising or personifying beauty. Beauty itself remains abstract and unattainable."

"So perfection and beauty are both unobtainable ideals," said Lionel. "What other unobtainable ideals can we think of?"

"Goodness," suggested Emmeline.

"Innocence," Lionel offered.

"Not at all," Cynthia objected. "Innocence is a disability."

"All right then," said Lionel, "how about truth?"

"You honestly think perfect truth is unattainable?" I asked him.

Lionel smiled. "Possibly," he said. "We could discuss it."

"Happiness," Cynthia suggested.

"OK and what is your unobtainable ideal?" Lionel asked looking at me.

"Coffee," I stated, resting back in my chair.

Lionel reddened. "Oh, I am sorry," he said and hurried off to the kitchen.

Emmeline leaned over towards me. "You are a fool," she said.

"A perfect fool?" I suggested.

Caesar Answers

Caesar has developed a new trick. He has taken to answering the telephone. I suppose it is my fault; I should never have bought a speaker 'phone – or, at least, having bought one, should not have placed it on a low coffee table in the study, where Caesar can reach it. For a dog, he can be quite intelligent sometimes. Having watched me several times use the telephone without lifting the receiver, he decided to take over. It happened the second day after I purchased the machine. The telephone rang and Caesar rushed into the study to press the button. I was in the kitchen doing the washing up, my hands full of grease. I could only get near enough to watch helplessly from a distance.

Caesar pressed the speaker button, stood by the telephone, and gave a short sharp bark. I could hear something indistinct coming from the speaker. Caesar barked again and then pressed the button turning the telephone off.

"It wasn't for me," he announced.

"It might have been for me," I complained.

"You think so?" he asked in a surprised voice. "I never thought of that."

"It is usually for me," I told him.

"How can you say that?" he queried. "It is a new telephone. Norms have not yet been established."

"It is only the receiver which is new. The line is the same."

Caesar shook his head sadly, as if to say that either I didn't know what I was talking about or else I was very bad at explaining things.

"Do you not understand that?" I asked.

"I am going to be using the 'phone much more now," he said, ignoring my question. "I hope you don't spend too long gossiping with your friends. You might stop me getting important calls."

I had finished my work in the kitchen and dried my hands. Caesar followed me as I walked into the study. I chose my words carefully, lest there should be any ambiguity.

"I never gossip," I said. I said it evenly and without emotion or emphasis. Nothing could have been clearer.

Caesar coughed and hid his face.

"What important calls?" I asked, moving on to safer territory.

"In future," Caesar replied, "I shall be organising much more of my business by telephone."

"You don't have any business."

"One has to move with the times," Caesar went on obliviously. "You may not realise it, but we live in a technological age."

The telephone rang again. Once more Caesar ran to answer it. Once again he barked. I could hear Emmeline's voice. She ignored Caesar; she doesn't believe he exists.

"Hello," I said.

"I'm sorry," she answered, "I shall be late home."

"Any problem?" I asked.

"No," she said. "Everything is fine. I am going to meet Cynthia for coffee after work. We will probably take the opportunity to do a little shopping together."

"I see," I said coldly. I don't like Cynthia.

"Can you get yourself something to eat? I won't want anything when I come in."

"You see," said Caesar, when Emmeline had rung off. "Even you can find the telephone useful." I had moved back into the kitchen to put the kettle on for a pot of tea.

"Of course I find it useful," I snapped. "I bought it. It is my telephone. I wouldn't be without it. I have always had a telephone."

"Even when you were a puppy?"

"I was a boy not a puppy."

"Of course," Caesar apologised. "I was forgetting; you had a deprived childhood."

I sighed. Caesar is quite impossible in this sort of mood. It is pointless trying to reason with him.

"OK," he said. "Since you feel so strongly about it, I will let you use the telephone without restriction. We will have to see how things work out."

I was about to let him know what I thought of his generosity, when the telephone rang again. Again Caesar bounded into the study to answer it. I heard him bark twice. By the time I reached the study, he had pressed the button and the 'phone was quiet.

"It was for me," he said. "I have to go out."

After Caesar had left, I picked up the 'phone to identify the identity of the last caller. The telephone number was not one I recognised. I pressed the appropriate button to return the call. The ringing tone lasted only for a few moments.

"Hello," I said.

From the other end, I heard a short, sharp bark.

Purrfect Rapport

I had not seen Cleopatra for some hours. She had disappeared in the late afternoon, some time after tea, and had not returned for her evening meal. This was most unusual. She seldom missed a meal unless ill. In the evenings, when there are no visitors and I am reading or listening to the radio or watching the television, she likes to curl up on a rug near my chair. I was about to go to bed, before I heard her come into the house. She came straight into the living room and stood looking at me, somewhat unhappily I thought.

"I have been worried about you." I said. "Where have you been?"

"Miaow," said Cleopatra.

"You've been next door?" I was surprised. My neighbours had always made it clear that they did not like cats.

"Miaow."

"I see," I replied, "they weren't in the house. You were in the house alone. How did you come to be there?"

Cleopatra gave me guilty look and said "Miaow."

"You went into the house through the front door, when they were loading the car and weren't looking. Then they both went out and shut the door, locking you in the house. They hadn't seen you and didn't know you were there."

"Miaow."

"I'm not surprised you were upset," I replied. "All alone in a strange house. So you went looking for a way out. You went into all the rooms where the doors had been left open but couldn't find any door or window open to the outside."

"Miaow."

"Nor a cat flap. As the people next door don't keep a cat, you wouldn't expect to find a cat flap. I can understand you think that inconsiderate but from their point of view it is quite sensible. They didn't expect you to come calling. I hope you didn't make a mess anywhere."

Cleopatra was offended and said "Miaow."

I apologised. "Of course you wouldn't do that. So you searched all the rooms and wondered what to do next. You went into the kitchen to see if there was any food lying about but you couldn't find anything."

"Miaow."

"Not even a biscuit. You thought they kept a very tidy house and you didn't like it. You prefer lots of little things left lying about on the floor – small rubber balls, bits of string – things like that to play with. So you were very bored. I didn't know cats got bored."

"Miaow."

"I suppose you're right. All sentient creatures can be bored. It was just that so often I see you doing nothing that I assumed that you never get bored. You say there is a difference between doing nothing and having nothing to do. I can see that. You can only really enjoy doing nothing if there are plenty of things to do. The act of doing nothing must be deliberate. When you have made a positive decision to do nothing, then you can luxuriate in the comfort of your relaxation. It is the difference between leisure which is enjoyable and unemployment which is stressful."

"Miaow," said Cleopatra.

"I hadn't realised you were so perceptive. So what did you do next?"

"Miaow."

"Yes, I suppose you would be tired after the trauma of finding yourself imprisoned in a strange environment. For all you knew, the owners could have gone away on holiday and might not be back for weeks. So you just settled down on the floor, underneath a table in the dining room, and went to sleep. When you awoke it was dark and you could hardly see where you were. You found your way into the living room in the front of the house. The curtains had not been drawn and a little light from the street lamps penetrated the room. Being able to see the strange shapes of unfamiliar objects gave you no comfort and you retreated to the dining room and re-established yourself under the table, where you felt safe."

"Miaow," Cleopatra affirmed.

"Did anything else happen?" I asked. "How long were you there?"

"Miaow."

"It *would* seem like a long time," I agreed, "when you don't know how long you are going to be on your own. You just stayed under the table and waited. Eventually you heard the door opening. The light in the hallway went on and you could see the neighbours removing their coats. They didn't know you were there, so you told them. What exactly did you say?"

"Miaow."

"They must have been surprised," I said.

"Miaow," said Cleopatra.

"So you just ran out of the door and left them to their own devices. Welcome home."

"Miaow," said Cleopatra. "Can I have some milk now and I'd like some of that fresh salmon, if you have any left – and please don't talk to me about what curiosity does to cats."

Truth Will Out

(A Consultation from the Casebook of Dr Magnus Fell)

- Good morning Dr Fell.
- *Good morning. What can I do for you today?*
- I don't know if you can do anything but I thought I had better ask, just in case.
- *What seems to be the trouble?*
- I don't understand it. I feel a bit of a fraud coming to see you at all. I feel quite well.
- *You are looking very well.*
- The problem is, doctor, I cannot stop telling the truth.
- *Why should you want to stop telling the truth?*
- Truth is very dangerous. It is ruining all my relationships; it is ruining my life.
- *Perhaps you had better start at the beginning.*
- It started two weeks ago. I was on my way to work and listening to Prime Minister's Questions on the car radio. I couldn't help thinking how much better it would be if the Prime Minister would actually answer the questions occasionally. I thought how refreshing it would be if he said something like, "Yes, we did make a mistake. We realise that now. We are doing something to put it right."

- *I don't think it is the Prime Minister's style.*

- It isn't anybody's style. Anyway, quite foolishly I was thinking how much life would be improved if everyone told the truth, and then when I got to work it started.

- *What started?*

- I started. I started to tell the truth.

- *Have you never told the truth before?*

- Of course I have, but not always, not all the time. Like everyone else, I have told the truth in moderation.

- *Tell me what happened.*

- My first appointment of the morning was with one of the other solicitors in the practice. We had an important case to discuss. He came into my office and asked if I would like to see him now to discuss the matter. I replied that I would like never to see him again, I couldn't stand the sight of him but as we had to work together on this business the sooner we got our discussions over the better.

- *Have you ever spoken to him like this before?*

- Never. Our relationship has always been thoroughly professional and polite. I have never liked him as a person. I've avoided socialising with him but I have never given him even a hint of this. We have to work together. Neither of us is going to leave the practice.

- *What prompted you to speak to him in this way on this occasion?*

- That is what I don't know. He asked me a question and I felt compelled to answer it honestly, keeping nothing back.

- *What happened then?*

- He looked surprised, told me I was mad and stormed out of the office. Later in the morning, I had a note to say that he was withdrawing from any involvement in the case and that in the absence of a written apology, he would ask for a meeting of the partners to discuss my behaviour.

- *What did you do?*

- I sent a written apology. I was sorry. I didn't want to talk to him that way.

- *But what you had said, you meant?*
- Yes, but I didn't want to say it.
- *I see. What else happened that day?*
- My secretary asked if I would like a nice cup of coffee. I said that I would but that, if she were making it, there was as much chance of its being nice as there was of my getting a Christmas card from the leader of Hezbollah.
- *Not a good way of motivating her.*
- She cried all day. Then a client asked if I thought the demands she was making for her divorce settlement were reasonable and, instead of suggesting that they might with advantage be moderated somewhat, I told her that she was a disgusting bloodsucker and that her husband was well rid of her.
- *Anything else?*
- When I got home, my wife asked if I liked her new hairstyle. I said it looked as if it had been created by dyslexic magpies.
- *You were right to come to me. You are suffering from a fairly rare complaint called TRS, or Truth Response Syndrome. Whenever you are asked a question, you have no choice but to give a completely honest answer. It is quite unpleasant while it lasts. I am afraid there is no cure but it usually goes away by itself after a few weeks. I suggest you take a holiday until it passes.*
- I haven't yet told you all. Even at the beginning it was very serious. My tennis partner's wife told me her husband had seemed very edgy lately and asked if I was aware of anything that might be worrying him. I told her the truth; he was afraid she might find out that he was having an affair with her best friend.
- *You gave an honest answer.*
- She showed no signs of being grateful. Then, after a few days, my symptoms got much worse.
- *How much worse could they get?*
- I found I could not help telling the truth, even when I wasn't being asked a question. By the way, that is a really hideous tie you are wearing.

- *I like the tie. Your condition may be more serious than I first thought.*

- I think so. My wife gave a dinner party the other evening. I told her there was too much salt in the soup and that the lamb was overcooked. I told my sister-in-law that the way she played with the onions on her plate was evidence of distinct sexual repression. I started to tell my clients exactly what I thought of their attempts to defraud shops with compensation claims, to avoid paying appropriate maintenance to estranged wives and children, or to pretend they had been libelled and subjected to serious mental injury from innocuous and true newspaper articles.

- *You began to lose clients?*

- Indeed I did and it got worse. I started going up to complete strangers in the street and telling them that they shouldn't slap their children, or that they shouldn't throw litter on the pavement.

- *I've done that. That's how I got this cut over my right eye.*

- I'm not surprised. I can't stop myself from accosting complete strangers and commenting on their mode of dress or telling them that they should get their hair cut and, probably, washed. I wave down motorists and tell them how badly they are driving.

- *I get the idea. It seems that though you started with Truth Response Syndrome, you have now developed TTS or Total Truth Syndrome. I am afraid this is much more serious.*

- Does this go away by itself?

- *Not as far as we know. There is no record ever of anyone's being cured but nor do we know of the condition lasting for more than six months.*

- I don't understand.

- *I am sorry to have to tell you that no one with TTS has ever survived for more than six months.*

- What causes their deaths?

- *They were all murdered.*

The Message

"This is Steven Morris speaking. I am sorry but I am not available at present. Please leave a message after the bleep and I will endeavour to call you back, as soon as possible."

"Steve? This is Brian. Lucinda cannot make it tomorrow. Do you still want to come for dinner – you are very welcome, if you do – or would you rather leave it for another time? She said she was really sorry and is looking forward to meeting you."

Brian put down the telephone and went to join Janet in the kitchen.

"I 'phoned Steve to tell him," he said. "He wasn't home yet. I had to leave a message on the answering machine."

"It is such a shame," Janet replied. "I was looking forward to seeing if they would hit it off. I think they will, you know. Steven is a good catch by anyone's standards – what they used to call a very eligible bachelor – and Lucinda is quite pretty and no fool."

"Lucinda is a dish."

"Oh, you think so, do you?" Janet responded archly. "Perhaps you should have married her instead of me."

"Perhaps I should have done," he said, taking hold of her and kissing her roughly on the lips. "Perhaps you should have married Steve."

"I might have done," she replied thoughtfully, "if he had

asked me." Janet had been going out with Steven, when she met Brian. Steven was still a student then, just a little younger than Janet, not ready for a commitment. They had been, and remained, good friends.

"I know Lucinda isn't everyone's cup of tea," Janet said, extricating herself.

"She can't be, or she would be married by now."

"She has had plenty of chances but she wasn't interested. It took her years to get over Robert. After they broke up, she wasn't interested in anyone."

"But she's OK now?"

"I think so. She does seem to be quite excited about meeting Steven. She was really upset about having to take her boss's place at that conference in Birmingham. You and I have both given Steve a big build up. I hope it comes to something."

"For his sake as well. She would be good for him."

"So would anyone other than that floozie he is going with at the moment."

"Miaow."

"You don't like Samantha any more than I do."

"He likes her."

"He likes what he can get. She is what you might call, accommodating. Anyway, he cannot be too smitten; otherwise he would not have been so ready to meet Lucinda. What message did you leave on his answerphone?"

"I just said Lucinda was very sorry she couldn't come tomorrow, but he was welcome all the same. I said she was still looking forward to meeting…" Brian stopped in mid-sentence. "Oh, crikey."

"What's wrong?"

"Samantha will be with him when he gets home today. She will hear the message."

"Are you sure?"

Brian was sure. It was Thursday and Samantha was almost

certain to stay the night in Steven's flat. She had to get to work early on Thursdays and pretended it is easier to get to her work from Steven's flat; it saved travelling. Brian could not understand why she thought it was anyone else's business, why she thought she had to tell them, or why she bothered to find such a silly excuse. The point was that today was Thursday. She was leaving tomorrow evening to spend the weekend with her parents in Grimsby. She was bound to want to be with Steven tonight.

"He'll be furious with me," Brian muttered.

Maybe not. What difference did it make? They were not engaged. There was no commitment. Anyway, Lucinda could be anyone. Steven could simply say she was the publisher Brian had promised to introduce him to, the one who might be interested in publishing his thesis. He could say she was Janet's cousin from Australia. It was neither here nor there that Janet did not have a cousin in Australia. Samantha would never know. There was any number of stories he could make up. There was nothing to worry about.

"There is nothing to worry about," Brian told Janet. "There are any number of stories Steve can tell her."

"He won't," said Janet. "Steven is a bad liar."

"So what will happen?"

"Samantha will be furious. She will accuse him of carrying on behind her back."

"So they'll break up. That will be good for him, won't it? After a few weeks, he will be thanking us."

"No he won't and that is not what will happen."

"What will happen then?" Brian asked.

"Samantha will cry. Steven will say he is sorry and, of course, he really loves her. He will promise not to see anyone else. In no time at all, you'll find they are making plans to get married."

"That will be terrible."

"Indeed it will and Steven will say we have been interfering."

"Well, haven't we been interfering?"

"Of course we have. That only makes it worse."

"But with the best of motives – just for his sake."

"Perhaps I can get in touch with him," suggested Brian. "Perhaps I can warn him about the message, so he doesn't play it when Samantha is there."

"How will you do that?"

Brian considered the possibilities. He remembered Brian's telling him about a very important client meeting he was to attend in Reading this morning. He had expected to be able to get away soon after lunch and did not expect to go back to the office. Either he would be home early or he might stop in at the University gymnasium for a workout. It was seven o'clock now; it was possible Steven was still there. He went into the hallway to look for the telephone directory, quickly found the number he was looking for, and then remembered having tried once before to telephone the gymnasium, only to be told that they could not put calls through.

Janet called to him. "Steve might be at the gym," she said brightly.

"There is no way of 'phoning him there. I tried once before."

It will be his own fault, Brian thought. In this day and age, there was no excuse for his not having a mobile 'phone. Brian had tried to persuade him. What would he do with a mobile 'phone, Steven had asked. He had seen the effect on other people's lives. Either friends and colleagues telephoning him at inconvenient times would plague him constantly, or he would have to keep the handset almost permanently turned off. He might as well not have it. For his part, he was never that desperate to contact someone, that he could not wait until he was at home. Steven had pontificated to the effect that mobile telephones were the curse of the modern age. In more civilised times, people had kept their private affairs to themselves. Today, you can hardly travel on a bus or in a train without being invited – nay, forced – to listen to mobile telephone users making or cancelling appointments, apologising to their spouses or partners for being late, making assignations, calling taxis or checking on football results. On every street corner, in every supermarket shopping aisle, someone is busy in audible conversation with business colleagues or clients. Smoking had been banned in many public places, why not mobile telephones?

"We should persuade Steve to get a mobile telephone," Janet suggested.

"Why not?" Brian replied. "It would be no more difficult than coaxing the Chief Rabbi to have a bacon sandwich. In any case, it won't help us get in touch with him now."

Perhaps I could contact one of his neighbours, Brian thought. What is the name of the chap who lives in the next-door flat? Guy? No, George. Singleton or Middleton – something like that. Their front doors were right next to each other. Perhaps he could persuade George to keep his front door open so he could waylay Steve and tell him not to listen to the messages on this answerphone, while Samantha is around. No, I can't do that. I can't involve him in Steve's private affairs. I could tell him to get Steve to telephone me as soon as he gets in, before he does anything else. Hold on. Samantha is bound to hear the message. She would want to know why it was so urgent. He might even use the speakerphone and she would hear everything that was said. What is the use?

"I've got an idea," Janet announced, coming into the sitting room. "You know Steve's next-door neighbour, Peter Marshall?"

"Isn't his next-door neighbour called George Middleton?"

"You are thinking of the man he works with, George Mornington."

Brian nodded sadly.

"Why don't we telephone Peter Marshall and ask him if he will pop round to the gym and give Steve a message to telephone us. It is only ten minutes' journey by car."

"Do you think we could ask him to do that?" Brian asked doubtfully.

"We can ask. He can only say no."

"I'll ring Directory Enquiries for his number."

"No, don't bother," Janet sighed. "He will say no. I remember his telling me he doesn't have a car."

"There is nothing we can do then?"

"Not a thing. Really, Brian, that was a stupid thing to do."

"What?"

"Leaving that message."

"I didn't think."

"Exactly. Fancy doing something like that. You might as well have told Samantha to her face that we were trying to break up her relationship with Steve."

"I wouldn't put it like that. We are just trying to give Steve the opportunity to compare her to someone else."

"I don't know why I let you make important telephone calls. You always say something wrong." Janet shook her head in annoyance.

"No I don't," Brian shouted. "And this wasn't an important telephone call."

"Not until you messed it up, it wasn't."

"It is not my fault Steve always has Samantha round his neck. I can't be expected to think of everything."

"It would be very nice, if you just thought of something – just for once."

"This is entirely uncalled for," Brian said savagely. "If you go on like this, you will be having a tête-à-tête with Steve, if he comes tomorrow evening. I am not sure I will want to be here."

"That is fine with me," she shouted back.

The telephone rang. Brian answered. It was Steven. He was telephoning from Reading. His meeting had gone on all day and he was going out to dinner before returning home. He just wanted to check that everything was OK for tomorrow evening. Oh, what a shame Lucinda couldn't make it. Was he still welcome on his own? Yes he'd love come. He had lots to tell them about his bust up with Sam.

God's Direct Line

From our Religious Correspondent

News has just reached me of an announcement soon to be made by the highest of all authorities. God is to issue His first ever press release and will announce the most important change since the resurrection. And, unlike the resurrection, this change will affect all religious practice in the developed world. I understand that a transition period will be allowed for third world countries. This will last for three or four decades but, by the middle of the century and possibly before, we can expect a major shake up in religious observance, making it more effective and much cheaper. A change is to be announced, which will bring people closer to God by cutting out the middlemen.

Until now, priests and mullahs and rabbis have provided us with our line to God. No more. In the electronic age, God is going on-line on the Internet. We will all be able to speak, or for the time being write, directly to our God and get a reply. We will be able to read or hear it straight away or save it to be read or listened to at a convenient time.

Priests will no longer be required and, within ten years, no more will be recruited in North America, Europe and Australia. Natural wastage will operate in the period before electronic communication is available universally but, in addition, there will be a programme of planned redundancy with priests of all denominations being retrained for employment as housing managers, social workers, teachers, sports centre managers, singers and stand up comedians. It is expected there will be a particularly large demand from rabbis for retraining in this last category.

There will no longer be any need for churches, mosques, temples or synagogues. Some of these will be converted into theatres or leisure centres. Others will become public computer centres, where the public will be able to pray, play or work, using the latest hardware and software and will be able to get a cup of tea or a light meal. Yet others, where there is the need, will be converted into low cost houses and flats for the homeless. The accumulated wealth of the churches and other religious bodies will be used to finance these conversions. All new centres created in this way will be registered as charities and will be run by trained professionals on a non-profit making basis.

God feels that His infinite mercy and compassion previously have been demonstrated mainly to individuals. The great communal benefits flowing from the changes to be announced will provide the grand gesture that, perhaps sadly, is needed to draw waverers and unbelievers back into the fold.

Nevertheless, important and beneficial as are these by-products of the move to the worlds of electronic mail and the World Wide Web, it is the ability that everyone will have to be in two-way communication with their God that will be the revolutionary aspect of this development. Catholics will be able to confess (*confessions@catholic.godinhvn.com*) and receive absolution without the intervention of priests, who (one expects) have no direct experience of the sins committed. Jews, who will no longer need to attend synagogues on the Day of Atonement, will submit their prayers via *atonement@jewish.godinhvn.com*. While there will be these and other such specialised lines of contact, a general help line (*prayers@godinhvn.com*) will be available to all.

A Web site (*http://www.godinhvn.com*) will provide access to information and educational material about all religions. Worried parents, by judicious use of passwords, will be able to ensure that their children are not exposed to information that they would consider as blasphemous. Thus, access to the Web site can be controlled, so that the user's religion appears as the true religion and other religious views are reported accordingly.

In an important sense, this is going back to basics. A reading of the Old Testament shows how, in the beginning, God spoke directly to man. As our numbers have increased and as life on earth has grown more complex, so He has ceased to do this. He admits this is a matter he has long regretted. Individual advice will be available to all (*advice@godinhvn.com*). All messages will be answered within two working days.

In addition, the Almighty is letting it be known that He has had nothing to do with Pastor Sanyangore from Zimbabwe who, it was reported in *The Times* on 24 May 2017, claims to be in regular telephone contact with Him and can contact Him at any time. God has no telephone and does not intend to obtain one.

Tell Me Why

- *Good morning.*
- How do you do?
- *Very well thank you. May I ask you a few questions?*
- Why?
- *I am an Opinion Seeker.*
- What is an Opinion Seeker?
- *It's a bit like an Opinion Former, only less creative.*
- Like a second rank politician?
- *I suppose so.*
- Do you enjoy the work?
- *Very much. One gets to meet some very interesting people.*
- And does it pay much?
- *Quite well. Hold on, I am supposed to be asking you questions.*
- Why did you choose me?
- *I have just started and you are the first person to come this way.*
- Why did you take up your position in this spot?
- *It seems to be a fairly central position in the town square.*
- Were you looking for a particular cross section of the community?
- *Not at all. I want a random sample.*
- Do you think this is a good place to get a random sample? Do you think you will meet a lot of people here, who don't go shopping?

- *I will be quite happy to concentrate on shoppers.*
- Do you assume I am a shopper?
- *It doesn't matter. May I ask you some questions?*
- Why don't you?
- *I seem to have trouble getting started.*
- Is this often a problem for you?
- *It has never happened before.*
- Does it happen to other people in the same line of business?
- *I have not heard of the problem.*
- Does it worry you?
- *It could make it difficult for me to interview my full quota for the day.*
- Then why don't you get started?
- *May I?*
- What is your first question?
- *Thank you. Do you live in this town?*
- Why do you want to know that?
- *It is the first question on my questionnaire.*
- Why should anyone want to know?
- *We want to know to what extent people come from out of town to shop in this town centre.*
- Do you know if I am a shopper?
- *Not yet. That will be another question.*
- Didn't you say it didn't matter whether or not I am a shopper?
- *Whether you are a shopper or not, I still have a lot of other questions to ask.*
- What sort of questions?
- *Are you going to let me ask them?*
- Do you think that I am the sort of person who would try to stop you doing your job?
- *No, of course not.*
- Was that not implied, by your asking if I were going to let you ask your questions?

- *I am sorry if you took it that way. I did not mean to be rude. I trust that you will believe me.*
- Is there any reason why I should not believe you?
- *Of course not.*
- Why don't you just ask your questions?
- *That might be best. Do you come frequently into this town centre?*
- What do you mean by frequently?
- *Say once a fortnight.*
- Isn't that a fairly arbitrary definition?
- *It has to be?*
- If I lived ten minutes' journey away and were coming to see my aged mother who lived alone in the flats here, would you say that to visit once a fortnight was to come frequently?
- *Does your mother live in those flats?*
- Is that question on your questionnaire?
- *It is not.*
- How do you think that you are going to get through this interview, if you keep deviating from the subject?
- *Shall I start again?*
- How much time do you think I have to stand here chatting to you?
- *I am sorry. May I ask you just one more question?*
- Have I said that you could not?
- *Why is everything you say in the form of a question?*
- Why not?

A Downside to Everything

"I have another complaint."

Clifford sighed. "I suppose it is that I ignored your previous complaints."

"Not at all," I said affably. "It is what I have come to expect."

He sighed again and closed his eyes.

"You are not bored, I hope?" I said.

"No more than usual."

"That's life," I commented.

"No. Actually, it is you." This was more enigmatic than usual. I moved quickly to the cause of my concern.

"Why is it acceptable to say something is upside down, when it is considered skittish to say it is downside up?"

"Is that what is worrying you?"

"It is."

"Then you must lead a particularly uneventful life."

As usual, Clifford failed to see the importance of the issue I was raising. I explained: when the top or the upper part of something is more important – or more our focus of our interest – than the lower part, then it is perfectly reasonable to make this the subject of our sentence. When the opposite is the case, then the lower part of the object or entity should be given pride of place and should be put first.

Pedantic creature that he is, he asked for an example. I offered a compact disc. The underside of the disk contains the recording. The top contains only details of what is recorded.

"And perhaps a pretty picture."

"Indeed, but my point is that the usefulness of the disc would not be in any way impaired, if the top were scratched, whereas if the underside were damaged, the disk would be unplayable. It is the downside we really care about and if it were all up with the downside, we would want to know immediately and not discover it by inference."

"Very interesting," Clifford said, stifling a yawn, "how about another example?"

I had to think about this for a few moments. "An iceberg," I suggested.

"An iceberg! It is impossible for an iceberg to be upside down."

"They said manned flight was impossible. Just think about it. If an iceberg were inverted, it would be headline news all over the world – and not because the relatively small upper section was now under water, but because the gigantic downside was now uppermost. It would be downside up; no question."

"Humph."

"You are not enjoying this evening, are you?"

"I enjoyed the meal, but there is a downside to everything."

"That is another thing about which I wish to complain."

"That everything has a downside?"

"Why do you call it a downside? What goes up must come down. It is one of the laws of nature. There is nothing intrinsically superior about going up. If you have two escalators, you do not regard that for going down as inferior to that for going up. That the word, downside, should be regarded as having pejorative connotations, is a stain on the English language. Just think about it. If you calm down, that is a good thing."

"If you calmed down, you might cheer up."

I ignored this intervention. I was giving the examples. I

continued. "To write something down is no worse than writing it up; indeed, the latter almost certainly involves the former. I could go on and on."

"Please don't." This was said with real feeling. I must have made an impression.

"I don't know what to put it all down to, but I don't think it is something I should put up with. What do you think I should do?"

"That is up to you."

"It is not down to me?"

"It will be, if you decide to do anything."

"I suppose there is a downside to everything," I said carelessly.

Here's Looking at Euclid

It was only when George Raft turned down the opportunity that Humphrey Bogart got the offer to act in what was to become his most famous film.

"Capablanca?" he exclaimed. "One of my heroes." Bogart was inconsolable when he discovered he would be going to Morocco – or rather pretend he was going to Morocco – and that he would not be impersonating the nineteen-twenties world chess champion. Chess, along with mathematics, was his lifelong passion and this is as good a time as any other to celebrate the great man's achievements as a chess player and mathematician. It is strange how the world forgets.

Chess came first. Bogart's father, a Manhattan surgeon, taught him to play chess when he was a young boy. Forever after, he would play at every opportunity, famously playing Alfred "Gloves" Donahue *All Through The Night* in 1942. His celebrated opening gambit, *The Maltese Falcon,* developed when playing Sam Spade in 1941, is much copied, as is his defence, *The African Queen,* used against Charlie Allnut ten years later. Highlights in his chess-playing career included his *Dark Victory* in *Virginia City* against *The Oklahoma Kid.* Admirers said he was good enough to *Beat the Devil.*

Back in 1938 he had studied at the feet of *The Amazing Dr Clitterhouse* and now Mathematics took over his life. Clitterhouse was working on an arithmetical conundrum he nicknamed the *Dead End* and enlisted Bogart's assistance. Just *Knock on Any Door* when you arrive, Clitterhouse had told him.

Bogart committed himself *Body and Soul*. They were *Two Against the World*, for the race was on to solve the conundrum and win the *Treasure of the Sierra Madre*. These were *The Desperate Hours*. Bogart travelled *Up the River*, was lost for some time in *The Petrified Forest*, booked a *Passage to Marseilles*, crossed the *Sahara* on foot, and was spotted briefly *In a Lonely Place* on the *Road to Bali* before he returned to America *Across the Pacific* on a *China Clipper*.

He arrived home at *Midnight* and, after having enjoyed *The Big Sleep*, embarked on a *Love Affair* with *The Barefoot Contessa, Sabrina*. They swore to be *Always Together* but it was not to last. Bogart was absorbed day and night in his mathematical calculations. "*Men Are Such Fools*," Sabrina declared. She had the *Big City Blues* and departed for New York with her *Bad Sister*. He never saw her again.

There was another *Dark Passage* in his life – *Conflict* with his *Brother Orchid*. From the time of his schooldays: his brother had been *A Holy Terror*, always pretending to be *The Big Shot* and *A Devil with Women*. In *The Roaring Twenties*, he got himself involved with *Kid Galahad*; it was like going to *Crime School*. If he had dreams of becoming *King of the Underworld*, these were smashed when the *Racket Busters* moved in. Orchid would serve a term in *San Quentin*. Released just before the outbreak of war, he joined the Marines and first saw *Action in the North Atlantic*. Transferred from one *Battle Circus* to another, he was wounded in Okinawa, an "*Isle of Fury*," as he described it in a letter home. He stayed on there with the American Administration after the war. "*We're No Angels*," he wrote, "but there is a job to be done." At last he settled down, married and *Tokyo Joe* became his brother-in-law.

Bogart was alone and lost for inspiration, his hopes of fame as a mathematician almost at an end. He was saved by *The Return of Dr X* from the *High Sierra*, who had worked with the *Black Legion*. They were *Angels with Dirty Faces*, he declared. Dr X told him the story of the *Two Guys from Milwaukee* and how *They Drive by Night* guided by *Invisible Stripes*. It was the clue he needed – rather too technical to be described here – and Bogart was able to write to Clitterhouse, "We dreamed of success and *It All Came True*."

They won the prize and *Women of All Nations*, including *The Two Mrs Carrolls*, threw themselves at his feet. Bogart was unmoved. It was not what he wanted. "*To Have and Have Not*," he mused, before winning the *Love Lottery*, meeting Lauren Bacall, a *Marked Woman* from the moment they met and whom he married in 1945.

While Bogart embarked on no further serious work in Mathematics, he did enjoy a short stint as *Stand-In* for a friend who set mathematical puzzles for "*Chain Lightning*", a weekly magazine published in *Key Largo*. One of his puzzles, *Three on a Match*, was so ingenious that even *The Great O'Malley* confessed himself unable to solve it. He had earlier boasted that he could solve anything Bogart could produce. "*Thank Your Lucky Stars* Bogart is not the regular problem setter," they told him.

Asked to comment, Bogart would only reply, "*The Harder They Fall*." It was his last movie.

***

For those who are interested in such things, of the 82 films in which Bogart appeared, 69 are mentioned above. The others are:

Broadway's Like That
Bullets or Ballots
Dead Reckoning
Deadline – U.S.A.
In This Our Life (cameo)
Sirocco
Swing Your Lady
The Caine Mutiny

The Dancing Town
The Enforcer (aka Murder, Inc.)
The Left Hand of God
The Wagons Roll at Night
You Can't Get Away with Murder

Alternative names of films included:

Battling Bellhop – Kid Galahad
Call It Murder – Midnight
One Fatal Hour – Two Against the World

A Secret Life

The words were out of her mouth before she could stop herself. I raised my eyes and stared at her in surprise.
"Would you say that again?" I asked.
"It was nothing," Xanthe replied.
"No," I insisted. "Tell me again."
We looked at each other in silence for several moments.
"Zula vik oom keeva," she murmured at last. "Little do you know."
We had been sitting quietly after having watched a news programme on television. Scientists had been discussing the likelihood of intelligent life somewhere in outer space. I said we would never know for certain – the distances were too vast. Even if someone...
"Or something," Xanthe had interjected. It was a fair point.
"Even if someone or something were out there," I continued, "by the time it received a message from earth and replied we would be extinct."
"Astronomers say we might pick up radio signals emitted long ago by other civilisations," Xanthe said, "signals quite unconnected to any of our attempts at communication."
Then they would come from long dead civilisations, I had replied. It was then she said it. It just slipped out.
"Tell me," I said soothingly.

"I can't," she answered. "I would like to." She paused. "Can I really trust you?"

"We have been married for twenty-eight years," I reminded her. "I thought we had no secrets from each other."

"No secrets," she sighed. "Oh, if only that were true."

"It can be. You know I love you, and I know you love me. Just tell me about it."

"I suppose I must now."

"I think so."

"Yes. Whatever the consequences, I cannot live a lie any longer." Xanthe sat very still. She looked down at her hands. She clasped them together. "I don't know where to begin."

"You told me you were born in India," I said. "It is not true, is it?"

"No. It is not true."

"From where do you come?"

"From much, much further away."

"Tell me."

"Will you believe me if I do?"

"I have always believed you before."

"That's just it," she said, "but will you believe what I tell you now, when you realise that our whole life together has been built on deception? I wanted to tell you but I couldn't. I was not allowed to. I am not allowed to tell anyone but," she paused and looked at me, "but I can't keep it to myself any longer. I have lived so long as an ordinary human being, I now think and feel as if I were exactly what you have imagined me to be."

"They say that people who live together for many years gradually grow to be alike," I said.

Xanthe smiled sadly. "It cannot be," she said. "It can never be. I am not like other people."

"That is why I married you," I smiled. "You are more beautiful, more wise, more honest and more fun than anyone I have ever known."

"Ah, yes," she said dreamily. "They did a good job."

"Tell me."

Xanthe stiffened and turned her eyes away from mine. She began to talk very quickly and in stilted tones. "I come from far away, from a distant planet." She told me the name of the planet; I had not heard of it. She continued. "I come from a far off galaxy. I was sent here nearly two hundred years ago. I took human form and have lived in different guises in several parts of the globe. Before we met, I was indeed in India. I wasn't very happy there."

"You are not human?"

"No."

I could not help remembering how, many years ago, when I had introduced Xanthe to my friends, they had told me she was too good to be true. I smiled.

"Your friends were right," she said. "It was all a pretence."

"You can read my thoughts?"

"I can read most people's thoughts. Your thoughts I can read only sometimes. When you smile I know what you are thinking."

I sat quietly thinking about what she had told me. It is not every day your wife divulges that she is not human, that she comes from outer space, from an alien civilisation. It is difficult to know how to react. I smiled again – just checking.

"The children? They are as human as you are," she assured me. "We chose the DNA very carefully. In so far as they have inherited genes from my eggs, they are free of all inherited diseases and should live healthily into old age."

"You say you have been on earth for nearly two hundred years?"

"Yes. This is my eighth body. It is the first time I have been a woman. I rather like it. I have you to thank for that."

"It is good of you to say so."

"I wouldn't have liked being a woman in my earlier lives here. Until very recently, life was much harder for women and men had all the fun. Your system of sexual reproduction is unfair."

"How do you reproduce yourselves where you come from?"

"Oh, we have sex," Xanthe said, "but we are much less specialised. We have six different sexes and we can change at will from one to the other. We can all – how shall I put it – interact with each other, and all at the same time if we wish. You really can't imagine."

She was right. I couldn't imagine – and not for want of trying. We have nothing like that in my world.

"Why are you here?" I asked.

"We like to keep an eye on you," she replied. "This planet has the potential to disrupt the entire universe. At soon as Hargreaves invented the Spinning Jenny, we could see it coming. We knew the revolution in the cotton industry would soon lead on to nuclear weapons and genetic manipulation."

I nodded. "I suppose it was obvious."

"Not obvious at all," she retorted with a flash of anger, "Only a superior people would have realised."

"So you were sent to keep an eye on us."

"Not only I. There are lots of us. We check on what is happening and are here ready to act, if things get out of hand."

"Act in what way?"

"Oh, I would just do what I was told. I am not very important in all this. It is just a temporary posting for me, a bit like a Voluntary Service Overseas scheme. Most of us spend between two hundred and two hundred and fifty years here. It is not a long time in our lives. Being your wife was always going to be my last job here."

That she should regard being married to me as a job, was not flattering. I smiled wistfully.

"You know what I mean," she said. "I have said I like being married to you."

"Are you a scientist?"

"Where I come from, everyone is a scientist."

"Of course," I said and she gave me a curious glance. There was another pause.

"Whatever else we do, we are all scientists," she said.

"So you were only pretending not to be able to programme the video recorder?"

She nodded, clearly ashamed.

"And you didn't really need me to change the plug on the iron? You could have done that yourself?"

"I wanted you to believe I was who I said I was. I admit I enjoyed your doing these things for me. It was an innocent pretence."

"That is a very human attitude."

"One learns to adapt. After a while it becomes quite natural."

"You've gone native," I commented.

"I suppose I have. I have enjoyed it. Primitive societies are so quaint."

"Primitive? We are in England," I reminded her.

"How little you know," she smiled, "but somehow I have never minded. I am so sorry it has come to an end."

"An end?"

"Now you know about me, I shall have to leave."

"Why must you leave? I don't want you to leave."

"And I don't want to leave, but no one was supposed to know about me. I will be recalled. If only…"

I could tell she was minded to resist. I had to do something.

"Refuse to leave," I said. "Tell them you won't go. Don't you see? This is wonderfully exciting. You can make yourself known. You will be famous. Every world leader will want to meet you. You'll be on breakfast television. I'll write a book called, 'I Married an Alien'. We will be rich," I paused for a moment before adding an afterthought, "and you can probably save the world from nuclear destruction and global warming." That should have the desired effect, I thought.

"It's no good," she replied with tears in her eyes. "I have no choice. I have to go."

"What, now? Immediately?"

"I am afraid so. Goodbye, my dear. Thank you for everything." Smoke began to come from the top of her head. In a few moments there was nothing left but a pile of her clothes.

"Oost zig lechter," I breathed softly. "It is just as well, or my cover would most likely have been blown."

The Tearaway

QUESTIONER: I see you left school last year.
TEARAWAY: Yeah. You could say that.

Q: You didn't like school?
T: Didn't go much, did I?
Q: But I see you attended five different secondary schools.
T: Yeah. Kept getting the DCM, didn't I?
Q: The what?
T: The DCM, the Don't Come Monday.
Q: You mean you were excluded from all of these schools?
T: Yeah, expelled, excluded. Maybe they didn't like my face.
Q: I don't see why. It's quite a nice face.
T: Nah. I mean they didn't like my business.
Q: You mean you started a business while you were still at school? That shows great initiative. I am surprised you were not encouraged. What was the business?
T: I used to ask people for money.
Q: That's it? You would just ask them?
T: Yeah. Keep it simple. No overheads.
Q: And did people give you money?
T: You bet. They thought it would bring 'em luck.
Q: Did it bring them luck?

T: Who knows? But the two who didn't pay up had terrible accidents.

Q: Quite a coincidence.

T: Yeah. Wasn't it?

Q: And I see you set fire to your last school. Was that some sort of revenge?

T: Nah, strictly business. Revenge is a mug's game. I don't go in for gratooitus violence.

Q: You mean someone paid you to burn the school down?

T: Not likely. I planned it all alone. Everyone came out to see the fire. I knew they would. I was able to walk into five houses and help myself to anything I wanted. Dead easy.

Q: But the police found out you started the fire.

T: Yeah, but only the fire. I got put on probation.

Q: What did you learn from this experience?

T: To wear gloves.

Q: So, let's move on. After you left school did you get a job?

T: Nah. Went on benefit.

Q: No jobs at all?

T: Bits and pieces. Nothing legal.

Q: And then your father came back into your life.

T: Yeah. Hadn't seen him since I were seven years old. It turned out he were seeing the mother of one of me mates, so we got together. Got on like a house on fire.

Q: And he said you should sort yourself out.

T: Yeah. He said all this living from day-to-day was getting me nowhere. He said I should get myself a proper job with prospects. Join an organisation, he said, where they give you some training. But first, he said, you have to decide what it is you want to do with your life. Decide what you like doing, what you are good at.

Q: And this is when you finally decided to dedicate yourself to a life of crime?

T: Yeah. It gives me a buzz. I think I've got a real feel for it.

Q: Have you ever used a gun?

T: No.

Q: Well, never mind. That is something we can teach you. We can start you off in Protection and see how you go. If you show the right spirit, the prospects are unlimited and the world is your oyster. Now are there any questions you would like to ask me?

What Is This Thing Called Love?

"What is this thing called love?" Caesar asked.

For one horrible moment, I thought he was going to break into song. Caesar has a voice that is a cross between a low-pitched growl and a high-pitched whine. His interest in music has never extended far beyond a seeming appreciation of television advertising jingles and never has there been any indication that he shares my love of Cole Porter. When he repeated his question in slightly different form, I breathed a sigh of relief.

"What is it," he said, "this love thing? I keep hearing about it on television, but I don't understand what it is all about."

It is unusual for Caesar to admit there is anything he does not understand. Once I remember he gaily chatted for ten minutes about the importance of the theory of relativity, before it emerged that he thought it was something to do with uncles and aunts. It is all because he has such a poor attention span. He is a strange dog.

"Love is the sweetest thing," I told him.

"You mean you eat it?" he asked with serious concern. "How comes you have never let me have any?"

"You don't eat it," I told him. "Love is a feeling – the feeling a man and a woman experience, when they are very much attracted to each other."

"Oh, I know about that," Caesar said, wagging his tail. "I do that all the time. I didn't think humans were interested in that sort of thing. I've never seen them at it."

"I am talking," I said archly, "about a feeling of tenderness, of attachment, of the feeling that the other person is the most important being in the universe, the feeling that his or her welfare matters more than anything else in the world."

"What?" he barked. "No desire, no lust?"

"Of course," I replied. "Sexual attraction, desire, longing – these are all part of it."

"But you don't actually do anything? You just have these feelings? It's all in the mind is it?"

"Of course it is not all in the mind."

"You mean humans do it just like dogs?"

"If you mean what I think you mean," I replied primly, "it – as you so delicately put it – is a normal human activity, but we are not like dogs. We can control our urges."

Caesar looked puzzled. "Why should you want to do that?" he asked.

"It is all about being civilised," I explained. "That is what distinguishes the man from the beast."

"So when you are civilised, you get less fun. I think that is rather sad." Caesar walked up and down the room, shaking his head.

"It is not at all sad," I retorted. "Civilisation brings one to a higher moral and emotional plain. It brings education and enlightenment; it gives one the opportunity to appreciate the finer things in life."

"Pretty poor compensation, if you ask me," Caesar sniffed.

"I don't expect a dog to understand," I said. "What do you know of art and literature and beauty?"

"Ah!" he snapped. "Now I know I am right. When you believe what you are saying, you don't start insulting me. It is perfectly clear to me: either, what you call your urges are very mild or you must be very frustrated. I think that must be why so-called civilised peoples are always going to war with one another. It gives them an outlet."

"You are talking nonsense," I insisted. "Civilisation provides a framework for society in which people can respect one another."

"I respect the bitch down the road. She is hot stuff."

"That is not what I mean," I said sharply.

"It seems to me," Caesar sighed, "you are having great difficulty today in saying what you mean. I ask you a simple question, 'What is love?' and you start mumbling on about art and literature. That is your trouble. You don't do anything. For you, everything exists only in the mind. You watch tennis on television; you can't be bothered to play. You would rather watch a cookery programme on television than cook a meal. Even your professed interest in politics is exercised from the comfort of your armchair."

"I once wrote to my Member of Parliament," I said defensively.

"Once," he snorted. He eyed me disdainfully. I hate it when he does that. It is not how a dog should regard his master.

"You are being disrespectful," I admonished him. "This is not the way a dog should speak to his master."

"Master!" He almost choked. "Where do you get this idea of a master from?"

"That," I told him, "is the nature of our relationship."

"You poor man. You are living in cloud-cuckoo land. Do I go out to the shops to buy *your* food? Do I prepare and serve it for *you*? Do I give *you* a bath? Master indeed!"

"I am in charge," I insisted.

"If it pleases you to think so," he replied casually, "that is fine with me."

"Good."

"But I still say you can't explain what you mean by love. As you talk about it, there is no excitement, no passion."

"Of course there is passion. Love is like a dying ember; love is like a flame."

"I think you have got your images in the wrong order," he said crudely.

"Love is a many splendored thing," I countered. "A man will do anything for the woman he loves."

"Do you love Emmeline?" he asked suddenly.

"Of course I do, she is my wife."

"Then why don't you clean the drains? She has been asking you to do that for weeks."

"You," I told him sharply, "are beginning to sound like Emmeline. I don't like it. Characters in fiction must be clearly delineated. Emmeline is my wife; you are my dog. It wouldn't do for people to mix you up."

"That is your problem," he told me. "You write this rubbish."

"If you go on like this," I warned him, "you are in danger of being written out of the script."

"No chance," he replied. "You need me too much. Still, just to show there is no hard feeling, how would you like me to take you for a walk?"

Fine Words Butter No Parsnips

(A Consultation from the Casebook of Dr Magnus Fell)

- *Good morning. You have not been to see me for many a day.*
- An apple a day keeps the doctor away.
- *Indeed, it helps. What brings you to see me now?*
- All roads lead to Rome.
- *I must say that you are looking very well.*
- Never judge by appearances.
- *A doctor can tell a lot from appearances.*
- Things are not always what they seem.
- *Perhaps you will tell me why you have come to see me?*
- Truth will out.
- *Eventually.*
- Two heads are better than one.
- *I will try to help.*
- Many hands are better than one.
- *That is often true.*
- Scratch my back and I'll scratch yours.
- *That will not be necessary. Just tell me what is troubling you.*
- Walls have ears.
- *You need not worry. With the door shut, no one can overhear what we are saying.*

- When one door shuts, another door opens.
- *Not here. Just tell me what is wrong.*
- He that lives long suffers much.
- *But you are still a young man.*
- Forewarned is forearmed.
- *Of course, but I am sure you have nothing to worry about.*
- Health is better than wealth.
- *Exactly.*
- Half a loaf is better than no bread.
- *Why did you say that?*
- What must be, must be. Necessity is the mother of invention.
- *Do you mean that you couldn't help yourself and that you did not intend to say, half a loaf is better than no bread?*
- The road to hell is paved with good intentions.
- *I think I begin to see your problem. Can you speak other than in proverbs?*
- We must learn to walk before we can run.
- *And I presume you would like to be able to run. You want to be cured?*
- Prevention is better than cure.
- *First we had better get you cured, then we can worry about preventing a recurrence.*
- A drowning man will clutch at a straw.
- *How do you cope at work?*
- Least said soonest mended. Absence makes the heart grow fonder.
- *I see. You are absenting yourself from work. Do they know the nature of your problem?*
- Bad news travels fast.
- *I suppose your reputation is suffering.*
- After a storm comes a calm. Out of sight, out of mind.
- *That's not too bad then.*
- It is no use crying over spilt milk.
- *I am glad you take it so philosophically.*
- All good things must come to an end.

- *I am sure you would like to know more of this condition you have.*

- Ask a silly question and you'll get a silly answer.

- *You are suffering from* Proverbial Diarrhoea – *literally, the free flow of proverbs. It was quite common in rural societies in the eighteenth century. It has always been extremely rare in urban communities.*

- It is never too late to learn.

- *I think we can cure you.*

- Actions speak louder than words.

- *It may take time.*

- Better late than never.

- *You will need to spend two hours each day reading philosophy. I suggest you start with Bertrand Russell's History of Western Philosophy, as much for the elegance of the writing as for the content.*

- Fine words butter no parsnips.

- *Perhaps not, but you need to be exposed to language that eschews trite and hackneyed phrases.*

- Old habits die hard.

- *You will have to try. It will help if you avoid speaking altogether for the next seven days, after you leave here.*

- The first step is the hardest.

- *Indeed.*

- Where there's a will there's a way. Nothing ventured nothing gained.

- *It is the only way.*

- There is more than one way to skin a cat.

- *Not in this case.*

- There's many a slip 'twixt cup and lip.

- *That is why it is important you follow my directions. Come back and see me again in ten days' time.*

- Time is a great healer.

- *Exactly. Good morning.*

Great Moments in History: How to Make Fire

The first great moment in History was the discovery of how to make a fire. Unfortunately, the cameras were not rolling at the time, nor did anyone think to keep a record of it or make a diary note. Consequently, the circumstances surrounding the discovery can be only the subject of conjecture. My recipe for such conjecture is a good bottle of burgundy topped off by a double whisky, after which it is fairly easy to reconstruct what must have happened. It is important to remember that the quality of the burgundy is crucial in this reconstruction of the past while, as far as the whisky is concerned, I recommend a good single malt, particularly... [*Any distiller who wishes to purchase this advertising space should contact my agent. I am sure it will be possible to reach an agreement.*]

The first thing to understand is that fire was around for a very long time before anyone realised how to make it. It sprouted from volcanoes and fell from the sky in thunderstorms but, unless you happened to live next to a volcano, fire was never available when you wanted it. Consequently, few people wanted it. What experience most people had of fire was unpleasant and suggested fire was dangerous, destructive and vicious. Men feared it with superstitious wonder. No wonder then that it was a woman who first saw the value of taming it. From the earliest days, while the men were out hunting and gathering, women were the homemakers, cleaning and tidying, looking after the children, organising the playgroups and preparing the food. One such was our heroine.

Mrs Ug was a short woman of striking appearance. Both front teeth were chipped, her nose was broken in two places, and she had abundant hair growing under her armpits, on her back and under her nose. Her legs were bowed and her breasts limp and wrinkled. She was aged twenty-five years and looked sixty, though in those days no one lived to the age of sixty. Her husband, Ug the Unfortunate, hunted and gathered like the best of them, and would then relax in the evenings with a group of his cronies. Each evening he would tell them his joke and they would always laugh dutifully, as if they had never heard it before. They were not particularly bright and it is possible they had forgotten it since the previous evening and thought they had never heard it before. Even those days it was a very old joke, ending in the line, "That was no lady; that was my wife."

The previous summer had been hot and dry when, during a storm, fire came from the sky and set the forest ablaze. The wind was high and flames spread quickly, driving animals before them and obliterating shrubs and bushes in their path. When the fire had burnt itself out, there was little food to be found and Ug had thought himself lucky to discover the charred carcass of a deer. He carried it home and threw it before his wife and children. The fur had all been burnt away and skinning the animal was much easier than with a fresh kill. The absence of blood would most likely have turned the children off their food – they usually made a fuss about something at mealtimes – but on this occasion they were very hungry and they each ate three portions without any fuss. Everyone agreed the meat was uncommonly tasty and for weeks afterwards the family would grumble that they were not again given such an appetising meal.

On several occasions thereafter, Ug would return home after a successful day's hunting, present his wife with the carcass of a wild boar or a squirrel and say, "Here, grill this."

"And just how do you expect me to cook anything without a fire?" Mrs Ug would scream at him.

"It is your job to look after the home." Ug would declare imperiously. "You never do any cooking; if you need fire, go and find some. Don't expect me to do everything. I don't know why I married you." Then he would storm out of the cave, thinking it would be nice to invent some sort of door he could slam on such occasions.

Similar complaints had been received by Mrs Og, Mrs Ig, Mrs Ag and Mrs Kettleby-Forsyte. Mrs Kettleby-Forsyte was one of the highland Kettlebys. During the rainy season, she had descended from the mountains and married beneath her. After some initial difficulties, she had been accepted by her neighbours, had got used to their eating berries with a knife, and was now a valued member of the community. It was she who called them together to discuss the problem.

They started with a brainstorming session and the best ideas to emerge were that they should pray to the sun and should sacrifice a wild animal. Mrs Og and Mrs Kettleby-Forsyte agreed to compose a suitable prayer. Mrs Ig and Mrs Ag were deputed to find a suitable place for the sacrifice. It was left to Mrs Ug to tell her husband to hunt for some animal they could sacrifice.

"You stupid ***," he said when she told him – the men of that time could be quite crude in their language. He picked up a rock and threw it at her head. The rock missed its target, hit the wall of their cave with a glancing blow and created a shower of sparks that landed on a heap of dried grass and sticks lying nearby. Soon there was a fire big enough to attract a crowd of onlookers.

"I can make fire by throwing rocks at my wife," Ug told his admiring neighbours.

It took until the end of the summer before Mrs Ug was able to demonstrate that two rocks could be used for the purpose and her life need not be put at risk every time the family wanted a cooked meal.

Long Life

"I was wondering whether to subscribe for it," I said.

"Eternal life, you mean."

"Yes."

"We don't know how long it will last," said Albert.

Albert Onejug was my Independent Scientific Adviser. I had called him in as soon as I heard the subject in the news.

"You mean the offer," I asked. "You don't know for how long the possibility of eternal life is going to be on offer."

"It is not actually on offer yet," he replied, "but that is not what I mean."

"Do you mean you don't know how long eternity is going to last? Won't it last for ever?"

"Not on this earth it won't. We know that the earth will cool some day and we know that some day the whole galaxy will get swallowed up in a black hole."

"I am not very well up on black holes," I confessed. "Would you like to tell me about them?"

"No," he explained.

I thought about this.

"It is probably an exaggeration," he continued after a pause. "We doubt that the ageing process can be stopped for ever."

"I didn't think you scientist fellows ever said something you didn't really mean," I complained. "My faith in science is being shaken to its very roots."

"It wasn't scientists who talked about eternity. It was journalists."

"Ah," I said, glad he was on a retainer rather than an hourly rate, "then you had better start again at the beginning."

"You mean the big bang? I don't think I should. Shall I start with the recent developments?"

"Please do," I said.

"We have to start with George Roth of the National Institute of Ageing in Baltimore?"

"I've never heard of him," I admitted, "nor of the Institute."

"The important thing is what he told the American Association for the Advancement of Science."

"I've never heard of that either but I'm sure you're right."

"Dr Roth told the association that we scientists have done something quite remarkable."

Albert often talked like this – *we scientists*. I had learned to live with it.

"What exactly have *they* done?" I asked.

He gave me a disapproving stare.

"My American colleagues," he said grandly, "have found that mice fed permanently with a low calorie diet will live much longer – perhaps seven times longer – than mice fed on a normal diet."

"So what," I said. "Mice don't live very long in any case."

"The important thing," he pointed out, "is the percentage increase. It is as if a human being were living for five or six hundred years."

Now I don't want to blow my own trumpet but if I have one great psychological strength it is the ability to make a quick decision when it is needed.

"Put me down for it," I said immediately.

"I am afraid it is too late," Albert told me.

"I feared as much," I said sadly, "though it is a great disappointment."

"You should have consulted me earlier."

"I suppose it doesn't matter now but when would have been the best time?"

"A few months before you were born would have been ideal," he said with assurance.

"Would that not have been a little impractical?"

"I suppose so. Probably it would have been OK if you had come to me before you were six months old."

"I am several years older than you."

"There are often difficulties in the practical application of scientific theories."

I sat quietly for some moments. There were times when my trust in Albert's professional judgement was less than complete.

"So I won't be able to live even for five or six hundred years," I said at last.

"It is unlikely," he replied. "I doubt if it is even a remote possibility."

"And just because I came to you too late."

"That is not exactly what I said," he objected. "The experimental work is still going on. If you had been a mouse, your chances would have been better."

"It was not something that I could arrange," I confessed.

Albert grunted non-committedly.

"Dr Roth was telling the American Association of Science about current work with monkeys," he continued. "So far it appears that they can increase their life span by fifty per cent with a low calorie diet, about seventy per cent of the normal intake."

"I suppose I could try cutting down on calories," I suggested.

"You probably eat too much, so that would be a good thing," he said rather rudely. "It might help you to live out your allotted years but it won't extend your life beyond normal expectations.

All the research done so far suggests that a low calorie diet is necessary throughout life."

"It would make me healthier?"

"Undoubtedly," Albert confirmed. "At every meal you must stop eating while you are still feeling hungry."

"You must be joking," I said – but I was wrong.

Lord of the Flies

"Other people come to me with prayers," God said one day, after I had been particularly direct in my criticisms. "You come with complaints."

"You have only yourself to blame," I said resolutely. "You should not have created flies."

"In point of fact, one of my most successful creations," He responded. "Did you know that there are more than eighty thousand different species of flies? They are the fourth largest animal group. Virtually indestructible and they live everywhere in the world."

"Too damned successful, if you ask me," I said.

The sun was eclipsed briefly and there was a roll of thunder in the distance. I sensed that I had expressed myself too bluntly.

"If you want to use the language of damnation," He said sternly, "you should direct your remarks in the opposite direction."

"People would like to be rid of flies," I continued after making the appropriate apology. "They do no good to man or beast."

"You are quite wrong, as so often," He laughed.

I couldn't see the joke but I let it pass. There were worse things He might do than try to make fun of me.

"Flies spread disease and they dirty the wall paper," I said.

"They have a very important role in balancing the ecology of the planet. They speed up the decomposition of dead animals, animal dung and vegetable matter."

"Maybe," I replied, "but…"

"They eat other insects that you probably dislike equally or even more."

"OK but they do these things only because you decided that they should. You could have arranged things differently but, oh no, you had to create flies to make life miserable for the human race."

"Flies came first," He said. "Perhaps the flies should complain because I created Homo sapiens to persecute them."

"You are not being serious," I complained. "Surely you created the whole caboodle just for us."

"Not at all," He said. "You were an afterthought."

"I don't believe it."

"I would have thought that it was perfectly obvious. If I had had you lot in mind from the start, do you think I would have created a universe that is so unfriendly to you? Large parts of the earth are either uninhabitable or will support human life only in the most uncomfortable of conditions. Hurricanes, earthquakes, avalanches and floods make life uncertain for millions. The earth itself has been designed to have a strictly limited life."

"But you gave man dominion over everything."

"Yes, I did but as an afterthought."

"I still don't believe you."

"Think about the sequence of events. First I created the heavens and the earth. Nothing special. Dark and formless."

"OK."

"Then I introduced light, so that there would be a difference between night and day, and after that I created Heaven. I thought by then I had done pretty well. It was all new. No one had done anything like it before. Even so, I was not satisfied."

"And so?"

"You remember that, at this stage, the earth was entirely

covered in water. I decided that it would be more interesting if I moved some of the land from under the water and had some of it sticking up in the air. It was only a short step from there to putting in some plants and vegetables, just as you might do, if you moved into a newly built house without an established garden."

"So you were the world's first gardener?"

"Of course."

"How long did all this take?"

"So far three days."

"Pretty quick."

"When I say a day, I don't necessarily mean what you would mean by a day."

"You don't?"

"There is a little poetic licence involved here. These days were distinct periods of time but they may have lasted for what you would think of as millions of years."

"It doesn't help me to understand you."

"You are only mortal."

I could not really argue with this.

"What happened next?" I asked.

"That's when I introduced your earthly days. I added the sun to mark the day and a moon to signal the night."

"Then you created man to look after it all."

"Hold on. I did nothing of the kind. So far, I had put together a very pretty world. I enjoyed it at first but then I realised that it was too static. Watching plants grow got to be pretty tedious after a while. I wanted more movement."

"And so?"

"I introduced fish and reptiles and birds."

"And dinosaurs?"

"And dinosaurs. Even so, it was not enough. After another day – one of my days that is – I added animals and creepy-crawly things."

"Five of your days and now you were ready to introduce man to look after it for you."

"I keep telling you," He said, "that was not what it was all about. I thought I had finished."

"Finished?"

"Naturally. I had created a beautiful world, gorgeous scenery, four seasons with vegetation constantly changing in appearance, animals with their varied life cycles. I could sit and watch them for ever, the way you watch nature films on Television."

"No people?"

"They just hadn't occurred to me."

"What changed your mind?"

"I'll tell you. After a few million years – your years, just one of my days – I realised that there was nothing to make me laugh. You need something to make you laugh and that is because I fashioned you in my image. I needed something to make me laugh. Animals didn't make me laugh. They act predictably and, within the limits of their intelligence, quite logically. Human beings are different. They are crazy, man."

"Are you telling me that you created man to make you laugh?"

"Can you think of a better explanation?"

Ewe and I

"Are you busy?" Emmeline asked.

"I'm writing," I replied.

"Anything in particular?"

"I'm trying my hand at a short story. I don't suppose you'll like it."

"Try me."

"It is called *Animal Husbandry*; it's a fictionalised autobiography by one Ivor Ramsbottom."

"What does he do?"

"He marries a sheep," I announced.

"How stupid," she said encouragingly. "How can he marry a sheep?"

"He simply proposes by asking, 'Will ewe marry me?'"

"That is not funny."

"You haven't seen it written down."

"I don't need to. I think the whole thing is rather sick."

"I don't write that sort of thing," I objected. "I am writing about the sort of sheep that you could take home to your family. In fact that is exactly what Ivor Ramsbottom does."

"Absurd."

"Not at all. Ivor's father quite takes to the ewe; he thinks she is a little lamb, probably because she makes sheep's eyes at him."

"Do you think anyone is going to want to read this nonsense?" Emmeline asked, going for the jugular.

I looked at her sheepishly.

"All my regular readers," I insisted.

"You mean Clifford and that other person whose name you didn't tell me?"

"Emmeline," I said, "do you realise that, if people overheard you talking like that, they could quite easily think you were serious?"

She sighed.

"Anyhow," I continued, "my readership is increasing all the time."

"Where do you get these stupid ideas?" Emmeline asked, ignoring my boast.

"Actually," I said, "you gave me the idea."

"I did?" She seemed offended. "I remember saying that you were behaving like a silly old goat. I don't recall mentioning a sheep."

"You said the lawn needed cutting."

"And so you thought it would be nice to have a sheep?"

"It is nice to have a wife who understands me," I said by way of confirmation.

"I am glad you think so," she said with a threatening edge to her voice.

"I thought how nice it would be to have a sheep to eat all the grass."

"I am not going to have a sheep here," Emmeline declared. "That is final."

"I was thinking generally," I explained. "I wouldn't have a sheep here either – it might do things in the garden that we wouldn't like. In any case, I don't think the neighbours would approve."

"Never mind the neighbours," she said inconsiderately, "I wouldn't approve."

"Still," I continued, "I thought it would be interesting to explore the life of someone who did take a sheep into his home."

"And got married to it," she added sarcastically.

"It's only respectable. You wouldn't want me to write about people living in sin."

"No one talks about anyone living in sin these days," Emmeline reminded me, "and one man and a sheep do not comprise *people*."

"That is true," I said making a quick note. "The point is that Ivor Ramsbottom is a very conventional sort of bloke."

"Bloke?" she exploded. "Where do you get these expressions? Nobody says *bloke* anymore."

I made another note.

"OK," I said, "but he is very conventional, a dyed in the wool conservative."

"As illustrated by his marrying a sheep?"

"No! I mean he was very conventional up to the point when he met Cynthia."

"Where does Cynthia come into this?"

"I don't mean your friend Cynthia. Cynthia is the name of the sheep."

"In your wool-gathering, where do you imagine your conventional and conservative Ivor Ramsbottom will meet his sheep?"

"I thought they could meet in Woolworths – before it closed down." I suggested.

"This gets worse and worse," she said encouragingly.

"I don't see what is wrong with it," I murmured.

"It is like most of what you write," she told me. "It's woolly-minded."

Insolence and Effrontery

"I believe your post is unique."

"You know damn well it is. It said that in the blurb we sent you before you arranged to come and interview me."

Frank Gall had recently been appointed Lecturer in Insolence and Effrontery at Duffborough University, in the Department of Communication and Inter-Personal Skills. The University was famous for its unusual and innovative degree courses and I was interested to know the background to the appointment.

"I understand you will be giving lectures to all the undergraduates in the Department," I said.

"Are you telling me or asking me?"

"I was seeking confirmation."

"I knew this was going to be a bloody waste of my time. Actually, I will give lectures to all the undergraduates in the University."

"May I ask a very simple question?"

"It is what I expect of you," he sighed.

"What exactly will you be teaching?"

He looked at me suspiciously. "Can you really be more stupid than I took you for? You know what insolence is, I suppose?"

I held my temper and nodded.

"And you know what effrontery means."

"Yes."

"Then you know the answer to your own question."

"No. I mean what is the theme? Will you be examining your subject in an historical context? Will you be looking at insolence and effrontery from the point of view of linguistics? Will you be looking at their significance in Literature or in different societies or cultures?"

"Don't be daft. You could get any number of fools to teach those things. As is appropriate in one of the new Universities, I shall be running an entirely practical course, teaching students the skills they will need in the modern world."

I laughed involuntarily. "The way you put it, it sounds as if you are going to teach students how to be insolent and how to act with impudent presumption."

"Exactly so. Has it not entered your tiny mind that I might mean precisely what I say?"

"Why should you want to teach students how to be rude and obnoxious?"

"If it were not for your crass stupidity, you would see immediately. Don't you see the immense advantages it will give them in interpersonal relationships?"

"I would expect the opposite to be true."

"As one of life's losers, you would. I will have to explain it in very simple terms for you. First let me ask you, haven't you been feeling uncomfortable while interviewing me?"

"If I have, it is your fault."

"That is the first sensible thing you have said. Of course it is my fault. Insolence always puts your adversary at a disadvantage. He doesn't know how to react. While worrying how to cope, his defences will be weakened. My lectures are going to show how to gain advantages in negotiations. Business Studies students will find the course invaluable, but it will be useful to everyone."

"Hold on." I said. "You have been incredibly rude to me,

since I arrived. So you were just pretending, demonstrating the effects of being rude?"

"Not at all. You really are a pillock."

"And you are a pain in the neck."

"Thank you. I hope so."

"I can hardly believe the University would employ someone to teach students how to eschew all the normal rules of etiquette."

"Oh, not just that. It may not entirely have escaped your notice that insolence and effrontery have been demonstrated throughout the ages. I may give my students superior skills in their practice. They may develop particular expertise in giving offence but they will meet others, who will give offence to them. My lectures will teach students how to defend themselves against such verbal attacks. Someone like you would have a lot to learn from this part of the course. Perhaps if you were to attend, you wouldn't go so red or sweat so much."

I had to restrain myself again, as I asked when he would be giving his first lecture.

"That is uncertain," he replied wistfully. "At present I am under suspension."

Why was that?

"I told the Vice-Chancellor he was a pompous prat."

Just Give Your Name

Scene: ANYWHERE ANYTIME

Two men are talking.

- I have arranged for you to be able to get into the meeting tomorrow. Just give the lady on the door your name and she will let you in.
- *I can't give her my name.*
- Why can't you give her your name?
- *I need it.*
- You can still give the lady your name.
- *I like my name. I have grown very attached to it.*
- That is very nice for you.
- *No one would be able to write to me, if I lost my name.*
- There is no need for you to lose your name.
- *I wouldn't know who I was, if I lost my name.*
- I understand what you are saying.
- *I won't give it up.*
- No one wants you to give it up.
- *I regard it as a basic human right to be able to keep my name.*
- I have no argument with that.
- *You haven't?*

- No.

- *So what do I have to do to get into the meeting?*

- Just give your name to the lady on the door.

- *Hasn't she got her own name?*

- Of course she has her own name.

- *Then why does she want my name?*

- She doesn't want your name.

- *It wouldn't suit her. It's a man's name.*

- Of course it is.

- *Then I can keep it?*

- Of course you can keep it. Nobody wants to deprive you of your name.

- *I'd be lost without it.*

- So you have implied.

- *And the lady on the door doesn't want my name?*

- Of course she doesn't want your name.

- *Then why do I have to give it to her?*

- So that you can get into the meeting.

- *Let me see if I understand this. I can keep my name?*

- Certainly.

- *But I have to give it to the lady on the door?*

- Absolutely.

- *Even though she doesn't want it?*

- You'll need to give it to her, if you want to get in to the meeting.

- *I don't like this. I don't want to be without a name.*

- But you won't be without a name. You will still have your name.

- *Even after I have given it to someone else?*

- Of course.

- *Have you ever given your name to anyone?*

- Hundreds of times.

- *How did you get it back?*

- I didn't have to get it back. I was never without it.

- You mean you just offered to give people your name, but they didn't accept it?

- Of course they accepted it. I offered my name to various people and they took it.

- How did you get it back?

- I didn't need to get it back.

- So each time you gave your name to someone, you were able to get a new name?

- Why would I want a new name?

- To take the place of the name you had given away.

- I didn't give my name away.

- You didn't?

- Of course not. I just gave it to someone. I was never without it.

- Not at all?

- Not even for one moment.

- So you can give your name to someone and still keep it?

- Of course.

- And still have full use of it. You still own it absolutely?

- Certainly.

- It sounds like a very good trick. Can you show me how to do it with a twenty-pound note?

A First Glimpse of Second Sight

As I came into the room, Caesar was standing near the window, wagging his tail. He had that sort of self-satisfied look that dogs often have after having accomplished something disreputable.

"I knew you would be home now," he said.

"I always come home about this time."

"Not always. Even if you are going to come in at a different time, I can tell."

I removed my jacket and carried it upstairs into the bedroom. Caesar followed me.

"The other day, you returned in the middle of the afternoon. I knew you were coming."

"I came back to get my briefcase," I answered, washing my hands. "You probably saw it in the hallway."

"I often know what you are going to do before you do it," he insisted. "You are just about to go and put the kettle on."

"When I get home from work, and after putting my jacket away, I always put the kettle on. You don't need to be a soothsayer to guess that I am likely to put the kettle on now."

"I didn't say I can foretell the future," said Caesar, "but I can read your mind. I must have been doing it for a long time but I only just realised it. I heard about it on the radio; I think I am psychotic."

"It sounds like it – but I think you mean psychic. If you were psychotic, you would need treatment."

"Psychic, that's it," he said excitedly. "This chap on the radio said that lots of dogs are psychic. We have extra sense, he said."

"He obviously hasn't seen the way you behave. Extra sense is the last attribute you would be credited with. I think you are claiming extra-sensory perception."

"That's right," Caesar said, following me downstairs to the kitchen. "There's a Dr Rupert Sheldrake who has been doing research on it. He used to teach at Cambridge University, so you have to take him seriously."

"And he says that dogs have extra-sensory perception?"

"He says that they got in touch with over four hundred dog owners at a place called Random in Greater Manchester and lots of them said their dogs knew when they were coming home."

"There is no such place as Random."

"Dr Sheldrake said they chose them at Random."

You can see why it is difficult to have a serious conversation with Caesar. Sometimes I wonder why I don't just ignore him and let him go and chase pigeons. I explained the theory of random selection.

"When they did scientific tests," Caesar continued undeterred, "nearly half the dogs tested could tell when their owners were returning home."

"There is probably some perfectly reasonable explanation."

"You're just a septic," Caesar muttered.

"You mean sceptic. If something is septic, it means there is rotting flesh."

"Well I think you are pretty rotten to make fun of me."

"Your problem," I said, "is that you get all your information from the radio and television."

"And other dogs."

"I suppose so."

"Cleopatra tells me about some of the things she reads in the newspaper."

Now I confess I have no direct evidence that the cat can read. I have never seen her reading the newspaper – or anything else for that matter. On the other hand, she does seem to pick up a lot of information that is difficult to explain in any other way. I told this to Caesar.

"It's a bit like extra-sensory perception," he commented happily.

"There is no such thing."

"Yes there is and I've got it. Wasn't I standing at the window, as you came up the path today."

"You were," I admitted, "and every day this week."

"There you are then," he said triumphantly. "That proves it."

"Stuff and nonsense," I retorted. "You've been standing at that window all week for most of the time I have been inside the house. You always do, when the bitch next door is in heat."

"That's the trouble with you," said Caesar. "You put everything down to sex."

The Big Idea

My Lords, Ladies and Gentlemen, you will have read in the media that I intend to use this occasion to make a keynote speech focusing on a major issue of policy. I have to tell you that, for once, the rumours are correct. Tonight I intend to discuss new policies and approaches to one of the great issues of today and to propose actions more radical than previously have been put before any electorate.

While I am about to reveal policies that are completely new, they are, nevertheless, firmly based on past experience and activity both in this country and abroad and draw heavily on the ideas of... Old Labour.

Yes, indeed. I intend to go back to the ideas of the post-war Labour Government and to use these ideas to solve, once and for all, one of the greatest problems of modern society.

Too often have politicians been driven by dogma. My government will not be driven by dogma. We will do what is right for the country.

What I ask you was the great idea of Old Labour? I will tell you. It was Nationalisation: Nationalisation of the means of production, distribution and control – the great industries, transport, the banks. A great idea... totally misdirected.

What do we all know about Nationalisation? What did we

learn slowly and painfully in the years after 1945? I will tell you in two words: it failed. It was bound to fail. Public Corporations were heavily bureaucratic, rigid in the performance of their duties, unimaginative in their vision; inflexible and ill equipped to cope with a changing world.

Nationalisation is the most inefficient form of organisation yet developed in the non-Communist world. (*Pause here.*) It may yet have its uses.

What, I ask you now, is the greatest problem facing modern society? What, when asked, do people say most concerns them? It is crime. The figures may change from time to time but, no matter which political party has been in power, the truth of the matter is that crime has remained at quite unacceptable levels.

My friends, tonight I have to tell you that all previous approaches to this problem have been wrong. Governments concentrated their efforts on increasing the efficiency of the police, on punishment and on trying to reform prisoners. None of these has been successful nor, in my view, could hope to be successful. Instead of trying to make the forces of law and order more efficient, we must make the criminal less efficient.

We know what the most inefficient form of organisation is. It is Nationalisation. My Government will nationalise crime.

A National Crime Corporation will be responsible for all major criminal activity. It will establish a strategy for crime and determine its distribution across the country. The Head of the Corporation will be responsible to a new Minister for Crime, who will sit in the Cabinet and will be responsible for setting regional targets. Just as the Chief Secretary to the Treasury meets annually with other Ministers to agree Spending Limits, so the Home Secretary and the Minister for Crime will meet to agree national targets for crime, detection and conviction, as well as the grant to be made from the Crime Ministry towards the cost of policing.

It will be recognised that a certain minimal level of crime is desirable for each community. The need to protect one's self from crime engenders a sense of responsibility, which is important for the individual. At another level, the development of joint approaches to fighting crime can lead to the growth of community spirit. I particularly commend the growth of Neighbourhood Watch Schemes, whose success is just as great, or even greater, in areas with minimal crime rates, as in areas where crime levels are intolerable.

It may be objected that some criminal enterprises will be too small to be governed by a National Corporation. We agree with this. It may be remembered that when Road Transport was nationalised by a previous Labour Government, small businesses were exempt. This seems obvious sense. However, our strategy could be ruined, if we were to leave even small crime in the hands of private businesses. These are the engines of economic development and their prospects for efficient operation would be favourable. Indeed, with large-scale crime emasculated by Nationalisation, unregulated small-scale crime might get quite out of hand.

Our problem was to find another form of organisation, which might rival the incompetence of the Public Corporation. I am pleased to say that we have found what many will see as the perfect solution. All criminal organisations, with more than seven employees or associates or with a turnover of more than £750,000 per annum, will be the direct responsibility of the Public Corporation. All other crime will be the responsibility of... elected Local Authorities.

Our Party believes in the theory of local democracy. One has to admit, however, that the practice has often given grave cause for concern. Clearly, local democracy can be respected only if local government has significant and important areas of responsibility. The mistake in the past, the mistake of all political parties, has been to give them responsibilities, where it was important to be efficient. This put unwarrantable pressure on the good people, who are willing to give up their time for the good of their neighbours. Far kinder and better to give them an area of responsibility, where their inefficiency will be positively appreciated.

The Minister for Crime will be responsible for overall Local Authority policy in these activities and will consult with Local Authority Associations to agree crime targets by category and area. The Minister will have reserve powers for Crime Capping, though we expect that there will be little need to use them.

At the introductory stage, all practising criminals will be required, within a period of twelve months, to register with the Registrar for Crime, at the local office of the Public Corporation. They will be assessed for, among other things, length of previous service and intended years of future employment and for suitability for different categories of crime, such as armed robbery, forgery, shoplifting, etc. There will be a special category for computer crimes. They will be assessed also for willingness to undergo periods of imprisonment and, where the public mood demands it, police brutality.

After assessment, criminals will be allocated to either the office of the National Crime Corporation or to the Local Authority Crime Department. All further recruitment will be through local job centres, thus giving a useful boost to the activities of those valuable institutions. The Minister for Crime will monitor the division of responsibilities between the Corporation and the Local Crime Departments and will from time to time propose changes.

Criminals will be salaried or wage earning and will be liable to income tax on their earnings. We can expect the numbers of those registered as unemployed to drop as a result.

Now I think that I see some of you looking a little doubtful. How, you are saying, will we ensure that crime is committed only by employees of the Crime Corporation or of the local Crime Departments? It is here that we show our willingness to learn from experience overseas and again from the history. Based on practices developed in the nineteen-twenties by Al Capone in Chicago, we will establish *Capone Clubs*, directly responsible to the Minister. These clubs will offer protection to criminals prepared to be employed by the central or local body operating in the area. They will indeed make offers that cannot be refused. We can expect that, within a very short period of time, there will be very little freelance activity. These "Clubs" will, of course, be entirely self-financing, as will the Corporation and the Local Authority Crime Departments. In fact, the former will use surplus income to subsidise the police forces and the latter will provide an important new source of local government revenue.

In our first week in office, the new Home Secretary will introduce our Crime in the Community Bill.

For the first time, a government will have tackled crime at its roots. We may expect the following results:

- A reduction in the incidence of crime and the elimination of its more objectionable features.
- Easier, less stressful and cheaper policing.
- Less strain on the legal system.
- An end to prison overcrowding, as the number of convictions can be targeted to the number of places available.
- A boost to local democracy, as local government is invested with important new responsibilities and is given a new source of finance independent of central government.
- A reduction in unemployment and a greater role for job centres.

Within a relatively short period of time, the financial savings to the Treasury should be very considerable. Large sums of Government expenditure will be available for redirection.

I can give you a pledge, here and now, that the money released by the reforms I have proposed will be used to transform provision in the areas of Education and Health.

The ―――― Party has a vision and an agenda for the future. A big idea.

Respect for the Aged

The telephone rang. I answered.

"Is that you?" enquired the voice from the other end of the line.

"I think it must be," I confessed.

"How terrible for you."

"What?"

"To be you. I suppose you had no choice in the matter."

"Not that I remember."

"Nevertheless," said Clifford, for it was he, "nevertheless, you have no excuse."

"You cannot be sure of that."

"There is no excuse for your not telephoning me yesterday."

"Why yesterday? I have not telephoned you for some time. What was special about yesterday?"

"Have you no feelings?" Clifford spoke with deep, synthetic emotion. "Have you no respect for your elders and betters?"

"Did you get out of bed on the wrong side, this morning?" I asked.

"Where I got out of bed is none of your business," he replied sharply, "and is certainly not something I am prepared to discuss. Why will you not answer my question?"

"I am not aware that you have asked a question."

There was a short pause before he admitted that there might be some truth in what I had just said. "The question was implicit," he asserted. "Why did you not telephone me yesterday?"

"Why should I have done?"

"Why?" Clifford exploded. "Why? Do you not know what day it was?"

"It was not your birthday."

"Of course it was not my birthday. It was Respect for the Aged Day."

"How do you know things like that?"

"It is in my diary."

"Really?"

"It is an American diary, but none the worse for that."

"I see."

"And you did not show any."

"Any what?"

"Any respect. You should have telephoned."

"Are you eligible?" I asked.

"I am older than you are."

"Two and a bit weeks."

"You will understand when you reach my age."

"Tell me what you know about Respect for the Aged Day," I said.

"It is on September the fifteenth. It is very important."

"To whom?"

"To the aged."

"And what else do you know about it?"

"I know it is a day when people like you should treat me with respect. Respect for one's elders is a traditional Confucian value."

"Exactly so," I told him, "and you are not eligible. In the first place you are not yet seventy years of age and, in the second place, you are not Japanese."

"Neither of those things is my fault," Clifford asserted, "but why should they matter?"

"Yesterday, as clearly you do not know, was *Keiro No Hi* – a Japanese national holiday. It was established in 1966, when the Law concerning Welfare for the Aged was enacted."

"Would I be eligible if I could learn to eat sushi?" Clifford wondered.

"Certainly not. At one time, you would have qualified at sixty but nowadays, because so many people live so much longer, seventy is regarded as the key age."

"Perhaps it was psychological. If you tell people they are old, they start to feel it."

"Marx said a man is only as old as the woman he feels."

"Karl?"

"No, the other one."

"Tell me more about *Keiro No Hi*." Clifford was issuing a challenge, clearly believing I had exhausted my fund of knowledge.

"One's sixtieth birthday used to be regarded as very important, partly because it marked the completion of the cycle of the Zodiac – that is twelve animal signs matched with the ten element signs."

"But now they forget about the Zodiac?"

"Yes and now, all over the country in towns and villages, they give gifts to people over the age of seventy."

"One day," said Clifford, "I shall think that an idea worth importing into this country. Tell me," he continued. "How do you know things like this?"

"Easy," I replied. "I expected you to telephone. I looked it up on the Internet."

An Eventful Day

Mr Simkins lived in a small cottage at the foot of a hill. He lived alone, his wife having died three years earlier. His married daughter lived in the same village and on most days he would take the ten minutes' walk to visit her and play with his grandchildren. Although he missed his wife very much, his days were full and he was happy and contented.

One morning very early, while Mr Simkins was still in bed, he heard a very loud noise. It reminded him of a bomb, of which he had a very hazy memory from the war when he had been a child. The house trembled. He sat up in bed and wondered what it could have been. As he got out of bed he looked for his slippers and saw that they were not under the bed, where he always placed them, but had made their own way to a spot under the dressing table by the window. He observed with surprise that the floor of the bedroom was slanting towards the window, something he had never noticed before. There were large cracks in the wall, something else he had never noticed. He thought that he had better see if anything else was amiss.

He showered and shaved more quickly than usual but took some time to select one of his new shirts, having a feeling that this might be an eventful day and not knowing whom he might meet. When he was satisfied with his appearance, he made his way downstairs.

The front door was hanging from its hinges and there was a large lorry in the front lounge. On closer inspection, it appeared that only the front half of the lorry was in the lounge, the other half sticking out into the front garden. Looking past where the walls and window had been, he could see the flowerbeds had been completely destroyed. He was thinking about this when he heard a voice.

"Good morning."

Mr Simkins turned round and now saw a man sitting in the driving seat of the lorry. He was fair-haired and his face was covered in blood.

"Good morning," Mr Simkins replied politely. "I didn't notice you sitting there. Have you been here long?"

"For about half an hour," said the man.

"I am sorry to have kept you waiting. I wasn't expecting a visitor."

"It's my fault," said the man. "I should have let you know I was coming. I don't usually drop in on people unexpectedly."

"Please don't worry about that," said Mr Simkins gently, "not many people call. I like company. Can I offer you a cup of tea?"

"I wouldn't want to put you to any trouble."

"It's no trouble. I am going to make one for myself."

"In that case, thank you. It is very kind of you."

"Not at all," said Mr Simkins as he moved towards the kitchen.

One wall of the kitchen had collapsed, burying the dresser where he kept the crockery, but he found two clean cups on the draining board. While he was waiting for the kettle to boil, he made four slices of toast and together with butter and marmalade put everything on a tray. He made the tea and took the tray into the lounge.

"I am sorry it took so long," Mr Simkins said.

"Not at all," replied the man.

"I thought you might like some toast."

"Thank you."

"Do you take milk and sugar?"

"Yes please, just one lump."

"It is a very pleasant day," said Mr Simkins, looking out through the wall and noticing a small crowd of people standing on the pavement. He waved to Mrs Dawes, his next-door neighbour.

"I say," said the man, "do you think you could help me with the tea and toast."

"Help?"

"Yes, I can't move my right arm. I think I've broken it."

"Oh, that is tough luck."

"My left arm seems OK."

"I'll hold the saucer and the plate for you."

"Could you put some butter and marmalade on the toast?"

"Of course."

Mr Simkins stood on the step of the lorry to pass the tea and toast to his guest. He felt the lorry move slightly and watched plaster fall from the ceiling.

"I am afraid I broke a vase as I came in," said the man. "It was on the coffee table that used to be in the middle of the room. I am afraid it made a dreadful mess."

"No matter. I have a woman who comes into clean later today and it was only a cheap vase."

"By the way," said the man, "my name is Jedediah Klugman. My friends call me Jed."

"Then I shall call you Jed and you can call me Mr Simkins, as befits the difference in our ages and our stations in life."

"That is only right and proper. My station is Kings Cross."

"I am not at all surprised."

"Have you lived here long?" Jed asked.

"For about twenty-five years. We moved here, my late wife and myself, to get away from all the traffic in the town. I have always liked it."

"It was a pretty cottage," said Jed.

"Do you come through here very often?"

"My first time."

"You must come again."

"I'd like to."

"It's a nice lorry," Mr Simkins said admiringly.

"Quite nice but it is small as lorries go."

"It looks quite big to me."

"On the continent they have forty-four tonne lorries."

"You wouldn't have managed to get in here with one of those," Mr Simkins said jokingly.

Jed laughed. "I suppose not."

There was a sound of falling masonry.

"I think that was the dining room," Mr Simkins said.

"Too bad."

"Are you quite comfortable in sitting in the cab? Wouldn't you like to move?"

"I don't think I can," Jed replied. "I seemed to be pinned in by the steering wheel."

"It's strange the way the people meet."

"Yes, isn't it?"

They sat in silence for some time, thinking about the part that chance takes in all our lives.

There was a knock at the front door.

"Come straight in?" Mr Simkins shouted. "We're in the lounge."

The newcomer looked warily at what was left of the hallway ceiling and stepped gingerly into the lounge.

"I'm sorry to disturb you when you have a visitor," he said.

"Not at all," said Mr Simkins. "Let me introduce you: Gerry McFingal, Jed Klugman."

"Excuse my not shaking hands," said Jed.

"Any relation to Philomena Klugman?"

"My sister."

"You are Phil's younger brother? I remember you when you were in short trousers. Phil was my childhood sweetheart."

"You used to give me sweets to bribe me to leave the two of you alone."

"That's right. How nice to see you after all this time. How is Phil these days?"

"She's married with three kids, lives in Australia."

"Send her my regards."

"I'll do that."

"And how have you been keeping?"

"Very well until this morning," said Jed. "I've had an accident."

"Oh, I am sorry. Are you hurt very badly?"

"I think so."

"He has broken his right arm," said Mr Simkins.

"Tough luck," said Gerry.

"That's what I said," Mr Simkins commented.

"You were right," said Gerry. "Oh, by the way, I had better tell you why I came. Doris won't be able to come in today to do the cleaning. Lisa isn't well and Doris has to stay in to look after her."

"I hope she gets better soon."

"I don't think it's too serious. Lisa will probably be back at school tomorrow. Perhaps Doris could come in then."

"I fear it might not be convenient tomorrow," Mr Simkins said, listening to the fall of more masonry and watching the wall between the lounge and the dining room collapse. "Perhaps she could check with me first." He looked out through the dining room into the garden.

"My wife always said that a through room would have been nice," he said. "It does give a more spacious feel."

"Would you mind if I have a cigarette?" Jed asked.

"I'm sorry," Mr Simkins answered, "I have a very strict rule about that. I don't want to appear inhospitable but, if you want to smoke, you will have to go outside."

"I can't do that."

"I suppose not. I'm sorry."

"I don't really blame you. It's your house."

"One has one's standards."

"I suppose that's right."

"I'd better go now," Gerry interrupted. "Doris will be wondering where I am."

"Of course," said Mr Simkins. "It was nice of you to drop by."

"It was nice meeting you again," Jed said.

"My pleasure," said Gerry. "Goodbye."

He walked out of the house through the space where the door had been.

Mr Simkins felt the house shake. There was a sound of breaking timber and his bed fell through the ceiling, landing on the lorry, just missing the cab.

"What was that?" Jed asked.

"My bed landed on your lorry. I think it is broken."

"The lorry?"

"No, the bed."

"It won't be much use then."

"I suppose not. Did you feel it?"

"I think the jolt may have broken my ribs."

"Tough luck."

"These things happen."

"I suppose they do."

"It never rains but it pours."

"It's not raining now," Mr Simkins commented. "The sun is shining."

"Are there still people outside? I can't see from where I am."

"Quite a crowd. I wonder why."

"Probably they want to know what will happen next."

"I was wondering about that myself," said Mr Simkins.

Life Is What Happens

"I've been thinking," I remarked to my wife one day.

"Really?" Emmeline replied. "How unusual."

"I have been thinking about life," I continued.

"Oh," she said casually, "is that all? You would do better to think about cleaning the drains."

"I did, yesterday."

"You cleaned the drains yesterday?"

"No. I thought about cleaning the drains. A bit of a waste of time, if you ask me. Life is much more important."

"Really?" she said. The tone of her voice suggested profound disagreement.

"It is something we all experience, you know?"

"What is?"

"Life. We can't help it. Here we are and there it is. We go through it from the moment we're born until the moment we die, all the time, awake or asleep, no matter what we do or plan to do. Have you ever thought of it? Every life is different. Every life that was ever lived was different from every other life – no matter how similar. That is the way it is. There is nothing you can do about it. If two people wanted to live the same life, they couldn't."

Emmeline made no reply but looked at me sadly. I don't like

to criticise her, but I don't think she can handle philosophy. She is very good at shopping lists; she is an excellent cook and a fine lawyer, but she is not at her best with abstract ideas. Ask her to explain the meaning of life or why London buses always arrive in pairs, and she is completely stumped. She turned her attention to a begonia sitting in a pot on the sideboard. It is the sort of thing she does, when getting out of her depth in discussion. I think it was a begonia; one flower is much the same as another to me but someone had mentioned we had a begonia and that could well be it. I am not an expert on plants; if it is not edible, I am unlikely to be able to put a name to it.

Emmeline shook her head at the begonia. "If I left the plants to you, they would all die," she said.

I thought about this. "You see," I said eventually, "you too are thinking about life. Even plants have life. Every flower and every vegetable is a living entity, even if not a thinking being."

"If you were a thinking being," she retorted, "you would think about doing some gardening."

"I have no wish to vegetate," I replied wittily.

Emmeline showed no appreciation. She has no sense of humour and gave me a withering look – something she is very good at. Her withering looks have a certain magisterial quality that no one else can equal.

"Your withering looks are magnificent," I complemented her.

"I give up," she replied, and stalked out of the room. I think she stalked; it was a bit unexpected and I had to think about it afterwards. It may be that she flounced out of the room, or merely strutted or marched – I cannot be sure any longer – but she left the room; of that I have no doubt.

I sat alone in the lounge and considered her words. She had given up. That was sad. If it signified acceptance of defeat, almost tragic, but what had she given up? She did not say. How can a lawyer be so imprecise, so vague?

Of course Emmeline is not really a lawyer any more than

Emmeline is really her name. It is just that she wants to remain anonymous and not be mixed up with what, for curious reasons of her own, she calls "the rubbish I write". She does not want to be identified, so I have to pretend her name is Emmeline and she is a lawyer. It becomes difficult when she acts so out of character. That is a burden I have to bear. That is life.

But now she had said she had given up. What had she given up? I gave up something once. Emmeline said it would be good for the soul. I gave up self-denial. It made no difference: Emmeline was willing to deny me everything that might have tempted me. She is a wonderful wife, always looking after my best interests. I got up from my chair and went into the kitchen to where, as I guessed, she had retreated.

"What are you doing?" I asked.

"Making myself a cup of coffee." She emphasised the word *myself*.

"I thought I should tell you," I said. "You are a wonderful wife."

"You can make a cup for yourself, if you want," Emmeline replied gratefully.

I decided against the coffee and returned to the lounge. I needed time to think. Life, what is it all about? It seems to have a sort of accidental quality. There may be such a thing as planned parenthood, but no one ever heard of planned childhood. None of us asks to be born. It just happens and, for better or for worse, there we are. Most of us try to make the best of things. We acquire some basic skills in communicating with other people. We discover that incontinence is unpleasant and learn to avoid it. We dream and plot and life just happens while we are planning to do something else.

That was it – not an original thought but none the worse for that. I rushed into the kitchen to tell Emmeline.

"Be careful," she called to me as she saw me approaching.

"Life is what happens," I called back excitedly, as I slipped on the newly washed floor. I landed flat on my back, having hurt my dignity more than a little.

"What on earth?" I exclaimed.

Emmeline smiled sweetly.

"That's life," she said. "It has a sort of accidental quality."

The Wreath Lectures

The Wreath Lectures at Duffborough University are this year to be given by William Wastrel Professor of Planned Obsolescence and Conspicuous Consumption. Broadcast on Radio Duffborough and relayed to stations throughout the developing world, the lectures have helped to make the town and the University world famous.

I was talking with Professor Wastrel in his study at the University, looking out over the town centre with its remarkable statue of Boudicca aiming an arrow at an apple on the head of a child.

"The statue was presented to the old College of Technology by George Brass, mayor of Duffborough in the early nineteen-fifties. He left school at fifteen," Professor Wastrel told me, "and made a fortune in scrap metal. He knew nothing of history. The statue stands as a constant reminder to our youth of the importance of a good education."

I accepted a large mug of black coffee as we both sat down in futuristic and somewhat uncomfortable armchairs by the window. I grimaced involuntarily.

"No, they are not very comfortable," he agreed. "Luckily they are not made to last. I'll get new ones next year."

Were it not that Lady Shanksbottom suffered from chronic

hay fever and was allergic to flowers, there might have been no Wreath Lectures. As Principal of the College of Technology, Sir Primus Shanksbottom had been responsible for the growth that had propelled his institution to University status. A grateful staff commissioned a famous alumnus of the Art School to paint his portrait and, while Sir Primus watched it being hung on a wall high above his head, it fell and struck him between the eyes. He died instantly. It was less than three weeks after his inauguration as the University's first Vice-Chancellor. His widow's edict that there be no flowers provoked the Governors and the staff to deep thought. Instead of flowers, a somewhat more permanent memorial might be appropriate. Having rejected proposals for a Shanksbottom wing added to the library as too expensive, or for a new Shanksbottom Room as an extension to the bar, which while appropriate to the deceased's predilections might have seemed essentially trivial, all concerned agreed that an annual programme of broadcast lectures would pay due tribute to Sir Primus's memory. Radio Duffborough was delighted to agree but cavilled at the idea of calling them the Shanksbottom Memorial Lectures. Something more marketable was needed. Remembering that their first thought was to send a wreath, one of the staff Governors suggested they call them the Wreath Lectures, and so they became.

"Doesn't the University worry that they might be confused with the lecture series on BBC radio," I wondered.

"Not at all," Professor Wastrel smiled. "The College has grown rich on the lectures. If the BBC picks up a few extra listeners, we don't mind one little bit."

I focused first on that characteristic for which William Wastrel was most famous. His was a towering presence in the University.

"You are very tall," I said.

"Six-foot four and a half inches in my stockinged feet," he agreed. "A curious phrase that; personally I never wear stockings, only socks. Being tall has given me great advantages. There is abundant research to show that tall people are more successful at interviews. I find it quite easy to intimidate my colleagues and, most importantly, I always get a clear view of the field." He is renowned as a passionate supporter of Duffborough United.

"Which brings us to the subject of your lectures this year," I said. "I believe this is the first time football has been the subject of the Wreath Lectures."

"Only one of the lectures will be specifically about football. The series is entitled *Sport – the Religion of the Masses*. I shall deal with football in Brazil, cricket in Jamaica, sex in…"

I interrupted him in mid-sentence. "Surely sex is not a sport?"

"It is if you do it right," he assured me, "though it has not been recognised as a sport by the Olympic Committee – not yet."

"You think that will happen?"

"Most things do."

We sat for some moments in silence, each deep in his own thoughts. I had no intention of revealing mine.

"I am surprised your lectures are not on a theme related to your work in the University," I said at last.

"Oh, but they are," he replied. "You forget: I am based in the School of Secular Religions and the two most popular secular religions are Shopping and Sport. My principal research interests are in the field of Consumerism, but I am interested in all the other secular religions."

"So, Consumerism is a secular religion?"

"Shopping is a religion. Why else should the shops be open on Sundays? Then again, shopping is also a sport, particularly at sale times. It has the essential elements – competition and bodily contact. Queuing comes into it as well. Of course, queuing is a sport is its own right – one of the few without religious overtones. In this lecture series, though, I intend to confine myself to the more traditional sports: football, cricket, sex, war…"

"This is intolerable," I exclaimed. "War is horrible and cruel; it causes untold misery."

"It does indeed, more than any other sport – and it is more popular than another other sport."

"People hate war."

"So they say, particularly if they are on the losing side, but it is played all over the world. All sports increased in popularity in the twentieth century, but none so much as war. My third lecture will examine war as both sport and as religion. I will show how, in war, the two are almost interchangeable."

I was appalled. I told Professor Wastrel I regarded his ideas as a sick joke.

"Do you think so?" he asked brightly. "Please tell people. It could help us attract a whole new audience."

Catocracy

"Miaow?"

"Since you ask, I think the Government's economic strategy is quite wrong."

"Miaow?"

"No, I am not claiming to be more intelligent than the Prime Minister."

"Miaow?"

"No, I am not better educated nor can I claim to be better informed."

Cleopatra then suggested that perhaps I had access to information not available to the Prime Minister and I had to admit this was not the case and nor was it likely I had read more on the matter.

"Miaow?"

"No, I am not better advised."

"Miaow?"

"Yes, he does have lots of advisers."

"Miaow?"

"I don't know what advice he gets from them. I judge by what he says and does."

"Miaow?"

"Yes. I still think he is wrong."

"Miaow?"

"It is common sense."

"Miaow."

"No I am not saying he has no common sense. What I say is he is wrong in this matter."

"Miaow?"

"Yes and in other matters."

"Miaow."

"Not always but I suppose it is fair to say I disagree with him on most things."

"Miaow."

"I agree with him about some things. I can't think of examples at the moment."

But on the matter under discussion, Cleopatra surmised, I could claim to be an expert. Alas, I had to disabuse her of this assumption. She shook her head sadly and asked what gave me the nerve to voice an opinion against someone who, quite obviously, knew much more about the subject than did I. I explained that this was the nature of democracy. Everybody has a right to an opinion.

"Miaow?"

"If you put it that way, yes even if they are totally ignorant of the issue under discussion."

Cleopatra's summing up of the matter was that, with unaccustomed modesty and total accuracy I was not claiming to be more intelligent than the Prime Minister; in fact, she added with unnecessary cruelty, I was certainly less intelligent. I was not better educated. Gratuitously she threw in that he got a better degree. It was evident that he had access to far more relevant information, would have studied any matter of policy more deeply and was surrounded by a large team of expert advisers. My views, she chortled – Cats don't often chortle. I think this was a first – my views were based on ignorance and prejudice. Rather than waste my time giving worthless opinions, I would be better employed talking to an imaginary dog.

That is the last time I discuss politics with a cat. Cats have no understanding of the democratic process.

What About Tennis?

I stepped naked onto the bathroom scales. Emmeline looked at the scales, as if willing them to humiliate me.

"You are willing those scales to humiliate me," I said.

"Scales will do what they have to do," she replied. She continued staring at the scales. When we were first married, she would have looked at me but that was long ago. Such is life.

"You are grossly over weight," she said fiercely.

"Perhaps a little."

"I chose my words carefully."

"The passing years," I explained enigmatically.

"You should do something about it."

"There is nothing anyone can do. Year follows year without any reference to any wishes I might have one way or the other."

"This is serious," Emmeline said following me into the bedroom. I started to dress. "You should think about taking some exercise."

"I think about it every day," I told her. "It doesn't do any good."

"You should do something."

"I am doing something," I countered. "I am getting dressed."

"You should get yourself out into the garden."

"While I am getting dressed? The neighbours might object."

"You should do something about the state of the garden. That would provide you with plenty of exercise."

"Advertising for a gardener isn't very strenuous."

"You should look after the garden yourself. You could do it now. Go and pull out all the weeds in the flower beds."

Why Emmeline said that I will never know. She knows I am allergic even to the idea of gardening. The thought of it gives me intense backache, brings my skin out in a rash and makes me so tired I have to sit down immediately. I sat on the bed.

"You shouldn't say things like that," I complained. "You know how it affects me."

"You need shaking up."

"I am not going to a funfair."

"Try going for long walks."

"That's no fun. I always end up in the same place."

"Where?"

"At home. Where I started from."

"What about tennis?" Unconsciously, Emmeline had stumbled upon one of the great questions of the modern age.

The rules are easy to understand. In its simplest form, the game is played by two men. The reader should understand that the word men is used here loosely and it could as easily be two women playing – even two loose women – or even children of any gender but old enough to play tennis. How old is old enough, you may ask and you would incur no blame for asking, but you would get no satisfactory reply. No one knows the answer to this question but only that there is no minimum age of consent.

The game, then, is played by two persons. In certain circumstances – as for instance when there are more people wanting to participate – four persons may play but never three unless they are just pretending. When two people play, it is called singles; when four people play, it is called doubles. It is important to note that two singles do not make a double although in the opinion of many authorities this should be the case. We will concentrate our attention on the game of singles, as this is more straightforward and raises all the important issues we need to discuss. The principal difference in doubles is that the ball is allowed to bounce between the tramlines. Trams are banned from both games.

In singles, one person stands on one side of the net leaving his opponent, as the other player is called, with nowhere to go but to the other side of the net. The net is three feet high in the middle, though most people do not know this unless they take the game seriously. Each player holds a racket and the object of the game is to use the racket to cause serious damage to a small round cloth-covered ball. The player who causes the most damage to the ball probably wins the game, although this is by no means certain, as he has to accumulate more points than his opponent. The battle for each point begins when the first player, or it may be the second, goes into service. Whichever it is, he stands at the back of the court and hits the ball as hard as he can into the right-service court. Sometimes the right service court is the left-service court, which confuses both players. If this is an ordinary friendly game being played, then they just carry on beating hell out of the ball and occasionally saying "Well done," to each other.

The trouble starts if there is any money hanging on the result or if ranking points are involved. When this is the case, there has to be an umpire. It is probable you do not have any ranking points, so you may never meet an umpire. Umpires make tennis into a whole different ball game. Now, when the first player – or it may be the second player – goes into service, it is service like no other. In the real world away from the tennis court, service implies giving assistance or help; it carries connotations of civility and good manners. In the game of tennis it is somewhat different. As in the friendly game, the server hits the ball as hard as he can in the direction of the service court but this time the umpire calls out in a loud voice, "Fault." The server glares at the umpire and serves for a second time.

"Fault," calls the umpire and then, to add insult to injury says, "Game Bloggins," Bloggins being the name of the other player.

"You cannot be serious," says the server.

The umpire ignores him and calls out the score, something like, "Bloggins leads four games to three."

"There is no way that was out," the server says but the umpire continues to ignore him. The server approaches the umpire and speaks animatedly to him for several minutes. No one can hear what they are saying. Bloggins, who was expecting this, walks up and down reciting Kipling's poem "If." He just gets to the lines, "If you can force your heart and nerve and sinew / To serve your turn," when the umpire repeats that it is his turn to serve and play resumes.

Tennis players are not like other people. We all of us have forearms; tennis players have forehands and backhands. Soldiers will fire a volley; in tennis they play a volley and, if they do not have a volley, they play a half volley. They drive without licences, they lob and they smash – and no one seems to mind. The successful player loves to play games and plays games to love.

This reminds me of Emmeline. "What do you think of this?" I call to her.

She comes into the study and looks over my shoulder at what I have been writing. She reads in silence for a few moments. "I still think you are grossly over weight," she says.

Ignarus Quaestio Repitito

(A Consultation from the Casebook of Dr Magnus Fell)

- Good morning, Dr Fell.
- *Good morning. What can I do for you today?*
- What can you do for me today? I hope you can help.
- *What is wrong?*
- What is wrong? I wish I knew.
- *Can you describe your symptoms?*
- Can I describe my symptoms? I don't think I can. I don't know what they are.
- *Then what do you want me to cure?*
- What do I want you to cure? I don't know. I want you to cure whatever is wrong with me.
- *Why do you think something is wrong with you?*
- Why do I think there is something wrong with me? Everyone tells me so. My friends are telling me constantly, "Something is wrong with you." They cannot all be wrong.
- *I think I see. Why do you always repeat any question I ask you?*
- Why do I always repeat any question you ask me? Do I? I was not aware of it.
- *When talking to other people, do you repeat their questions before answering?*

- When talking to other people, do I repeat their questions? I don't think so. I don't know. Perhaps I do.

- *Think carefully. Can you think of any occasion when someone has mentioned it?*

- Can I think of any occasion when someone has mentioned it? Now I think about it, I can remember my friend Bernie asking why I was developing the habit of repeating what he said before responding. He must have mentioned it more than once, because I can recall his getting quite upset about it. He suggested it was a defence mechanism I was adopting to give me more time to reply to what he was saying.

- *And was it?*

- And was it? And was it what?

- *A defence mechanism.*

- Was it a defence mechanism? I don't think it could have been. I was not aware I was repeating what he said. If it was a defence mechanism, it was entirely unconscious.

- *I am afraid I must tell you, you are suffering from an extreme case of* Ignarus Quaestio Repetitio *or Unconscious Question Repetition.*

- Unconscious Question Repetition? Why the Latin name?

- *It sounds more impressive. Patients often like to impress their friends with important sounding maladies. However, your friend Bernie was quite right in supposing this might be a way of giving you extra time to marshal your thoughts before giving your views on something. When employed in moderation and sometimes for rhetorical effect and combined with a pregnant pause, it can be an effective strategy. Are you with me so far?*

- Am I with you? I think so.

- *If you had the condition under control it would not be serious. Many people, when talking to others they know to be more intelligent than they are, deliberately slow down the conversation by this means in order to give the impression they are thinking seriously about what is being said or, indeed, to give the impression they can think.*

- The impression? I hope you are not implying…

— *My dear Sir, I am sure you are not paying me for an opinion that you are less intelligent than you like to think you are. I keep such opinions to myself. I would never dream of saying such a thing. I hope you did not take offence.*

— Did I take offence? I don't think so.

— *I am just trying to describe other conditions and behaviours that bear similarities to your problem and often may be combined with it. Shall I continue?*

— Shall you continue? Please do.

— *Sometimes — and this may be conscious or unconscious — people pretend not to hear something said to them or condition themselves to a reflex denial of having heard.*

— Pardon.

— *If this denial is ignored, it soon becomes apparent that they have in fact heard exactly what was said and can continue the conversation without having anything repeated. Do you follow me?*

— Do I follow you? I do indeed.

— *I thought you would. Now, as I was saying, yours is a very serious case of* Ignarus Quaestio Repetitio; *you are apparently quite unaware of the symptoms, which seem to be quite out of control.*

— Quite out of control. Can I be cured?

— *There are cures but also there can be side effects.*

— Side effects? I will risk side effects. I am prepared to try anything.

— *Serious side effects.*

— Serious side effects. I am ready to try most things.

— *Sometimes quite devastating side effects.*

— Devastating? I am willing to try some things.

— *Then, if you are prepared to take the risk and because your symptoms are so pronounced, the treatment most likely to be effective is for you to record your conversations and then listen to how you sound and to consider the effect this will have on others. Will you try that?*

— Will I try that? Of course I will. Why on earth should I not?

— *I have to warn you that a number of men — all men in this case —*

having heard what they sound like in conversation, have been so appalled that they have given up speaking and now converse only in writing.
  - Only in writing? I will let you know how I get along.
  - *I look forward to receiving your letter.*

Adam's Story

There were four of us in the garden. There was me, Adam. I must have been there for a very long time, as I had no sense of ever having been anywhere else. It seems strange now that it did not worry me. I could remember nothing of my childhood; I could conjure up no picture of parents, school or playmates – nothing except the garden. It was as if I had always been there and always would be there, though there would come a time when I would learn otherwise. Apart from having to look after the garden – which took very little time because the landlord had done such a good job in laying it out – I could spend my days watching the flowers grow and admiring the birds and the bees. There was not much to do but that did not seem to worry me. I was perfectly happy.

Then there was Snake. I never found out how long he had been there and frankly, if he had told me, I am not sure I would have believed him. There was something unsettling about Snake, some aura of unreliability, something disreputable that I could not define. I can say only that if he told me the time I would feel the need for some corroborating evidence, not that time had much meaning for us in those days. He and I would meet sometimes as we wandered about but I never sought his company nor, as far as I know, did he seek mine.

The third member of our community was Eve. She was a

relative newcomer. I woke up one morning with a pain in my chest such as I had never had before or since, and there she was. Where she came from I knew not and, if she knew, she never told me but I took to her immediately and we became great friends spending most of our waking hours together. Sometimes she would help me in the garden and we would pick fruit together. I was even happier now than before, particularly because Eve had a delightful habit of running about in the garden without any clothes on.

Lastly there was the landlord, Jay. He was a strange old cove, very old indeed, who would come and go as the mood took him. He was quite unpredictable but very full of himself and constantly going on about what a good chap he was and how important. To tell the truth, he was a bit scary but, I must say, he was generous to a fault and let us all live in the Garden rent-free. However, it did get on my nerves that he was constantly telling me how lucky I was and that he had made me what I had become. He actually said he had created me, which I thought was going a bit far.

Jay liked everything to be done his way and he wanted everyone to know it. As far as he was concerned, it was his world. Certainly it was his garden and he had erected a notice to say so: "Eden Gardens – Proprietor J. Hover". He made up rules, which he expected all of us to obey. Some of his rules seemed to me very silly. He said that as he never worked on the seventh day of the week nor should we. That was daft. Firstly, he had no right to impose his likes and dislikes and habits on us. Secondly, and I suppose more to the point, we never did any work in those days. We messed about in the garden a bit but that was more like play or a hobby. And then he decreed that on this seventh day, which he called the Sabbath, we should not play music (we had no instruments) or make a fire (we did not know how). I lived in the expectation that one day he would put up a notice saying only, "It is forbidden to deface this notice."

One of his rules concerned a tree in the middle of the garden. For some reason, Jay said we could eat the fruit from any other tree but not from this one. He never explained why. It was not as if he wanted to keep it all for himself; he never touched it. Birds and monkeys would eat some of it but most of the fruit, looking and smelling delicious, would be left to rot on the tree. Anyway, to cut a long story short, Snake persuaded Eve that this prohibition was just another of Jay's pointless rules, imposed on us to make us feel inferior. As she told it, Snake made fun of her until she picked and ate some of the fruit. It was as succulent as anything she had ever tasted and she hurried to give me some, which I consumed almost without thinking about it.

Jay went ballistic and gave us notice to leave the garden. We had very few possessions but Jay did give Eve and me some clothes he said we would need. As for Snake, Jay was even angrier with him than with us and the last I saw of Snake he was slithering out of the garden on his stomach.

Out in the wider world, it was more difficult for us to find food and we had to learn how to grow our own but Eve and I discovered wonderful and exciting ways of entertaining each other and got to know each other more deeply than ever before. Then, after some time, Eve produced a baby boy. We did not understand why this had happened and it was a very messy and, for her, a painful experience. Still, she seemed to have some instinct as to how to cope and we called the boy Cain. Some months after, she produced another boy, whom we called Abel.

Away from the garden, there seemed to be more things to do and we found things worked best if we instituted some form of division of labour. I did the hunting and foraging, while Eve looked after the home and the children. She did the cleaning and the dusting and prepared the food for the table. She did not have to do any cooking because we had not worked out how to make fire and had all our food raw. In order to avoid conflict, I made all the decisions and Eve did what I told her. This arrangement worked well and I was sure it would catch on. Jay agreed; he was in the habit of popping round from time to time – uninvited – and telling us how he thought we should behave. At first I was quite irritated by this but as time went by I began to be amused by this self-important old codger with his delusions of being responsible for everything in the world (even for the sun and the stars) and his claim that he could and should control everyone and everything. On the other hand, Eve seemed to believe everything he said. It was as if her critical faculties were deserting her and after the children were born her intellectual development ceased. As the years went by, we found less and less to talk about but she was an obedient wife and a good mother and she cannot be blamed for the terrible things that later happened between the children. That is not something I want to talk about. If Cain or any of the grandchildren want to tell the story, that is up to them.

A Great Turn-Off

I don't think there is a name for those remote control units you use to turn televisions or video recorders on and off, but you know what I am talking about and how they can be used to freeze the picture being played back. Thinking they can be rather fun, I have invented a similar control device for human beings. It sort of turns people on and off – it stops them moving and turns them into living statues. It doesn't hurt and there seem to be no after effects. I tried it out on my wife, when she was going on about something, while I was trying to hear a news item on the radio. She didn't even know I had done it. When I reactivated her, she resumed her complaining in mid-sentence.

I shouldn't have done that really but I knew it was safe. I had already tried it out on various animals and none of them came to any harm. Even the dog was not hurt when I zapped him in the act of marking his territory on a tree in the park. Since he was standing on three legs, he fell over and looked somewhat surprised when I unzapped him, but he suffered no other ill effects. I zapped a fly that was irritating me. It dropped like a stone into a pot of jam, which I then had to throw away. I tried it on a bird in the garden. It too began to fall out of the sky – but only for a second, as I then released it from its frozen condition and it was able to catch the wind and resume its flight.

I had learned somewhere about how we all have neurons which receive stimuli and conduct electrochemical impulses. That is how I got the idea for the device. I knew electric shocks could cause muscle spasms and it seemed reasonable that muscles might be affected or even controlled remotely. I decided to experiment.

In the event, it proved remarkably easy. I started with an ordinary television remote control unit and made a number of adaptations. The first of these was to – no, perhaps I had better not tell you. If one of these ever got into the hands of criminals or hostile armies, I would never forgive myself. Mind you, one of these People Freezers or Person Deactivators – I still can't decide what to call it – would be very useful for fighting crime. I know; I have tried it in a small way.

What happened was this. I was walking in the high street, just minding my own business – as I always do – when I saw a youth running towards me, dodging in and out between other pedestrians, and being pursued by two or three others shouting "Stop him!" I noticed the youth was grasping a lady's handbag. I took hold of my PD and froze him for a few seconds. He pitched forward and fell headlong onto the pavement. To any bystanders, it appeared he had tripped and he was apprehended without anyone knowing I had intervened.

If it were not for fear that the PD could fall into the wrong hands, many beneficial applications could be envisaged. Perhaps I can develop two versions. The first would be for military and police use. Without the appropriate code, it would be impossible to switch off, or protect oneself from the device. For the second version, there would be some sort of defensive shield people could wear. The shield could be removed when not needed. The potential in medicine would be immense if it could be shown to cause the loss of bodily sensation. I contemplate its being used in place of anaesthetics. It would be so much cheaper and safer. Ambulance crews could carry the device as a matter of course.

No special training would be required for anyone using it. A visit to the dentist would be transformed.

I admit that there is still a lot of development work to be undertaken. Firstly, the prototype PD is easily replicated and has no hidden code. If one unit switched you off, you could be switched back on by another. Secondly, the effects wear off very quickly. A double-glazing salesman called at the house a few days back. I froze him and then closed the front door and went to finish making a pot of tea. I went back to open the front door. He was still there but, before I did anything, he suddenly resumed his patter, as if there had been no pause. I conducted several more experiments – with my wife and with various unsuspecting members of the public – and in each case found the effects wore off after exactly three minutes.

Even if this limitation can be overcome, there appears to be a greater problem before my dreams of medical applications can be realised. I discovered this when experimenting on my wife to check her heart beat in a deactivated state. She was standing at the kitchen sink peeling carrots. I turned the PD on her and then put my hand over her heart.

"Not now," she said. "You always choose the wrong time."

It was a good thing I had not tried this experiment on a stranger. I could have got myself into a great deal of trouble. It seems that bodily contact reactivates the muscles. If I can get over that difficulty, I will have a new prototype ready to present to a grateful world.

On the other hand, it might be fun to play with it for a few months before anyone knows what I am doing.

The Speed of Light

Those scientists have been at it again. It is not right. They know how I feel about things like this, and I am sure I am not the only one who wants a bit of stability in my life. Until today, I thought Einstein – Professor Albert Einstein to you – had provided it. Until today, I would have said that if there is one thing I know – and that proposition is beginning to look very doubtful – it is that the speed of light in a vacuum never varies and that from the beginnings of the Universe it had remained, and must always remain, unchanged. The speed of light is 186,282 miles per second; it always has been and it always will be. That is what I thought. Well, it is not exactly what I thought – I had to look up the actual speed – but in essence that is what I thought. You get the general idea.

Now there are some chaps at Imperial College London who want to turn all this upside down. It does not seem to matter to them that Einstein built his whole theory of relativity on this idea. It is of no consequence to them that everybody has been very happy with the theory of relativity; they still feel the urge to publish their ideas. I know we all feel urges from time to time, but most of us refrain from rushing into print to tell other people about them. If we did, it could herald the end of civilisation as we know it. That is my opinion on the matter.

Ah, I hear you trying to say, how can I say everybody is happy with the theory of relativity when not everyone has even heard of relativity. I have to concede you have a point there. It is not a very good point, however, as even the meanest intelligence should be aware that, when I say everybody, I do not mean everybody. No, when I say everybody, I mean everybody who has heard of relativity and has some understanding of what it means – in fact, very few people. Such people do exist. I have it on very good authority.

Now where was I before I was so rudely interrupted? I know I was not intending to tell you all about relativity. You probably know as much about it as I do. To tell the truth, you probably know more about it than I do. No, it is the speed of light that concerns me. I think it should concern everyone.

These jokers at Imperial College have got the idea that light used to travel faster than it does now. They think that, when everything started – you know what I mean, just after the big bang – light travelled faster than it does now and it has slowed down. They think this is very interesting and are not at all worried. Well, I am worried. If light can slow down once, it can slow down again. Just think of the consequences.

Of course, it depends by how much it slows down. A five per cent fall probably would not affect us too much. That would worry fewer people than a similar fall in the stock market. But suppose the speed of light started to fall and kept on falling. The consequences would be severe. It is not the stock market that would be affected first, but something that concerns far more people – sport. I will give just a few examples. Motor racing would become a thing of the past, as the drivers would not be able to see where they were going until they had already got there, and by then it would be too late. Cricket would be banned, as the only chance a batsman would have of hitting the ball would be to swing his bat wildly while watching the bowler still moving towards the bowling crease. This would make the game too dangerous, as well as even more difficult for the uninitiated to understand. Eventually, the nature of soccer would be altered, as the premier skill required of players would be similar to that needed to spot the ball in a picture contest where the ball has been blanked out.

Now I think of it: if light were to slow down sufficiently, one sport would be improved, though it would probably appeal to a different clientele. In boxing each fighter, as he throws his punch, would try to guess where his opponent is now, while making a judgement about what punch has already been aimed in his direction. For the spectator, the effect might be similar to ballet and it would be much less likely that anyone would be hurt. As I have no interest in either boxing or ballet, I fail to see that this would offer much compensation for the general inconvenience caused by slowing down our light.

I have no confidence that these scientist chaps are going to do anything about this. They seem to regard it all as a great joke or, at least, as an excuse to publish more articles and books. However, if they will not actually do anything, I think it is not unreasonable that I ask them to keep an eye on things and, if the speed of light begins to slow down again, to let me know. I will then make my own arrangements.

In His Image

"I am having a difficulty with Creation," I said to God one day.

"I had a little difficulty with that myself," He replied – with more than a little touch of sarcasm, I thought.

"I mean I have difficulty understanding some of it."

"Ah!"

"I'd have thought you knew what I meant, your being omniscient and all that."

"Ah."

"It is not as if you were making a joke. There is no evidence of your having a sense of humour."

"Of course I have, you foolish mortal. Humans have a sense of humour. From where do you think you got what you are pleased to think of as your sense of humour? I created you in my image."

"That is it," I exclaimed. "That is the bit I am having difficulty with. What exactly do you mean when you say you created man in your image?"

"I mean what I say. That is the sort of God I am."

"That is as it may be, but you do not make yourself clear."

"I made you in my image. If I understand what I mean, then it should be equally plain to you."

I was tempted to reply there must be something wrong

either with the model or with the workmanship. I resisted the temptation. He would not have taken it in good part. When He is angry, He can get quite violent, throwing thunderbolts here and there, creating storms and, on a particularly bad day, producing plagues of frogs or locusts.

"You were wise to resist temptation," He commented.

I suppose He wanted to impress me after my crack about his supposed omniscience. I made no comment.

After a short silence, I offered a straw. "Perhaps it is possible you created a deliberate area of ambiguity?"

He clutched it eagerly.

"If you give the matter more than a moment's thought, you will realise that, had I not peppered my pronouncements with ambiguities, you would have had to invent them."

"To help maintain full employment?"

"Exactly. Priests, rabbis, imams and the rest of them would have nothing to do, were there not vast swathes of text for them to – as they would put it – interpret."

"And I suppose if someone doesn't like your message, as interpreted by one religious authority, he can always find another more to his liking."

"Exactly."

"So you end up with dozens, maybe hundreds, of different religions all claiming to be the true faith."

"Indeed. That is the way it works."

"And you don't intervene even when some interpretations of your teaching appear as quite the opposite of what you meant."

"I don't take sides."

"Yet they all claim you take sides, particularly when they start killing each other, and you still don't intervene."

There was a long pause.

"You said you wanted to discuss creation," He said at last.

"You claim to have created man in your image. Can I ask you about that?"

293

"I can imagine," He said. "You want to know if I have arms and legs, and how do I get exercise. Do I have a beard and who trims it for me? Am I fat or thin? What do I eat and how do I prepare my food?"

"Well, no," I said. "I just wanted to ask if you have ever had any prostate problems."

Parents Are People

Parents are not being prepared for the day when their children start school. Young children have come in for criticism from the chief inspector for schools, who claims they are ignoring their responsibilities and are not preparing their parents for the day when they, the children, will start full-time schooling and their parents will be left to their own devices for hour upon hour in the middle of the day.

The behavioural and emotional skills of this group of parents were at an all-time low, with many unable to settle and not ready to learn. In the absence of their children, some parents had no idea how to occupy their time – some even resorting to watching daytime television.

"Everyone wants children to start school at the age of five," said a spokesman for Ofsted [*the Office for Standards in Education, Children's Services and Skills*], "but we know that some children have not prepared the parents adequately. In the long run, this will rebound on the children. As time goes on, they will have to give more and more support to the parents, and will not be able to devote as much time as they would wish to the pursuit of their studies. Ultimately the whole family unit will suffer."

Children often have feelings of inadequacy when faced with their responsibilities and this leads them to organise and structure their parents' time, leaving the parents with few opportunities for undirected leisure activities. Anxious to make good use of every available moment with their parents, children are planning more joint play dates and formal family outings. A third of parents questioned said they did not get as much time for just mucking about as they had allowed their own parents.

A spokesman for PAP [*Parents Are People*] commented, "It is important for parents of four to six-year olds to be given the chance just to lark about and interact with each other in an unstructured way. It is how they explore what it is to be them. It is how they get the hang of being a human being."

Without proper guidance before their children start school, parents – particularly young or inexperienced parents – were likely to have difficulty organising their lives. In extreme cases, fathers have been known to develop an unhealthy interest in spectator sports and on Saturday and Sunday afternoons – times when they should be firmly under the control of their children – may be found watching football matches. Rising standards in schools are not being matched by similar improvements in the home.

A spokesman for the National Union of Students said these comments were "unhelpful". "Education is clearly a partnership between children, schools and of course parents," she said, "and if we start blaming children for doing a bad job, it becomes very difficult for them to know how to work in partnership with the schools or with the Social Services." In the modern world it was only realistic to realise that the needs of children were continually increasing. Advertising determined there were more and more things they must have. It was inevitable that many children would need to send both parents out to work. In the evenings the parents would often be too tired to follow instructions and might behave badly.

Under sixes come in for further criticism in a quite separate report about their dietary habits. The children's predilection for junk food is harming their parents. With the children refusing to eat proper balanced meals, parents are failing to learn or practise elementary cooking skills. Not needing to cook for their children, increasingly they are failing to cook for themselves, seeming to believe that if junk food, high in fat, salt and sugar, is sufficient for young developing bodies, then it is OK for adults. The result is that more than twenty per cent of the population is now considered overweight, costing the NHS an estimated £500m a year and the wider economy about two billion pounds in related illnesses and time off work.

The spokesman for PAP was scathing in his criticism. "At the end of the day," he said, "children owe a duty of care to their parents."

[First published in *Education, Public Law and the Individual (EPLI) – Vol. 7, Issue 3,* October 2003.]

Bilingual Dog

It had been a long day and I was looking forward to relaxing. Caesar was in the study pacing up and down on the rug and muttering to himself.

"Quiet boy," I said thoughtlessly.

"Boy," he snarled. "Since when do you call me 'boy'?"

He was quite right. It was a form of address I never used.

"Most people talk to their dogs that way," I said defensively.

"Most people don't expect a reply," Caesar declared, "which is just as well, because they don't deserve one."

"I wasn't wanting a reply," I countered off-handedly. "I just wanted peace and quiet to read my newspaper."

"I was here first," he stated bluntly, resuming his perambulation and incomprehensible muttering.

I sat down and tried to read. It was impossible to concentrate.

"I think it's even worse when I can't hear what you are saying than when I can."

"I said, *Qué es ese?*" Caesar informed me.

"What is that?"

"Exactly."

"What are you talking about?" I tried again.

"I am learning Spanish. I am going to be by local."

"What do you mean, *by local?*"

"It means I am going to learn to speak two languages," he said sniffily. "I thought you would know that."

"You would do better to learn to master one language," I said cruelly. "The word is bilingual."

"That's right," he said undeterred. "I am going to be bilingual."

"How can you learn Spanish?" I asked.

"My friend Red is going to teach me. You remember; I told you about him once before. He used to work in advertising for *Vogue*."

I did remember his telling me this. I had thought it one of his wilder flights of fancy.

"Are you telling me that your canine friend speaks Spanish? I don't believe it," I stated bluntly.

"He can if he wants to," Caesar claimed, "but he doesn't know any other dogs who would speak Spanish. He understands the language perfectly. His housekeeper speaks to him in Spanish. He learned it from her."

"Are you telling me that this dog employs a housekeeper?"

"I think the woman from his office, the one who lives in with him, actually employs the housekeeper, but it is the same thing." He paused. "I thought you might like to help," he went on.

"Help with what?" I asked suspiciously. It pays to be suspicious, when Caesar declares anything other than complete independence.

"I thought you might like to help me to learn Spanish. Not many people get the opportunity to hold conversations in Spanish with their dogs," he added truthfully.

"I don't speak Spanish," I said.

"Not at all?"

"Not a word."

Caesar gave me a disdainful look. It was a speciality of his. Not many dogs can do it.

"I could help you then," he suggested happily. "What Red teaches me, I will teach you. Then we will both learn."

"I do not think that is a good idea," I said firmly.

"Por qué no?"

"I beg your pardon."

"Why not?"

"I just don't think it is a very good idea."

"You think it would be embarazoso?"

"What's that?"

"You would be embarrassed if someone found out you were taking Spanish lessons from a dog."

"No, it's not that at all," I lied.

"I thought you would find it interesante."

"Interesting?"

"You see," he commended me. "You're catching on. Es divertido."

"Diverting?"

"Amusing. It is fun."

"How much Spanish have you learned?" I was intrigued.

"Siéntese."

"Pardon."

"I said, 'Sit down'."

"I am sitting down."

"So you are," said Caesar. "I'm telling you some of the useful phrases Red has taught me, for instance: déjeme en paz, no me gusta."

"What does that mean?"

"Leave me alone, I don't like it."

"It sounds useful for you," I said.

"Silencio."

"Are you telling me to be quiet?"

"Of course not," Caesar said patiently. "I am telling you how to say, *be quiet*."

"I think that will do for now," I said. "Why don't you go out and play with a bone?"

"OK," said Caesar, moving towards the doorway. "Adiós amoco."

"Amoco is an oil company that was taken over by British Petroleum. You mean amigo."

Caesar looked at me admiringly.

"Then you do speak Spanish," he said.

Fabian Memories

Sidney "the World Wide" Webb never owned a computer. This unsurprising truth is only one of the many trivial and insignificant revelations contained in the latest book by Georgio Fantasia, a maverick historian who eschews research in favour of folk memory. The technique made it inevitable that his *Fabian Memories* would be a short book. History, he says, belongs to the people but they didn't pay for it and, like many things that come free, is not always valued. Folk memory has to be nurtured by discussion and invention; it should be a living entity. Unfortunately, folk are much older than they were when significantly younger, and many of those most qualified to develop and distort these memories have passed the point from which none of us are destined to return.

In his early days, Sidney had been anything but World Wide and this began only when, dabbling in education, he had a hand in founding the LSE. (One should note that his hand was not caught under the foundation stone and, indeed, the purpose of Fantasia's short tribute is in part to lay to rest such apocryphal slanders.)

As a lifelong socialist, his wife Beatrice – the daughter of a potter – initially disapproved and said she would have nothing to do with the London Stock Exchange. Although childless, Beatrice was in labour for most of her adult life, occupying any spare time writing books about rabbits, which were popular, and a law report, which was poor and of interest only to a minority.

At first, Sidney could not find the time to tell her his plans for the London School of Economics, as he was too busy enjoying the society of his friend Fabian of the Yard, who lived in Scotland and was sometimes known as St. Fabian, after the Roman general Fabius Maximus Cuncator. In Fabian's society, everyone wrote Socialist pamphlets and spoke in Latin. This put another member of the group – George Bernard Shaw – in the mood to write *Caesar and Cleopatra*. Neither of them replied and Shaw blamed Shakespeare for this, as he did for nearly everything else.

Another friend was Tunbridge Wells, known as H. G. because he was very short. When he was still a young man, H. G. was a poor teacher – quite a good teacher but poor – and possessed only a second hand watch. Not being able to afford hour and minute hands he invented a time machine and became rich. He is remembered today for promoting the idea that science was a fiction.

They had all been introduced into Fabian's society by Edith Nesbitt and her bland husband Herbert. Later, Edith would devote herself to amusing children near the railway.

Meanwhile, it was by railway that Beatrice and Sidney travelled to Glasgow and Dublin on their honeymoon to investigate trade union records. As a good socialist, Sidney soon gave up his work with the civil service to live on the £1,000 a year Beatrice had inherited from her father.

Not everyone was a friend of Fabian. As a schoolboy, John Milton Keynes had nothing to do with them and, even when he reached manhood, he was too much too liberal for them and for his part he preferred the company of Woolfs.

Then came World War won – won by GB and her allies – and Keynes, to show how clever he was, worked out how much peace would cost. He too did not have a computer, but was able to calculate that the German people, if they did not have enough money, would not be able to pay their debts. This was controversial and everyone soon fell into a deep depression. Sidney and Beatrice fell in love with Stalin's Russia while Keynes, having a general interest in money and employment, soon developed a theory. [*The General Theory of Employment, Interest, and Money* – J. M. Keynes, *1935–36.*] Talking about this kept everyone busy until Japan invaded China, Germany invaded lots of people and everyone was involved in World War too.

By the time World War Two was won (a difficult concept for people who could not spell) an empty taxi had arrived at 10 Downing Street and Clem Attlee, once another of Fabian's young friends, had become Prime Minister. Had he still been alive today, he would have told the author of this study that a period of silence on his part would be welcome.

In the long run, as Keynes had predicted, they were all dead.

Rock-a-Bye Baby

(A Consultation from the Casebook of Dr Magnus Fell)

- *Good morning. You have not been to see me before?*
- Doctor Foster went to Gloucester.
- *I see. Did anyone recommend you?*
- Oh! The grand old Duke of York.
- *I don't think I know him. Never mind. What seems to be the trouble?*
- I see the moon, and the moon sees me.
- *It is perfectly normal to see the moon – you need not worry about that. It is unusual to think the moon sees you. When did this first happen?*
- As I was going to St Ives.
- *Are you married?*
- Little Polly Flinders.
- *A fine lady. Did you tell her about the moon seeing you? What did you say to her, when you got home?*
- Polly put the kettle on.
- *But when you told her about the moon, what did she reply?*
- Boys and girls come out to play; the moon doth shine as bright as day.
- *Then your wife didn't believe you? She didn't take you seriously? Did she think you had been drinking?*

- Hey diddle diddle.

- I see. I don't think you are experiencing hallucinations. My diagnosis is that you are suffering from something quite different.

- Oh dear, what can the matter be?

- I think you have a bad case of Nursery-rhymetitis. It is quite common for grandparents to get a mild dose, which manifests itself in their constantly quoting lines from nursery rhymes. Your speech seems to consist only of such quotations. We should be able to cure you.

- How many miles to Babylon?

- We shall have to see. I assume you have grandchildren.

- Mary, Mary, quite contrary.

- Just the one?

- Tom, Tom, the piper's son.

- It's nice to have a musician in the family.

- Sing a song of sixpence.

- Indeed. Now, in order to be able to suggest a remedy, I shall have to ask you a lot more questions.

- Who killed Cock Robin?

- Not that sort of question. I need to ask you things about yourself. What do you do for a living?

- Tinker, tailor, soldier, sailor.

- You travel quite a bit, then?

- Round and round the garden like a teddy bear.

- You don't get further afield?

- Round and round the rugged rock.

- And you meet a lot of people?

- My mother said I never should play with the gypsies in the wood.

- You were brought up in the countryside?

- I had a little nut tree, nothing would it bear.

- Did you keep animals?

- I had a little pony, his name was Dapple Grey.

- And now?

- I love little pussy, her coat is so warm.

- *This all seems perfectly normal. Is there any food you have started eating very recently that you are not used to?*

- Hot cross buns!

- *Plain or with anything?*

- Oranges and lemons.

- *Anything else?*

- Pease porridge hot, pease porridge cold.

- *It sounds revolting. Tell me, have your friends remarked on the peculiarities of your speech?*

- Bobby Shafto's gone to sea.

- *No other friends?*

- Solomon Grundy, born on Monday.

- *Then he is too young to have noticed anything. We don't seem to be getting anywhere. Let us go over this again. You said you were going to St Ives, when this all began. Did you meet anyone on the journey?*

- There was a little girl, and she had a little curl right in the middle of her forehead.

- *Did she remind you of anyone?*

- Old Mother Hubbard.

- *And did you say anything to her?*

- Where are you going to, my pretty maid?

- *What was her reply?*

- What are little boys made of?

- *You must have regarded this as some sort of a challenge. What did you say?*

- I'm the king of the castle.

- *I take it, this was not true. What was her response?*

- A frog he would a wooing go.

- *Quite a put down. I think I can see the problem. You have always thought of yourself a happily married man. Suddenly you found yourself making a pass at another woman. When she rejected you with a line from a nursery rhyme, you felt both guilty and ridiculous. You spend a lot of time with your grandchildren and you got an attack of Nursery-rhymetitis. It is not uncommon. What you need to do is buy your wife a bunch of flowers and keep away from nursery rhymes until the symptoms disappear. Come and see me again in about three weeks' time. When would suit you?*

- Please to remember the fifth of November.

- *I will see you then, at ten-thirty. Look after yourself. By the way, what is the weather like?*

- The north wind doth blow and we will have snow.

- *Then drive carefully.*

- London Bridge is falling down.

- *Then you had better avoid it. Goodbye.*

Premium Bond

"I have been looking at a number of guides to taxation and investments," I told Clifford. "The trouble is, they are all written by experts."

"Surely that is an advantage," he responded.

"Not at all. It means they all say the same thing. There is no variety; it is no wonder people find dealing with their tax affairs to be so much of a chore. If you compare the glossary of financial terms in one booklet with that in another, you will be hard pressed to find any differences."

"That does seem a shame," he agreed.

"What we need," I continued, "is a guide written by someone who knows nothing at all about it. Only then will we get any imaginative insight into the subject."

"You are just the man," he said. "Your ignorance on this, as on most things, is unparalleled. You write it."

"I will," I said, and I did, and here it is:

Accounting Period – The time during which a woman is not sure if she has fallen pregnant.

Additional Voluntary Contributions – Tax paid on cash payments received by plumbers, electricians and other such self-employed craftsmen.

Age Related Allowance – This refers to the fact that elderly people can get away with all sorts of behaviour, which would have been quite unacceptable when they were younger.

Annuity – To do with the way in which computer software companies make you think you need to buy a new version of their products every year. [From the Latin *annuus*, meaning annual, and *ity*, being a corruption of IT; a new IT.]

Basic Rate – Average speed.

Bear Market – A misprint for 'bare market'; where nudists buy their food. Regarded by some as a super market.

Black Economy – Night work.

Bull Market – Where animals are bought and sold.

Business Expenses – Those things you could be doing, if you were not going about your business. Similar to what economists call opportunity cost, e.g. the real cost of purchasing anything is the lost opportunity of purchasing something else.

Capital Gain – A mayor for London.

Covenant – A promise to God about money; e.g. *If I can't take it with me, I won't go.*

Discretionary Trust – When you trust people as far as you can throw them.

Dividend – I won't see Diana again. [Di + *Vidi* (Latin – I saw) + end.]

Endowment – A mechanism for giving away your money.

Equalisation Payment – A charitable gift.

Equity Income – A fair day's pay for a fair day's work.

Freelance Earnings – Undeclared income: a product of the black economy.

Friendly Society – The local drama club.

Fringe Benefit – A charity show put on during the Edinburgh Festival.

Gift Aid – Assistance in helping you to give away your money: this is usually provided by one's children.

Grossing Up – Most people put on weight when they reach

middle age. This is known as 'grossing up'.

Higher Rate – Tax levied on the income of the Monarch.

Income – The Oxford Dictionary defines income in many ways. Probably the most relevant is: *the coming in of divine influence into the soul.* Consequently, when you are asked to declare your income on your tax return, you are probably being asked how many times you went to Church (synagogue or mosque, etc.) during the last year.

Independent Financial Adviser – Someone who shows you how to invest in ways that will make him richer.

Indexation – Adding to the list of books Roman Catholics are forbidden to read. As publication of the list ceased in 1966, indexation no longer exists, and all references to it are based either on ignorance or religious bigotry.

ISA – Inexplicable Shaving Amount. The unexplained mystery as to why some men wear beards and others do not.

Inheritance – Passed down from generation to generation; in the genes.

Inland Revenue – A secret society.

Interest – This is what you have, if you have money. If you have no money, you are unlikely to be interested.

Investment Trust – Letting someone else fill in your coupon for the National Lottery.

Joint Expenditure – The cost of your Sunday lunch.

Kapital Gain – Short for *Das Kapital* gain. The benefit derived from reading Karl Marx.

Life Assurance – Before you are eligible to sign your own tax return, you have to provide proof that you are still alive. This is called 'life assurance'.

Listed Company – A guest list.

Market Maker – A town planner.

Married Couples Allowance – This is the compensation the Government used to give people for having got married. Gordon Brown thought it served them right and removed the allowance in his March 1999 budget.

MIRAS – A device for looking into the future. Hence: MIRAS, MIRAS on the wall, what is the best investment of them all? Gordon Brown did not like the look of the future, so he removed this as well.

Mortgage – An over-ripe fruit, particularly a rotten greengage. [From the French *mort*, meaning dead + gage.]

National Debt – Owed by each and every citizen to the footballer who scored the winning goal in the last World Cup match won by the National team.

National Insurance – The armed forces.

National Savings – Protected buildings.

Offshore Trust – Confidence in the Captain.

Overpayment – A misprint for 'over-pavement'; a bridge.

PAYE – A way of giving away your money before you receive it.

Pension – A cheap boarding house.

PEP – The energy you could display in your younger days in avoiding payment of taxes.

Personal Allowance – Those errors of judgement for which your friends may forgive you, because they like you.

Preference Share – More than the other fellow gets.

Premium Bond – Sean Connery.

Profit Sharing Scheme – This is a scheme by which any profits you make are shared out among all the family, while any losses are borne by you alone.

Proxy – A misprint of 'doxy'; a wench or mistress.

Quoted Company – A name dropped, as in: I was with X the other day and he said…

Redundancy Payment – Payments made for unnecessary work; e.g. to cowboy builders.

Retail Prices Index – How much more everything costs than you thought it would.

Scrip Dividend – An IOU written on a scrap of paper.

Self-Assessment – Autobiography.

Stamp Duty – The responsibility for making sure the correct postage rate has been paid on letters and parcels.

Tax Avoidance – Destitution. This is legal.

Tax Credit – A thank you letter from the Inland Revenue.

Tax Evasion – Death. This is a crime.

Tax Year – How long you have to work in order to earn enough money to pay the money the Inland Revenue demands from you.

Tessa – A civil servant first employed by Nigel Lawson to encourage people to save. She retired in April 1999.

Trustee – A convict to whom special privileges have been granted. Usually spelled *trusty*.

Underpayment – A misprint for 'under-pavement'; an underpass.

Unlisted Company – An uninvited guest; a gatecrasher.

VAT – A big barrel into which the Government requires you to put some money every time you buy something.

Working Abroad – Pimping.

X – A denial of liability.

Y – Who knows?

Z – Short for Zzzzz. Don't wake me.

God's Lucky Day

[In February 1997 God received an American Family Publisher's Sweepstakes entry mailed to Florida's Bushnell Assembly of God Church which began, "God, you may already be a winner."]

I had not conversed with God for some weeks. I really didn't have any excuse. I had just been busy with other things and never got around to Him. It was all a matter of one's priorities, as I had to admit to myself; one should not forget one's friends and I did have some feeling of guilt.

"I hear congratulations are in order," I said attempting to open the conversation on a happy note.

"To whom?" He asked grandly.

"To you," I said. "Did I not read that you are in line for a big prize?"

"Oh, that!" He exclaimed dismissively. "That's no big deal."

His language, I had noticed, was getting less and less formal and idiomatic as the years went by. How I missed the King James Version.

"One has to keep up with the times," He said, reading my mind; He can do that sort of thing when He wants to.

It took me a moment or two to catch the connection.

"Why?" I asked eventually. "Why do you have to keep up with the times? Surely you don't *have* to do anything?"

"It was a mere figure of speech," He answered casually. "It is a matter of style. I want people to realise that I am up with the times. To use the language of the moment, I want to get my message across, to spread the word – I am *relevant*."

"To whom?" I asked. "To whom do you want to be relevant?"

"To everyone," God declared, "to all people in all parts of the world."

"Just to people?"

"Of course just to people. In spite of what is sometimes suggested, I have not spread my ministry to dogs and cats."

"Or computers?" I suggested slyly.

"Naturally not."

"It was a computer that picked you out as eligible for this sweepstake that could win you millions of dollars. When I think of your agents going around with collection boxes and counting out the pennies, it seems to me that you could do quite a lot with a few million dollars; it seems to me – to use your language – to be a very big deal."

"You miss the point," He said. "It is the giving of the pennies that helps men to achieve salvation."

"And the receiving of them that makes someone rich."

"That is ungenerous of you," He chided me.

"I am more interested just now in the computer," I said. "Why did it pick you out for its sweepstake? Is it interested in salvation? Is this a sign that computers have developed souls that can be saved? After all, this was no mere chance. It wrote to you by name and said it had been searching for you and that you had been positively identified as being in the running for the big payout. I knew that computers were getting more powerful but I had thought that all this talk of artificial intelligence meant just what it said – that computers were developing *artificial* intelligence not *real* intelligence and personalities. Now we have a computer that believes in God and is sufficiently committed to you to find out where you live. Incidentally, I did not realise that you lived just outside Tampa in Florida. I think that will come as a surprise to a lot of people."

"It is only a forwarding address," God replied, "one of many thousands."

"What about the computer?" I asked. "If there is one computer that can find you, surely there will soon be hundreds or thousands or even millions that can. What is in it for them? Do they expect you to grant them eternal life?"

"That is a very interesting question," He said – conspicuously avoiding giving an answer.

"Perhaps, after all, you could not do that," I hazarded.

"I can do anything," God thundered. "How dare you suggest otherwise."

"I was only thinking that it is men's souls that you gather up for eternity."

"So it is."

"But surely computers haven't got souls, have they?"

"Not yet but, if at any time I decide that they deserve souls, I shall provide them. I decide who or what has a soul – and when. How do you think I managed evolution?"

As always, He had given me much to contemplate. I was grateful.

"It was kind of you to give me so much to contemplate," I said. "Would you object if I gave you a little advice?"

"Can I stop you?" God joked. We both knew He could stop me easily if He were so minded.

"If I were you," I started to say.

"Kindly rephrase that," He demanded imperiously.

"I think it would be better for your image," I said, "if you were to disclaim publicly any interest in or claim to the proceeds of that or any other sweepstake."

"Why do you say this?" He asked.

"It is normal in such sweepstakes for employees of the organisation responsible and for the shareholders of the organisation to be disqualified from taking part. There is a sense in which you could be said to be in control of this particular organisation, as you are in control of all organisations."

"I don't interfere in day to day management," God said defensively.

"Nevertheless," I insisted, "your omnipotence is well known. It is not enough that you don't interfere with the draw, it must be clear to everyone that you cannot interfere. Given your powers, it is impossible to do this. For the sake of your public relations, you have no option but to withdraw."

"I'll think about it," God said.

Harry Stophanes and the Birds

Fragments have been discovered recently of this first known international collaboration in the field of drama. The authors were Yuri Peadese 'and friends'.

Translated from the Latin'n'Greek.

Cast in order of appearance or not, as the case may be:

Classicus – a scholar
Julius Sneezer – a Roman geezer
Aggi Memnon – a widow
Helena Troy – her unmarried sister
Oedipus – the royal cat
Sextus Maximus – the owner of a large organ
Nero – an Indian Prince
Gigi of Troy – a Greek bearing gifts
Polygamus – a much married man
Pompey Circumstance – an Elgar statesman [Some authorities believe this to be a misprint.]
Harry Stophanes – a writer
Archy Medes – a man of principle

Act 1. Scene 1: The Market Place.

Enter from opposite sides of the stage, Classicus and Julius Sneezer.

C   Hail Sneezer.
JS   Hi there. Long time no see. Howya going?
C   Sneezer may not realise but something is rotten with the skate from Denmark.
JS   Never cared for fish myself.
C   It is time for something to be done. When will you be going to the Forum?
JS   I'm not sure. What's on?
C   Murder most foul.
JS   Sounds like fun. When shall I come?
C   Be there the Ides of March. *Classicus runs off.*

Enter Aggi Memnon with Helena Troy some yards behind.

AMem   Yon Classicus has a lean and hungry look. He reads too much.
JS   Aggi! Just the girl I wanted.
AMem   And which girl don't you want? I know your reputation.
JS   Ah! I thought I saw you with Polygamus the other day.
AMem   (*passionately*) He is a real man.
JS   And he has already had seven wives to prove it.
AMem   I'm on my way to hear Nero play the sitar and I want Helena to see Sextus Maximus's organ. It's time she got married but she only seems to be interested in launching ships – fifteen this week alone. So I thought, if music be the food of love and all that. Are you going the same way?
JS   Not I. I don't mind Nero but I always laugh when I see Sextus Maximus's organ.
AMem   I suppose you've seen it more often than most people.
JS   I suppose I have. *They leave together in opposite directions.*

Act 1. Scene 2: The Royal Palace.

Enter Oedipus, the cat. He looks about him slowly and deliberately and then crosses the stage and leaves.

Voice off   Where's that damned cat?

Act 1. Scene 3: The Market Place.

Enter Sextus Maximus and Nero. They are deep in conversation.

SM   Didn't we do well?
N   I did, of course, but what you were thinking about in the third movement, I have no idea. Your timing was impossible.
SM   I couldn't help it. I was put off by people laughing at my organ.
N   That always happens. You should keep it hidden. Look out, here comes Gigi.

Enter Gigi of Troy carrying a small parcel. He has been running and is out of breath.

G   I've been trying to catch you.
N   And now you have caught us; well done. Goodbye.
G   Don't be like that. I've got a present for you.
N   For me? What is it?

He takes the parcel and removes the wrapping. He holds up a large knife.

N   Is this a dagger I see before me?
G   It's a gift from Classicus. He says he will talk to you about it but don't forget you have to mark Anthony.
SM   Nothing for me?
G   Classicus says you don't need anything; you are already very well endowed.

They exit together talking.

Act 1. Scene 4: A Courtyard.

Enter Polygamus and Pompey Circumstance.

P   They will never keep it up.
PC As I understand it, they won't let it up in the first place.
P   I don't believe it.
PC Ask Harry; here he comes.

Enter Harry Stophanes.

P   Harry, is it true?
HS About the birds? I'll say so. They are all on strike.
P   Just because of the war?
HS That's it. They won't let us start until it stops. It's all the fault of that Lisa Strata.
PC He knows, you know. He wrote a book about birds.

Enter Archy Medes carrying a small paper boat.

AMed   It floats. Eureka.

Exit Archy Medes on a cloud.

Enter Cassandra singing.

C   Woe is you, woe is he.
Woe is everyone but me.
There once was a merry farmer.
So merry, so merry was he.
He mounted his horse, then his goat, then his sheep
And after the effort he needed a sleep.

Exit all on hands and knees.

Act 1. Scene 5: The Royal Palace.

The stage is empty.

Voice off   I still can't find the cat.

[*Editor's note: The middle sections of the play have been lost. Only part of the final Act has been discovered.*]

Act 92. Scene 4: The Forum.

Enter Classicus followed by Nero and Pompey Circumstance. Nero, with his sitar hanging over his shoulder, is carrying a dead cat.

PC This was the noblest Roman'n'Greek of them all.
C   Out, out damned spot. If only I had known, I should have become a watchmaker. Farewell the tranquil mind. (*Classicus falls on his sword.*) Ouch.
PC You want to be careful there. You could do yourself an injury.

Nero gently hands the cat to Pompey Circumstance and begins to strum on his sitar.

N   (*singing very softly*)
Archy and Aggi and Helena too,
Gone all my friends, not only a few.
Sextus and Gigi, they'd not even fighted,
Lisa is dead, my love unrequited,
Big Julie too, the best of the Sneezers
Nero stops singing. Classicus goes to the back of the stage and peers into the distance.
N   What rhymes with Sneezers?

C   Quiet a moment. Can you smell burning?

Pompey Circumstance joins Classicus at the back of the stage.

PC I can see flames.
C   There is a fire in the city. What shall we do?
N   We could try barbecuing the cat.

Exit all.